Dock Boss:

Eddie McGrath
and the West Side Waterfront

D1166822

Dock Boss:

Eddie McGrath
and the West Side Waterfront

BY NEIL G. CLARK

BARRICADE
BOOKS

Published by Barricade Books Inc.
Fort Lee, New Jersey 07024

www.barricadebooks.com

Library of Congress Cataloging-in-Publication Data

Clark, Neil G.
  Dock Boss : Eddie McGrath and the West Side Waterfront /
  by Neil G. Clark.
    pages cm
  Includes bibliographical references and index.
  LCCN 2017006265 | ISBN 978-1-5698081-3-9 (pbk.) |
    ISBN 978-1-5698082-0-7 (ebook)
LCSH: McGrath, Eddie (Edward J.), 1906- 1. Gangsters—New
    York (State)—New York—Biography. 2. Organized crime—
    New York (State)—New York—History—20th century.
    3. Stevedores—New York (State)—New York—History—20th
    century. 4. Stevedores—Labor unions—New York (State)—
    New York—History—20th century.
  HV6248.M46537 C53   2017
  DDC 364.1092 [B]—dc23   92-18776

10 9 8 7 6 5 4 3
Manufactured in the United States of America

For Mandy, Owen, Declan,
and any future beans.
You are my world. I would need to
write a thousand books to explain
the joy that you have brought me.

For Mom and Dad.
Love you forever and always.

CONTENTS

WATERFRONT GANG CHARTS

Dunn-McGrath Mob

 EDWARD MCGRATH *ALIAS* "EDDIE"

 JOHN DUNN *ALIAS* "COCKEYE"

   ANDREW SHERIDAN *ALIAS* "SQUINT"

JACK ADAMS *ALIAS* "JACKIE"

 ROBERT BAKER *ALIAS* "BARNEY"

 HENRY BELL *ALIAS* "BUSTER"

 JAMES BELL *ALIAS* "DING-DONG"

 LESLIE BELL *ALIAS* "LESTER"

 FRANK BONFIGLIO *ALIAS* "FRANK MARIO"

 THOMAS BURKE *ALIAS* "RED"

 HARRY CASHIN

 GEORGE DAGGETT

 BENJAMIN DIETZ *ALIAS* "BARNEY"

 JOHN DUFF *ALIAS* "DUFFY"

 AUSTIN FUREY *ALIAS* "AUSTIE"

 EDWARD GAFFNEY

 DANIEL GENTILE *ALIAS* "DANNY BROOKS"

 JOHN HUGHES *ALIAS* "PECK"

 MATTHEW KANE

 EDWARD KENNY *ALIAS* "THE SNAKE"

 FRANK KELLY *ALIAS* "U-BOAT"

 JOHN LA PORTE *ALIAS* "LITTLE JEFF"

 JOHN MCCROSSIN *ALIAS* "RED"

 JOHN MCLOUGHLIN *ALIAS* "MICKEY"

 HUGH MULLIGAN *ALIAS* "HUGHIE"

 CORNELIUS NOONAN *ALIAS* "CONNIE"

 EDWARD O'CONNELL

 VICTOR PATTERSON

 JAMES SKINNER

 ROBERT SULLIVAN *ALIAS* "FARMER"

 NICHOLAS TANZELLA *ALIAS* "THE BULL"

 LEON TOCCI *ALIAS* "LEO MASSI"

 WILLIAM VANDER-WYDE

O'Mara Group

  TIMOTHY O'MARA *ALIAS* "JAMES O'CONNOR"

 JOHN O'MARA *ALIAS* "JACKIE"

  CHRISTOPHER CALLAHAN

YANOWSKY GANG

CHARLES YANOWSKY
ALIAS
"CHARLIE THE JEW"

OTHER KEY GANG MEMBERS
- Ralph "Lulu" Clements
- John Harvey
- John "Fats" Manning
- Joseph "Joe Devine" McKenna
- John Ryan
- Philip "Philsie" Sheridan
- Joseph "Joe Portuguese" Silba

1941-1948

VINCENT BROWN
ALIAS
"BARNEY"

FRANK DILORENZO
ALIAS
"BIFFO"

GEORGE DONAHUE
ALIAS
"THE RAPE ARTIST"

ANTHONY LUCEY
ALIAS
"SLIM"

ANDREW POLO
ALIAS
"EDDIE POLO"

HAROLD MELTZER
ALIAS
"HAPPY

JOHN DE BIASIO

1934-1938

ALBERT ACKALITIS
ALIAS
"ACKY"

THOMAS ADOBODY

FRANK CAMPBELL
ALIAS
"SONNY"

MICHAEL KANE
ALIAS
"MICKEY HEALY"

GEORGE KEELER

JOSEPH KRESS
ALIAS
"JOSEPH JACOBS"

BERNARD MCMAHON
ALIAS
"THE BUM"

JOSEPH MURPHY
ALIAS
"HEELS"

FRANK PERASKI
ALIAS
"FRANK DALEY"

MICHAEL PICCARDO
ALIAS
"MICHAEL RENE"

THOMAS PROTHEROE
ALIAS
"TOUGH TOMMY"

JOSEPH POTTER

FRANCIS SMITH
ALIAS
"BUSTER"

JOHN STEWART
ALIAS
"ARCHIE"

STEWART WALLACE
ALIAS
"ONE ARM"

BOWERS' MOB

MICHAEL BOWERS
ALIAS
"MICKEY"

OTHER KEY GANG MEMBERS
- John Clinton
- Michael Kehoe
- Edmund Leahy
- James McNay
- Thomas "Tottie" O'Rourke
- John Potter
- John St. John

JOHN APPLEGATE
ALIAS
"APPLES"

HAROLD BOWERS
ALIAS
"BIG HARRY"

JOHN KEEFE
ALIAS
"KEEFIE"

DANIEL ST. JOHN

JOHN WARD
ALIAS
"BIG JOHN"

PROLOGUE:
GANG RULE — A LONGSHOREMAN'S STORY

ON A COLD February day in 1941, John Whitton, or "Mutt" as he was known around the West Side of New York City, unloaded the hatch of a docked cargo liner on Pier 14. A distinct odor, which was unique to the bustling waterfront, permeated the air. The sun had disappeared early, as a light snow covered the dock and a hard wind blew in off the water. The men on the pier pushed to complete their day's job and rushed to unpack the last of the ship's goods.

After the cargo had been unloaded, the longshoremen dispersed into the night. Some would head to the nearest dimly lit bar to drink and gamble away their free time. Others would march home to their nearby West Side tenement apartments, which were usually crowded with an abundance of children who relied on the day's wages.

For Mutt, the work wasn't easy, but it was still honest. Like a good number of men who worked on the piers, Mutt had been in trouble with the law before; however, since his release from prison, he had been trying to change his reputation. He still kept company with a number of unsavory childhood acquaintances, and he wasn't against making a quick buck with a small theft here and there, but he didn't intend on ever going back up north. Mutt had given enough of his life to the state, and he had made a promise to his elderly mother, Nora, that he would change his ways.

Mutt was born in 1905, now thirty-six years of age, and had a criminal record that dated back to 1913. His first arrest was as a juvenile, at the tender age of eight, and he had spent the bulk of his formative years in some of the state's most brutal reformatories. Back then, when he wasn't serving time, he was on the streets of his native West Side doing drugs and running with street gangs. Mutt got his nickname because he stood only 4'0" tall and weighed less than 120 pounds as a youth. The name stuck as, even as an adult, Mutt would grow to be less than 5'5" in height.

Mutt would rack up regular convictions for petty crimes until one eventful week in 1923. On March 30, Mutt and a lanky friend, Patrick Ahearn, needed a quick score, as the week prior Mutt had broken out of East View Penitentiary. At 9:00 PM that night, the duo donned blue workmen's garb, grabbed pistols, and headed toward the United Cigar Store on Lexington Avenue between 69th and 70th Street. The attempted robbery would alter the course of Mutt's life in a way he could never have imagined.

Both Mutt and Ahearn entered the store with guns drawn. The tiny shop consisted only of a small storage room, a cash register on a desk, and two glass display cases. The lone clerk in the shop knew what was taking place and complied with Mutt's request to put his hands up. Mutt popped open the cash register and grabbed $16.98 from the till. He then forced the clerk to the floor and demanded that he open the safe underneath the desk.

As luck would have it, an off-duty police officer named John Cordes, who had averaged nearly three hundred arrests in 1922 alone, had popped into the shop. Cordes had planned to buy a pack of cigars for his brother Freddie, who was waiting outside in the car. Cordes recognized something was amiss as, instead of the usual clerk behind the desk, he could only see two wild looking youths staring at him in surprise. As he got closer, he noticed a gun in the taller Ahearn's hand. Cordes recognized that he needed to get help, and he slowly backed to the door telling Mutt and Ahearn that "the store didn't carry his brand."

Mutt squealed, "You'll get your smokes!" and fired a shot directly at Cordes' chest. Instinctively, Cordes raised his right hand to shield himself. The bullet slowed down as it passed through the area near his right thumb and, what likely would have been a fatal bullet, lodged shallowly in his chest.

Cordes crouched to the ground as Mutt yelled to Ahearn, "Give it to that son of a bitch!" Ahearn ran up to the prone Cordes and leveled the pistol at his head. Before Ahearn could pull the trigger, Cordes sprang up, grabbed at Ahearn's weapon, and began to wrestle him for the gun. Cordes managed to turn it toward the lanky youth, and he fired a shot. Ahearn grasped at his stomach and slumped against the wall of the shop.

The injured Cordes turned Ahearn's gun toward Mutt. Mutt leveled his own gun, and he and Cordes exchanged wild gunfire across the small store. Cordes' bullets did not strike their target, but Mutt's shots found their mark in Cordes' right shoulder and left thigh. Mutt ran out from behind the counter to finish off the downed police officer, but Cordes leaped forward and tackled the much smaller Mutt. Cordes gained control of Mutt's gun, but Mutt quickly sprang up from the ground and shut himself in the stockroom behind the cash register. The bleeding Cordes stumbled out of the shop just as his brother Freddie, who had heard the gunfire, came sprinting toward it. Cordes advised Freddie to run to the nearest police station to get help.

In a scene straight out of a dark comedy, an off-duty police sergeant happened to be walking down the street. The off-duty officer, who was carrying his service revolver, heard the shots and noticed the bleeding Cordes, gun in hand, stumbling in front of the store. Assuming Cordes was a robber, the off-duty cop opened fire without warning and shot Cordes in the back of his right shoulder.

Cordes' body spun to the ground as the off-duty officer

continued to shoot wildly, striking the window of the cigar store, and also a neighboring business. Cordes fumbled for his police shield to identify himself to the approaching officer, but the off-duty officer fired another shot from close range that went through Cordes' right cheek and embedded in his jawbone. Cordes' brother Freddie, who had run back to the scene after hearing more gunfire, arrived just in time to see the downed Cordes kick the off-duty officer in the groin. The blow caused the off-duty officer to accidentally discharge his gun into the ground. The stray bullet ricocheted off the pavement and struck Freddie in the left elbow.

Cordes stumbled to his feet and, upon seeing the now bleeding Freddie, realized that no backup was coming. Cordes, who was suffering from five bullet wounds, took matters into his own hands and marched back into the store with Mutt's gun. He kicked down the storage room door and arrested the still-hiding Mutt. After sorting out the situation with the off-duty officer, the bleeding Cordes, his injured brother Freddie, and the belligerent Mutt marched down the street to the nearby Presbyterian Hospital.

Cordes arrived through the hospital's front door and was a fearful sight to everyone inside. Mutt was arrested by arriving policemen and Ahearn, who Cordes assumed was dead, was found by ambulance workers still slumped in the cigar shop. He was taken to Bellevue hospital where surgeons managed to stabilize him.

Amazingly, Cordes was discharged from the hospital only six days later. Ahearn, who recovered from his injuries, and did not have a long rap sheet, was sentenced to serve an indefinite term in the Elmira Reformatory. The troublesome Mutt received no leniency and was sentenced to fifteen years in state prison. The malnourished-looking youth was sent to Sing Sing and later Dannemora (otherwise known as Clinton or "New York's Siberia"), where he would be housed with the most hardcore convicts in the state. He was now a little fish amongst a sea of gangsters, sexual predators and murderers.

Mutt Whitton served all of his fifteen years, and when he was released in 1938, he was no longer a boy. He had lost his youthful ambition, and he no longer had the drive to live a life of crime. Mutt was burned out. Like many ex-convicts, Mutt sought work on the West Side piers after his release. Due to the casual nature of the employment, a man could blend in with the group and not stand out as a criminal. The dock workers didn't have to know how to read or write, and, as long as they weren't afraid of a hard day's work, they might be able to find employment.

Mutt had managed to stay off the cops' radar, but he was unable to change his past on one spring day in 1940. While Mutt was working as a longshoreman on Pier 45 he heard a familiar voice calling him. As he turned, he saw a face he could never forget—the face of John Cordes. The ambitious cop was now a detective in a unit that investigated waterfront crime. Cordes warned Mutt that he better be working an honest job and that he would be watching him closely.

Over the next few months, Cordes kept close tabs on Mutt, but all he found was that he was showing up for work every day and slinging cargo like the rest of the crew. Cordes visited Mutt regularly on the pier and gradually grew fond of him. He couldn't help but admire the way that Mutt seemed to genuinely want to turn his life around.

One day, Cordes heard through another longshoreman that Mutt had been fired by a shipping boss on Pier 45 after he learned of Mutt's criminal record. Cordes went to the shipping boss and tried to arrange for the pier to take Mutt back. When the pier would not rehire Mutt, Cordes left angrily, went and found Mutt, and drove him to Pier 14 on the Lower West Side. Cordes called in a favor with the boss there and had Mutt back at work by the next day.

Mutt was grateful. The work was good, and he was able to carve out a living.

Although Mutt was no longer committing crimes himself, he was still friendly with a number of the neighborhood's rougher characters, and he regularly overheard the latest gossip. One of the plans that Mutt had heard about involved the theft of a crate of machine guns off Pier 54 in February of 1941. A couple of workers had found that a hundred cases of unassembled Thompson machine guns, which had been purchased by the British Army for the war effort, had been stored on the pier. Two of the workers managed to swipe a case of ten unassembled guns, and they were now shopping them around to potential buyers. Word on the street was that the main dock mob on the Lower West Side was interested in purchasing them. Mutt had heard that the now-assembled machine guns were being stashed in a vacant lot, behind Tony's Barber Shop, near Pier 54. He also picked up that Edward Hooper, a longshoreman on Pier 54, had been responsible for the theft.

Cordes and his team of detectives maintained a phone at Pier 57, which was where their squad had an office. At 6:10 PM on February 22, 1941, one of Cordes' detectives received a call. "Any of Cordes' squad there?" asked the voice on the phone. Cordes was not around, but the caller said, "I heard Cordes was looking for something. He should head to Tony's Barbershop." The detectives, who had been frantically searching for the missing machine guns, knew exactly what the caller was insinuating. The detective asked who was on the other line, but the caller responded with a simple "Never mind," and the line went dead.

The police raced to the lot and found all ten guns concealed in a number of burlap sacks. The caller's tip was right on. Edward Hooper, who a watchman had earlier seen loitering around the guns, was arrested the following day. He blamed the crime on drunkenness and was convicted in April of that year. Buzz spread up and down the waterfront that Cordes' waterfront squad had a rat in their pocket. Although thousands of men worked on the piers, it was still a small world that was built on its own laws and rules, the main one being a strict code of silence. Along the waterfront, the longshoremen took care of their own problems, and they never squealed to cops.

The majority of longshoremen were honest and hardworking men, but if they couldn't get work for a week it was the neighborhood loanshark who would spot them the money, not a cop. Everyone knew the gangsters controlled things and, to most, it was an accepted part of life on the docks. The criminals lived on their streets, drank in their bars, and knew their families. For all the harm the criminals may have caused, many felt that they would rather deal with the devil they knew, than the outsiders on the police force.

Whether Mutt was the anonymous tipster didn't matter. Everyone knew about his history with Cordes and that Cordes had obtained a good job for Mutt. Mutt had the most reason to provide the tip, and therefore he was the most likely culprit. Such is the danger of being friendly with cops on the waterfront. Every longshoreman along the Lower West Side knew that someone would have to answer for ratting. The powerful gangsters who controlled the docks relied on fear. If people got away with speaking to the police, it would send the wrong message and could lead to others tipping off the cops. Examples would have to be made.

A couple of days after the weapons seizure, Mutt was on Pier 14 performing his normal day's work. Night began to fall on the afternoon shift, and most of the longshoremen were exiting the pier, when a heavy-set man, who Mutt knew as Andy "Squint" Sheridan, calmly walked down the dock toward Mutt. Following close behind was Joe Powell, a young strong-arm who worked for the mob on Pier 14 as a checker. There were a few men like Powell working on every gangster-controlled pier along the North River, and regardless of their official job title, their real role was to keep everyone in line for the waterfront mobs. Only six months prior, Powell had been cleared of the murder of one of his best friends. The friend, Charles T. Brady, was shot by Powell three times in the chest while sitting next to him in a car after a night of drinking and a petty argument. Powell and another man, who had been sitting in the car, testified that Brady was about to shoot Powell first. Powell's self-defense argument worked, and he was found not guilty by a jury.

Sheridan, who strutted in front of Powell, had slicked back hair and large thick glasses. Although he was wearing an expensive suit, he still looked sloppy due to the excess weight he carried around his waist. Mutt and Sheridan had missed each other by a year or so in Clinton Penitentiary, but Mutt knew of his reputation. This was the man who only appeared when the waterfront bosses, Eddie McGrath and Johnny Dunn, needed something important handled.

Powell identified Mutt to Sheridan with a passive head nod. The two approached. "Can I have a word, Mutt?" muttered Sheridan from behind the thick eyeglasses. Mutt had dealt with gangsters like this for years, and he knew not to be to be afraid in such a public place. If the man wanted Mutt dead, then it would have already happened. The pier was still scattered with a number of longshoremen who quietly pretended to not watch the exchange taking place. Mutt sighed in relief.

Sheridan motioned for Mutt to follow him into a nearby storage area that overlooked the freezing water at the end of the pier. The men, who were still working on the pier, watched as Sheridan, Mutt, and Powell entered the small the room, which contained a bathroom and a wash basin.

As Mutt turned to speak to Sheridan, he heard two loud pops. Sheridan had drawn a gun and shot Mutt twice in the chest. Mutt slumped to the ground. Sheridan then slowly approached and fired another shot directly into Mutt's forehead. Mutt had doubted the power of those who controlled the piers. These men had the clout to commit murder at will. Sheridan put his gun back in his pocket, and he and Powell dragged Mutt's bleeding body across the floor. The two men lifted Mutt's small corpse and deposited it into a deep urinal drain pipe that led directly into the frigid and icy waters of the North River. After carefully brushing himself off, Sheridan, who was now speckled with Mutt's blood, left the building. Powell remained behind to clean up.

Sheridan casually walked back to his car, in full view of all the longshoremen who still remained on the pier. He wanted them to know what had just taken place. The longshoremen kept their heads down, said nothing, and then dispersed like any other day. No one wanted to end up like Mutt.

Mutt failed to visit his loving mother that week. She went to his apartment and was told that he hadn't been around in days. She reported him missing, but the cops did not search very hard for an ex-con like Mutt. Cordes had heard the grim talk around the docks, and he knew there was no case to be made. Everyone on the waterfront knew what had happened to Mutt, but, officially, no one had seen or heard anything.

Every year when winter turns to spring, and the waters of the Hudson turn warm, floating bodies appear in the rivers around New York City. Mostly, they are drunks or suicides, but on May 12, 1941, the police fished out the bloated and decomposed corpse of John "Mutt" Whitton from a dock south of Pier 14. He was only able to be identified by fingerprint records.

The newspapers that day carried the story of another dead criminal who was working on the West Side docks. It was nothing new, and by the next day, Mutt's name was gone from the papers. Longshoremen spoke of his death in whispers, but it was usually just one name recited as part of a long list of others who had crossed the waterfront gangsters. Everyone knew who had killed Mutt, but why do anything about it? Who would want to end up like him?

This was a world controlled by gangsters.

This was Eddie McGrath's world.

Growing Pains

MANY PROHIBITION GANGSTER tales begin with remarkable stories of struggle, which are so often associated with the turn of the century immigrant experience. Future crime bosses deal with issues such as alcoholic and absentee fathers, sentences in brutal juvenile reformatories, and membership in tough street gangs. Conversely, the story of Edward John McGrath, who would later become one of the most powerful gangsters operating on Manhattan's waterfront during a time when the Port of New York was the epicenter of the shipping world, starts with more mundane beginnings.

The normalcy of McGrath's youth may provide answers as to how the sociable crook was able to smooth talk his way into the upper echelons of legitimate New York society, while at the same time leading a gang of convicted killers and strong-arm men. Most gangsters would have been lost in the formalities of a cocktail party, but McGrath possessed a charm and confidence that allowed him to blend in like a chameleon among the city's social elite.

Although McGrath did not come from wealth, his upbringing was relatively normal, given the tough area of the city in which he was raised. He had an unremarkable childhood, but the events and circumstances that followed his adolescence would transform him from an altar boy to a bootlegger, a robber, and finally to a waterfront racketeer who the police would claim was responsible for over twenty-five murders.

Edward J. McGrath Jr. was born on January 31, 1906, during a time when New York City had opened its doors to waves of new immigrants. Like so many others in Manhattan, McGrath was a first generation American citizen who was the child of two recent arrivals from the Free Irish State. McGrath's mother, Josephine, was born in Ireland in 1884 and had traveled to New York City alone in 1901. After arriving in America, Josephine settled in Manhattan and married McGrath's father, Edward McGrath Sr., who was then working as a laborer. The couple resided in a small apartment inside a humble tenement building around East 23rd Street, which was part of a neighborhood known as the Gashouse District.

Unofficially enclosed by 14th Street to 27th Street and Fourth Avenue to the East River, the Gashouse District was bordered by the affluent communities of Gramercy Park and Stuyvesant Square, where many rich New Yorkers had constructed mansions following the Civil War. Not nearly as nice as their wealthy neighbors, the Gashouse District was appropriately named after the massive gas tanks that had been constructed in the mid-1800s, alongside the rows of homes. Standing tall above the house tops, the gas tanks were known to leak and emit a putrid odor, and the area was considered one of the least desirable places in the city to live.

The presence of the gas tanks drove down the cost of living, and the neighborhood was flooded with recent immigrants from Ireland and Germany. The poorest residents took to living in crowded homes nearest to the East River, where they could find employment at the slaughterhouses, factories, and docks. Due to the enormous increase of arrivals in the early 1900s, the area was bursting at the seams and could barely accommodate the new residents; as a result, tenement homes were built to meet the demand of the growing population. The tenements typically consisted of five to six-story walk-ups that contained three to four apartments per floor, which was the style of home in which McGrath and his family resided.

For new unskilled immigrants, the conditions of employment were often treacherous, and many were attracted to dangerous jobs in exchange for higher wages. The McGrath family was no different, and tragedy would strike in 1909 when Edward McGrath Sr. was hit and killed by a trolley car at work.

The widowed Josephine was left to care for the young Eddie and his older sister, Mary. She remarried the following year to a twenty-two-year-old Irish immigrant named James F. Connors. Connors had arrived in New York City from Ireland on November 9, 1907, and was able to provide a stable environment for Josephine and her two children, through his work as a clerk. The new family settled into a home located at 315 East 88th Street on the Upper East Side of Manhattan. McGrath's devout Irish-Catholic parents sent him to Our Lady of Good Counsel Parochial School, and all available records suggest the young boy was successful in his studies. Eventually, McGrath and his sister were joined by a number of half-siblings. Two sisters came first, Marcella, in 1911, and Anna, in 1912; and then boys James, in 1914; Matthew, in 1922; and Peter, in 1923. In September of 1918, the family moved back to the peripheries of the Gashouse District to an apartment at 349 Third Avenue. McGrath transferred to St. Stephen's Parochial School at 141 East 28th Street, which taught both religious and conventional education.

At St. Stephen's, McGrath continued to excel. When not in school, he attended mass regularly at St. Stephen's Roman Catholic Church and was, for a time, an altar boy who sang in the church choir. McGrath graduated from the eighth grade on June 30, 1921, and the then fifteen-year-old decided to continue his education, even though during the 1920s only about twenty percent of students in New York State chose to continue school beyond the eighth grade. The practical choice for most was to find work and help contribute to their family's coffers.

In 1921, McGrath obtained his first part-time job working at Buhla and Company on 4th Avenue and 21st Street as a clerk. The following year, he was hired by the New York Telephone Company at the rate of fifteen dollars a week and left school, at around sixteen years of age, after completing the tenth grade. McGrath, who could read and write proficiently, found full-time employment, again as a clerk, at the Horton Ice Cream Company. In early 1925, McGrath left his job at the Horton Ice Cream Company in favor of a position at the 5th Avenue Auction Company.

Tragedy would again deal the teenage McGrath a blow, as in late 1925 his mother Josephine passed away. At the time of her passing, McGrath was still living at home, but Josephine's death left considerable strain on the family. The widowed Connors, who would not remarry, now had five young children to look after in addition to McGrath and his older sister. Not long after his mother's death, McGrath left the Connors' household and found lodging in a variety of different boarding houses around Manhattan and in the borough of Queens, which is where the Connors' family would later relocate. Prohibition in the United States was in full swing and, throughout the city, there was no shortage of rooming houses. The often small and sparsely furnished accommodations were full of youth who could not afford a permanent home, or by others who had come to the Big Apple in search of adventure and opportunity.

Due to the relatively cheap prices that the rooming houses offered, they attracted an eccentric clientele and, to cater to the residents, they were usually located in areas of the city that were nearest to bars and restaurants. McGrath continued to work at the Auction Company but also began to partake in the local nightlife scene with friends from his old neighborhood.

McGrath had grown up to be a good-looking young man, standing about 5'11" with a medium build, brown hair, and blue eyes. He had a slightly round face with outwardly pointed ears and was popular with the ladies due to his gift of the gab and taste for the finer things. Around the neighborhood, McGrath gained the reputation as a likeable smooth talker who did not shy away from a good time. At first, McGrath had no problem working as a clerk while spending his evenings drinking in the illegal speakeasies that dotted the New York landscape, but, by early 1927, McGrath stopped showing up for work and instead began to perform odd labor jobs that he found through friends.

An unemployed McGrath would have his first brush with the law on July 27, 1927, at the age of twenty-one, which made him a relatively late bloomer compared to other gangsters of his era. The crime is the first documented occasion that McGrath was caught by police, but it likely reflects a period when he was regularly engaging in minor criminality to subsidize his fast living.

The offence, which was anything but the crime of the century, involved the robbery of a local ice cream store in Queens. At 4:00 AM, two patrolling police officers heard the sound of glass breaking in front of the Tasty Ice Cream Company. The officers saw one individual standing out front, who, after spotting the cops, yelled to another man who had entered the store through the broken glass window. The second man bolted from the store and both he and his lookout took off sprinting down the dark and empty street. The officers gave pursuit and saw the two men enter a nearby vacant house. Entering with guns drawn, they found a drunken McGrath and another inebriated youth named Clarence Murray making a feeble attempt to hide inside a bathroom.

At the station, Murray admitted that he had smashed the glass, entered the store, and robbed the cash register of $9.47. McGrath was given $.47 for acting as a lookout. The failed bandits were charged with burglary in the third degree. The news of the arrests made the local papers and would have no doubt been an embarrassment to McGrath's straight and narrow family.

On October 3, 1927, McGrath and Murray pled guilty to the burglary charge. Fortunately for the duo, Judge Adel suspended the possible five to ten-year prison terms that they were facing, since it was both McGrath and Murray's first offence. The judge told the two youthful burglars that in the future they should "[. . .] associate with decent citizens" and that they should refrain from indulging in alcohol or fraternizing with the criminal element.

Both McGrath and Murray would not heed Judge Adel's warning and would instead continue with their reckless behavior, though to very different results. Murray would be arrested for another petty robbery in Manhattan, again while intoxicated, only five days after his conviction in Queens. His suspended sentence was reinstated by the General Sessions Court in Manhattan, and Murray was sent up north to serve a five-year bid in Sing Sing prison for a measly $9.00 take.

Let the Liquor Flow

MCGRATH MAY HAVE been late to the party, but by the time he began to explore the world of crime, Prohibition, the gangster's dream, was still in full effect. Passed on January 16, 1920, The Volstead Act prohibited the manufacture, sale, and transportation of any beverage containing more than .05% alcohol content. As history would show, the Act was ineffective as, despite what the temperance movement preached to the public, the average citizen still wanted to indulge in the occasional drink. Instead of creating a dry country, The Volstead Act would generate a booming black market run by organized criminals who readily fed the public's thirst for alcohol.

The ban on the legal sale of alcohol, and the immense profits associated with selling the illegal product, turned many street corner gangsters into wealthy bootleggers overnight. The available supply of booze could not keep pace with the public's demand, and those bootleggers who could get their hands on a steady flow of product flourished. Many local crime bosses turned into overnight celebrities, and stories of speakeasies, swinging dance halls, gang molls in fur coats, machine gun shoot-outs, and wealthy gangsters like Al Capone, Dutch Schultz, Arnold Rothstein, and Owney Madden dominated the headlines. Prohibition had made it acceptable for regular citizens to break the law in the simplest form, by indulging in a drink; even the rich and glamorous of society, such as film stars, musicians, and politicians, found it dangerous and exciting to be friends with the men who supplied their liquor.

Due to McGrath's age, and his late in life turn toward crime, he missed what would be considered the golden years of Prohibition. At a time when older and more experienced gangsters were creating their own empires, McGrath was still working in a respectable job as a clerk. However, like McGrath, unemployed and wild youth were not against turning to bootlegging to find lucrative work in a variety of entry-level jobs such as truck loading, delivery driving, and liquor sales.

Following his suspended sentence from Judge Adel on October 5, 1927, McGrath only racked up one more arrest before beginning his journey as a low-level bootlegger. No police records exist concerning the details of that crime, but on March 19, 1928, McGrath was arrested for the much more violent charge of assault and robbery with a gun. McGrath, who listed his address as 229 East 25th Street, was discharged with no further legal proceedings. The arrest was only four months after his conviction for burglary.

McGrath's regular companion during this period was a childhood friend, Nicholas Tanzella, who was known in criminal circles as "The Bull" due to his muscular build. Born in 1906, Tanzella was originally from Rhode Island. His family had moved to the Gashouse District when he was a boy, and he became friends with McGrath while the two were still in grade school. Tanzella, who had no record of arrests before 1928, had wavy black hair that he would slick back, and he was generally regarded as someone who was handy with his fists. With connections to the Italian community on the East Side, Tanzella had already been providing his criminal services to crime boss Joey Rao, a stocky gangster who ran a large piece of the bootlegging action in the Italian section of East Harlem.

Partnered with Tanzella, McGrath first found work for Rao as a delivery driver and salesman. The two novice thugs would ensure that product was delivered and would also encourage sales to speakeasies through gentle, or more forceful, coercion. McGrath quickly came to the attention of his boss Rao. Rao appreciated that the young Irishman always turned in a profit and that he could often handle situations by simply talking rather than resorting to violence. Unlike most of the bootleggers of the period, McGrath possessed formal education and work experience. With McGrath as the brains and Tanzella as the muscle, the two became one of the dozen or so men who were responsible for overseeing mid-level alcohol distribution for Rao's operation.

During this time, McGrath would meet a friend who would play an important role later in his life. Through Rao, McGrath was introduced to a young Italian-American gangster named Vincent "Jimmy Blue Eyes" Alo, or more commonly known as Jimmy Alo. Jimmy Alo was born in 1904 and had met McGrath after his release from state prison for an armed robbery conviction. Alo, who was born on the Lower East Side, was close to many up-and-coming gangsters such as Lucky Luciano, Joe Adonis, Frank Costello, Vito Genovese, and Luciano's partner, Meyer Lansky.

McGrath would later relate to a friend that Rao sent Alo to him so that Alo could get back on his feet financially and also learn the ins and outs of Rao's bootlegging operation. Alo was capable of committing violent crimes if needed, but like McGrath, he did not act at the drop of a hat. Both McGrath and Alo's preference for a low-key approach to business allowed the two to become friends.

The enticement of easy money had captured the young and impressionable McGrath. On a daily basis, he was interacting with men who had the type of wealth and power that he had never encountered while growing up in the Gashouse District. With the promise of money, women, parties, fancy clothes, and cars, it was clear that McGrath would never be employed as a clerk again.

1929: Robberies and More Arrests

THE STOCK MARKET crash of October 1929, or Black Tuesday as it came to be known, would signify the start of the Great Depression and would lead to millions of people around the country losing their livelihoods. For the fledgling gangster, Eddie McGrath, the year would begin with a crash of its own.

On January 28, 1929, McGrath, Tanzella, and two other men, hailed a cab on 2nd Avenue. As the cab approached 33rd Street, an oil truck soared through the intersection and struck the side of the cab. The cab was nearly destroyed by the accident. McGrath and friends were removed by emergency responders. All were all taken to Bellevue Hospital where, amazingly, they only required treatment for minor injuries.

If McGrath was hurt in any way, it did not stop him from getting up to his usual activities. On February 18, 1929, he was arrested after a pistol was found outside of a bar where he, and a large group of men, had been standing. McGrath, who gave his address as 45-01 40th Road, Corona, Queens, was released on February 21, 1929, after the weapon could not be tied to him.

For the next few months, McGrath and Tanzella continued their occasional work for Joey Rao, but according to police files, the two began to commit robberies in an effort to fund their increasingly extravagant lifestyles. During the 1920s to the 1940s, and long before the days of electronic banking, bags of money would routinely be delivered by courier to employers, who, upon receipt of the transport, would pay their employees with cash on payday. It made for a lucrative score for robbers but was regarded as a risky crime, as payroll companies often employed security guards, or off-duty policemen, to trail the deliveries. These men were instructed to shoot first and ask questions later.

According to police, on August 2, 1929, McGrath and Tanzella held up John J. O'Connell, a messenger for the Manufacturers' Trust Company. The armed O'Connell was in his automobile, and about to turn east on 37th Street, when another car pulled out from the curb in front of him and came to an abrupt stop. McGrath and Tanzella jumped out with pistols drawn. One rushed to the passenger side window and the other to the driver's side. With guns pointed at the car, the two screamed at O'Connell to turn over the payroll delivery and his pistol. The frightened O'Connell complied. McGrath and Tanzella then ordered O'Connell to get out of his car and to walk up 1st Avenue, or as one of the thieves phrased it to him, "Start walking or get plugged." The bag that O'Connell was carrying contained $5,664.50, or about $70,000 in today's currency, and was the weekly payroll for five different companies in the area. A police informer later pointed detectives in the direction of McGrath and Tanzella, and the two were arrested on August 27, 1929. Under questioning, McGrath admitted to working as a bootlegger but denied any knowledge of the robbery. O'Connell was unable to positively identify McGrath or Tanzella, and the two were discharged on the same day.

After the success of their last robbery, it did not take long for the gangsters to try again. Just nine days later, on September 7, 1929, McGrath and Tanzella joined a pair of experienced robbers to pull off another payroll heist. One of McGrath and Tanzella's new accomplices was John "Pinochle" Raffo, an ex-con with prior convictions for robbery. The previous year, Raffo had been one of six men caught with $32,000 worth of stolen aspirin. Rounding out the group was Raffo's partner at the time, Edward Gaffney, another well-known West Side hijacker.

The group targeted a payroll delivery that was scheduled to be made to the offices of the W.S. Gahagan Shipbuilding Company in Jamaica Bay, Queens. Arriving in a stolen car, the four stick-up men, who were wearing handkerchiefs over their faces, entered the building at 11:30 AM. At gun point, they subdued four clerks who were working in the office. The group then patiently waited inside for the payroll delivery to arrive.

The deliveryman, Hamilton Crowe, and a driver pulled to the curb in front of the building about fifteen minutes later. Three men approached the car and drew revolvers. The driver of the car was ordered out of the automobile and was tied up. Two robbers reached into the open car window and demanded the payroll from Crowe. Crowe feigned ignorance and pleaded that they must be mistaken about the payroll delivery. The bandits flung the car door open and began to savagely beat Crowe with the butts of their guns while repeating their demands for money. Crowe could do nothing to stop the onslaught and huddled down in the front seat of the car in a futile attempt to block the vicious blows. While two of the robbers were beating Crowe, the third climbed into the car and located the payroll. After finding the package, the robbers fled the area in a getaway car. Crowe was rushed to Rockaway Beach Hospital and was diagnosed with a fractured skull, a fractured right arm, and multiple internal injuries.

McGrath and Tanzella's next arrest was not directly linked to the W.S. Gahagan Shipbuilding Company robbery, but their successful score likely contributed to it. Following the Friday payroll robbery, the two were in a celebratory mood and decided to join a weekend-long party. Attended by other low to mid-level Irish and Italian bootleggers, the gathering was held at an apartment at 559 1st Avenue.

At some point during the festivities, an argument broke out, and two partygoers, Robert Burns and John Lyons, were shot by a single gunman who then ran from the party. Burns was hit in the left side of the chest, and Lyons, who was not the target of the shooting, was struck in the right arm. When Burns arrived at Bellevue Hospital, he told emergency room doctors that he had been walking to his truck on 1st Avenue when he heard a shot and felt immediate pain. Thirty minutes later, Lyons pulled up in a taxi and told a very similar story. Sticking to the gangster code of silence, both told police that they had seen nothing and that they did not know who shot them.

The following day, McGrath and Tanzella piled into McGrath's new car and drove to Bellevue Hospital to see how their friends were recovering following the shooting. With McGrath at the wheel, they pulled into the front parking lot of the hospital. A local patrolman, who had been made aware of the previous night's events, attempted to flag the suspicious car down. In response, the car made an aggressive U-turn and drove straight toward the front gates of the hospital. The patrolman ran into the car's oncoming path and yelled for McGrath to stop. At the last second, the patrolman dodged out of the way of the speeding car as it squealed past him into the street.

An APB was put out on the vehicle, and it was found, with its occupants still inside, a short time later. McGrath was charged with felony assault with an auto. He argued to police that he did not know about any party, that he took a wrong turn into the hospital, and that he did not see a police officer when he left. McGrath and Tanzella were held for further questioning about the shootings, but were released on September 16, 1929.

Along with Gaffney and Raffo, McGrath and Tanzella were back performing robberies within days of their release. On October 4, 1929, an automobile aggressively came to a stop in front of a trolley that was being navigated along Vernon Avenue in Long Island City. Three well-dressed young men hopped out of the car, while one remained behind the wheel. The driver of the trolley assumed that the men were making a rude attempt to catch the trolley, and he begrudgingly opened the doors for them. The robbers entered the trolley car with guns above their heads and yelled for everyone to lie on the floor. The gunmen then turned their attention to three passengers who were delivering a payroll. A robber struck the delivery man with the butt of his gun, while the other yanked the satchel of money from his hand. They then fled the streetcar. The final take from the job totaled $7,200. A tentative description of the robbers was provided by witnesses and would again lead back to the usual suspects—McGrath, Tanzella, Raffo, and Gaffney.

On November 24, 1929, the four were arrested and taken to Queens to be paraded in a lineup before witnesses from the W.S. Gahagan Shipbuilding Company. Later in the day, they were transferred to Long Island City, where they were put in another lineup in front of the trolley car riders. The group was then arraigned on charges of assault and robbery as a result of possible positive witness identifications. Each man denied the charge.

It must have been the luck of the Irish, as somehow the police were again unable to lay a formal complaint against McGrath. On December 9, 1929, McGrath, Tanzella, Gaffney, and Raffo appeared at the courthouse in Long Island City and were released after a judge decided that the identification statements taken by witnesses were not strong enough to hold up in court.

Although McGrath had been racking up numerous

arrests for robbery, he still continued to work as a bootlegger. McGrath had recently been working with an older gunman named Andrew "Squint" Sheridan, who had fallen under the umbrella of the Schultz and Rao gangs after being released from one of his many penitentiary stays. Sheridan was a tall, somewhat soft and frumpy looking man, with light brown hair, pale skin, and watery blue eyes, which were tucked away behind a pair of thick eyeglasses.

Sheridan had begun to lease his services to the Dutch Schultz Mob, and he also dealt with Joey Rao through many of the mutual connections that the two gang leaders shared. Whereas McGrath was valued for his people skills, Sheridan was only known for one thing—his ability and willingness to use a gun. McGrath, who had an uncanny ability to surround himself with the right people, recognized the need for a loyal and dangerous friend like Sheridan.

While McGrath did not have the textbook gangster upbringing, Sheridan was a criminologist's dream. If the bad seed theory applied to anyone—it was him. Born in New York City on May 8, 1900, Sheridan was one of eight children. His mother died when he was five years old, and his Irish immigrant father, Andrew Sr., was unable to care for his large brood. Andrew Sr. placed a handful of his children into the care of the Catholic Church, and young Sheridan was moved into St. Dominican Home, where he would reside from the ages of five to ten. The home housed some of the roughest orphans in the city, and sometime during his stay, another child threw a chemical substance into Sheridan's right eye. He was left with a permanent impairment to his sight, and he would forever have to wear thick glasses, which earned him the nickname Squint. Sheridan was incredibly bitter about his eyesight, and as the years progressed, his vision grew worse and his glasses grew thicker. Due to his terrible vision, he was unable to successfully perform the few labor jobs that he would have been qualified for, and as a result, he was regularly fired from various positions.

At ten years old, Sheridan was taken out of St. Dominican by his father, and his family was briefly reunited under the roof of Sheridan's paternal aunt at 57th Street and 1st Avenue. However, the damage had been done during Sheridan's five years away from the home, and the move back with his father proved difficult. It did not help that Andrew Sr., who was a hardworking man and a stern disciplinarian, did not know how to handle his unruly son. Sheridan had learned to hate authority and came to resent the beatings his father administered. At the age of twelve, Sheridan swiped and pawned his father's watch. Andrew Sr. then dragged his son to Children's Court on September 24, 1912 and had him brought up as a delinquent.

Sheridan was committed to the Catholic Protectory, which was more of a baby jail than a social service, for one year. After his release, he was shipped around to various relatives, but he was never able to adjust. He had only obtained sporadic schooling while at St. Dominican's Home and later dropped out of the sixth grade while attending St. John's Parochial School.

As Sheridan continued to grow older, his criminal record grew with him. On March 13, 1917, he was convicted of petty larceny and placed on probation. On April 21, 1917, he was sentenced to the House of Refuge, again for petty larceny. He was paroled on January 8, 1919, and, within a year, he was again convicted, this time for violation of the Sullivan Law after being caught possessing a pistol. Paroled on December 14, 1920, he was arrested three days later for holding up a clothing store. Sheridan was convicted of robbery and sentenced to seven-and-a-half to fifteen years in prison.

Prison psychiatrists, whose reports now seem comically unreliable when compared to modern science, found Sheridan would have been a dull and hardworking man had he not suffered constant embarrassment due to his eye injury. His mental age tested at twelve-and-a-half, which was likely a result of his lack of education, rather than his actual intelligence. Other words in Sheridan's report included average, simple intelligence, psychopathic personality, egocentric, and unstable. The prison psychiatrists were also troubled that Sheridan had a slight tic of the right eyelid, preferred to lean forward in an aggressive way when conversing, and possessed somewhat of a sickly smile.

Sheridan was paroled on July 26, 1926, but was arrested on December 19, 1927 for carrying a concealed weapon in the commission of a crime. The offense was discharged on the recommendation of the assistant district attorney prosecuting the case, but Sheridan was returned to prison for violation of parole. He was re-paroled on December 19, 1929. Within days of his release, Sheridan was on the streets and finding work in the employ of bootleggers like Schultz, who hired him based on the recommendation of Patrick Carroll, Sheridan's criminal brother-in-law.

Many people viewed Sheridan as dim-witted, but in reality, he was loyal to a fault. Having never experienced stability during his upbringing, Sheridan was steadfast to those he liked. McGrath did not share the same closeness with Sheridan that he did with someone like Tanzella, but he recognized the older gunman's usefulness. McGrath and Sheridan worked together throughout late December of 1929 and January of 1930. Later, McGrath was once overheard by police bragging that in December of 1929 he and Sheridan had been responsible for a delivery of Schultz's New Year's booze that was worth over $200,000.

Times were good for McGrath and his friends. The Great Depression had dampened the spirits of most Americans, but for McGrath, the Depression did little to diminish his business.

4

1930: The Gangster's Great Depression

IN LATE JANUARY of 1930, McGrath and Tanzella learned of a potential payroll job through a mutual friend named George Achinelli, an ex-convict with repute as a burglar and counterfeiter. The trio had been planning the job, but unbeknownst to McGrath, Achinelli had come to the attention of the police due to a series of loft robberies that he had been committing. In December of 1929, the police obtained a warrant for Achinelli's arrest on the charge of parole violation, but he had successfully evaded capture.

Detective Daniel Mahoney, a no-nonsense officer with the Safe and Loft Squad, and his partner, Detective James Kane, had been hot on Achinelli's trail for months when they received a tip on February 4, 1930, that Achinelli would be at his mother-in-law's house the following day. Detectives Mahoney, Kane, and a third named Detective Tannahey, began a stakeout in front of the home, at 120-30 Lincoln Avenue, South Ozone Park, Queens. Just before dark, the cops saw Achinelli emerge from the front door with Eddie McGrath in tow. The pair walked onto Rockaway Boulevard with the three detectives shadowing closely behind them. Mahoney walked up and grabbed at Achinelli, who managed to wiggle free and sprint down the street. McGrath dashed off in the opposite direction.

With Detectives Kane and Mahoney in pursuit, Achinelli disappeared around the corner of a building, froze abruptly, and hid against the corner of the wall. When Detective Kane ran past, Achinelli stuck out his foot and sent him flying headlong to the pavement. Detective Mahoney saw his partner lying prone on the ground, spun toward Achinelli, and fired one shot from his service revolver. The bullet traveled upwards through Achinelli's neck and into the base of his skull, killing him instantly. Mahoney would later say that he saw Achinelli reach for a gun, but no weapons were located on the dead man.

Further down the boulevard, McGrath had stopped running and surrendered to Detective Tannahey after hearing gunshots echoing from the other end of the street. McGrath denied any knowledge of planning a payroll robbery and told police that he had only met Achinelli that day. Police surprised McGrath by booking him on charges of felonious assault in connection with the robbery of a taxicab in Richmond Hill, Queens, ten days prior. The taxicab driver, Raymond Hoffman, had been held up and shot by a drunken man and a girl after the bars closed. McGrath fit a loose description of the assailant, but the charge was likely only a police ploy to keep McGrath in custody longer, as there was no basis on which to charge him in relation to the Achinelli incident.

Detective Dan Mahoney marched McGrath to the Queens Courthouse on February 7, 1930. McGrath's jaw must have dropped, as presiding over the court that day was none other than Judge Adel, the same man who had handed McGrath a suspended sentence on his first burglary charge back in 1927. Judge Adel examined McGrath's record and noticed that he had accumulated an additional six arrests since his first brush with the law. Judge Adel looked up from the bench and remarked, "When I suspended sentence on you, I told you to associate with decent citizens. Instead of following my advice, you have mixed with ex-convicts and other undesirables, and now I must send you away." With the swing of a gavel, McGrath's original five-year suspended sentence for burglary was reinstated. For the first time in his burgeoning criminal career, he would be off of the streets and doing hard time.

It wasn't much better during the early 1930s for the rest of McGrath's close friends. Three months after McGrath was arrested, Andrew Sheridan was sent back to his usual place behind bars. Sheridan had been sitting in a car with his brother-in-law, Patrick Carroll, when a probationary NYPD patrolman noticed them. The junior officer thought that the suspicious looking men may have been scouting out a potential robbery and approached the car. When he ordered them to step out of the vehicle, Sheridan, who was sitting in the back seat, reached for something under his coat. The officer opened fire without hesitation. A bullet passed straight through Sheridan's right shoulder, whizzed out of the car, and struck a nearby bystander who was only slightly injured. With a smoking gun trained on them, they quietly surrendered.

A fully loaded revolver, which happened to have the serial number filed off, was found in the injured Sheridan's coat; another gun was found on Patrick Carroll, and their car turned out to be stolen. The gangsters later conceded to police that they were waiting to ambush a rival bootlegger who had taken a load of beer from their employer—whom they would not name. Sheridan pled guilty to carrying a concealed weapon in the commission of a crime and was sentenced to seven years in state prison.

Nicholas Tanzella did not fare any better. From 1930 to 1932 he would rack up another three arrests for assault, assault and robbery, and again assault and robbery. On July 15, 1933, he was arrested under the alias of Michael Donardo while attempting to extort Jacob Wachsman, a prominent Brooklyn physician, along with fellow gangster Vincent Macri, who in the 1940s would become a top henchman of the Gambino crime family boss, Albert Anastasia. Tanzella and Macri had approached the doctor and threatened to kidnap him unless a $20,000 payment was delivered. Dr. Wachsman alerted the authorities, who planned an elaborate sting operation to trap the would-be extortionists. When Tanzella and Macri came to collect the ransom, they were given two fake packages and arrested.

While facing the extortion rap, Tanzella was also booked on a homicide charge as a result of the shooting of a watchman in 1932, after a bar fight. The district attorney's office eventually dropped the murder charge, but Tanzella had been caught red-handed on the extortion offense. Like his best friend McGrath, he also received a five-year sentence in prison.

New Friends

SING SING CORRECTIONAL Facility is New York State's most notorious prison. Located about thirty miles from New York City, it sits on the eastern bank of the Hudson River in the town of Ossining. The prison itself was built on top of bisecting railway lines, which connected the two main areas of the sprawling complex and, at the time of McGrath's arrival, the giant structure was the home of nearly three thousand of New York's worst criminals.

On February 10, 1930, McGrath was received at Sing Sing and assigned Prisoner Number 82750. He had only spent six days in the Queen's County Jail and would not be eligible for parole for at least the next four years. McGrath's reception documents from Sing Sing, which are the only surviving records from his incarceration, were similar to many of the other young men received by the prison. McGrath stated that his occupation was a laborer or clerk, and he was unable to provide any recent employment history. McGrath told the reception officer that he attended church occasionally, drank moderately, supported no one else financially, and was currently single. McGrath listed his only relation as his oldest sister, Mary.

McGrath enjoyed playing handball, and he fell in with a group of criminals from the West Side of New York City who had claimed one of the prison's courts. One of the West Side handballers, Dominick Genova, later identified to law enforcement that in February of 1931, McGrath met a new West Side inmate named John "Red" McCrossin. McCrossin was born on December 2, 1907, had a skinny build, fiery red hair and, before being sentenced to Sing Sing, had lived on West 20th Street in Manhattan. As a persistent offender and a natural thief, McCrossin often racked up arrests for assorted robbery offenses.

The crime that led to Red McCrossin being shipped up north occurred on December 27, 1930. McCrossin had waited in the lobby of the Graybar Building on Lexington Avenue and snatched a payroll parcel containing $401 from a manager of the Electro Sun Company. The manager alerted two nearby police officers who gave chase through a packed midday crowd while firing their service revolvers in the air. McCrossin did not stop, but the shots distracted him enough that he smashed right into the waiting arms of a third policeman, who had been coming the other way down the street. The botched robbery earned McCrossin a sentence of three and a half years, and he was scheduled to be released within months of McGrath's own discharge date. In April of 1932, with their sentences halfway completed, McGrath and McCrossin would meet another career criminal that would complete their budding gang.

John M. Dunn, known as Johnny Dunn to his friends, or the unsavory nickname "Cockeye" to his detractors, arrived in Sing Sing after also being convicted of robbery. Born in Queens on August 24, 1910, to a pair of poor Irish immigrants, Dunn's unaffectionate moniker, Cockeye, was due to a lazy left eye that had been present since his birth. Dunn's father worked on shipping boats that operated in the Atlantic Ocean but was lost at sea when Dunn was only four years old. The family moved to the West Side of Manhattan where his mother remarried a laborer named Thomas Cassidy, but Cassidy was also killed a short time later after a railway accident at work.

Dunn's twice-widowed mother now had four children

to support. She found work as an usher at Madison Square Garden, but Dunn and his younger brother Peter took to the streets to help fund the family's needs. Dunn's first arrest occurred in 1925, after he was caught shoplifting $.29 and a box of crackers from a store, and he was put on probation as a juvenile delinquent. The following year, Dunn was caught robbing a hardware store. On July 1, 1926, he was sent to the Catholic Protectory, where he served the better part of a year. On November 18, 1929, Dunn pleaded guilty to burglary after pilfering merchandise valued at $625 from a grocery store. That conviction earned him a sentence of two years in the New York City Reformatory. Dunn was paroled in late 1931 and went back to what he knew best — robbery.

Only standing 5'6", and weighing about one hundred and forty pounds, Dunn made up for his size with a tough attitude. He began to commit armed robberies around the West Side of Manhattan until April 15, 1932, when he and two other accomplices were arrested after attempting to stick-up a neighborhood card game. The three would-be robbers had made off with $9 from the players' pockets when they were arrested by a patrolman just outside of the building. Dunn was sentenced to a year and a half in Sing Sing.

Dunn's arrival at the prison reunited him with his neighborhood's more nefarious crowd who congregated on the West Side handball courts; this is where he first met McGrath. The two became inseparable. Both McGrath and Dunn had lost their fathers at a young age, were experienced hold-up men, and, most importantly, they shared an ambition to move up in the criminal underworld when they were released. The trio of McGrath, McCrossin, and Dunn spent their free time at Sing Sing lazing around, playing handball, and brainstorming criminal ideas. Meanwhile, outside of the prison, the underworld that the men planned to return to had gone through momentous changes since their convictions.

The Italian mobs in the city continued to grow. Following a war between two of the largest groups in the early 1930s, younger gangsters such as Charles "Lucky" Luciano, his partner Meyer Lansky, Benjamin "Bugsy" Siegel, Frank Costello, Vito Genovese, Albert Anastasia, and Joe Adonis had risen to prominence. The Italian gangsters were structured into five crime families, and at the time of McGrath's release, the leaders were Lucky Luciano (whose family became the modern day Genovese Family), Joe Profaci (the modern Colombo Family), Tommaso Gagliano (the modern Lucchese Family), Vincent Mangano (the modern Gambino Family), and Joseph Bonanno (the modern Bonanno Family).

Part of this emerging group of Mafia leaders included McGrath's old friend Jimmy Alo, who was now part of Luciano's crime family. In the late 1920s, Luciano had entrusted Alo to look after his key moneymaker, Meyer Lansky, and Alo and Lansky had become extremely close friends. Also a lieutenant in Luciano's family was McGrath's old bootlegging boss, Joey Rao.

The biggest change that occurred in the outside world, during McGrath's period of incarceration, was that Prohibition in the United States had been repealed. Gangsters had been cashing in on the sale and distribution of illegal alcohol for the last decade, and until 1933 it had remained the biggest money-making racket. On March 22, 1933, President Franklin Roosevelt signed an amendment to the Volstead Act known as the Cullen-Harrison Act, which made legal the manufacture and sale of 4% alcohol beer and light wines. After passing the amendment, Roosevelt uttered the famous remark, "I think this would be a good time for a beer."

Gangsters everywhere scrambled to reinvest their bootlegging funds into new rackets. Most focused on holding onto traditional illegal enterprises like gambling and loansharking, while others tried to get in on the ground level of legal alcohol production. A few even had the sense to retire with their riches. McGrath, Dunn, and McCrossin accepted that after they were freed they would be re-entering a competitive criminal landscape that consisted of out-of-work hoodlums scrambling for every buck that they could get their hands on.

The three decided that they would focus their criminal efforts on West Manhattan's profitable North River docks, in Greenwich Village and Chelsea, where Dunn and McCrossin resided. By the 1930s, the waterfront in New York City was the most vital shipping hub on the Eastern seaboard and serviced New York City's population of nearly seven million, who relied on the bustling waterfront industry to move both product and people. Stretching along the Hudson River from West Greenwich (between Houston and 14th Street), to Chelsea (14th Street to 34th Street), to Hell's Kitchen (34th Street to 42nd Street), and all the way to the Upper West Side (59th Street to 110th Street), the North River piers numbered nearly one hundred individual docks.

The Port of New York City was crucial to ensuring that business in the city ran smoothly. With over $900 million in facilities (or nearly $12 billion dollars today), the city had the world's largest and busiest port with annual revenues of over $146 million dollars (or nearly 2 billion today). Out of the more than seven hundred miles of New York City waterfront, over three hundred had been developed into piers. The port had roughly nine hundred piers operating in Manhattan, Brooklyn, and Staten Island; over one hundred ferry landings and tens of thousands of associated businesses, shipbuilding plants, and warehouses. Twelve major railroads connected to the waterfront, trucks constantly moved on and off the piers daily, and a quarter of Manhattan's food was brought in by boat.

Another distinctive factor that historically elevated the importance of the waterfront industry in New York City is that the most populous borough, Manhattan, is an island. As both the economic and cultural center of the United States, the tiny, thirty-four square mile landmass depended on the surrounding piers. Thousands of dollars' worth of valuable cargo passed through the West Side waterfront daily, and some of this cargo was bound to go missing, which is where experienced thieves like McGrath, Dunn, and McCrossin came in. Although never confirmed, it was believed that in the late 1930s, over $50 million dollars of cargo was "lost" annually, much of it due to theft. Since the New York City piers were so lucrative, most of the shipping companies chalked up the huge losses to the cost of doing business, and criminals were often free to steal with relative impunity.

The rough waterfront neighborhoods on the West Side, more often than not, consisted of tenement homes and seedy bars. The nearby docks had long attracted the criminal element, since claiming the territory around a particular shipping pier meant that a gangster would have guaranteed income, whether it meant loaning money at exorbitant interest rates to longshoremen, running gambling games, theft, or extorting local dock workers.

The other incentive for McGrath and company to focus on the West Side docks was the fact that it was one of the few places left in Manhattan that was not a stronghold for the increasingly growing Mafia. The ethnic makeup on the West Side was still predominantly Irish, and while many boroughs had begun to change by the 1930s, the Irish still maintained a majority in the neighborhoods of West Greenwich Village, Chelsea, and Hell's Kitchen. Droves of unskilled Irish laborers, who had arrived in New York City at the turn of the century, headed to the West Side to find work on the docks. Over time, many of these new immigrants permanently settled into the rows of tenements that lined the North River. Irish immigrants that followed chose to plant roots in the West Side communities, as these neighborhoods had now formed into enclaves that housed familiar traditions, religious institutions, food, and family and friends from their homeland.

Once residing on the West Side, families rarely left. The low wages and casual longshoreman's work did not provide enough financial stability for the, often stereotypically large, Irish Catholic families to move out of their cramped water-front dwellings. By the 1920s and 1930s, the bulk of the West Side of Manhattan was inhabited by second generation Irish-Americans who had grown up in poverty. The shared immi-grant experience created extremely tight-knit communities, which impeded the encroachment of other ethnic organized crime groups.

The fact that the West Side neighborhoods were so wary of outsiders was a benefit to any local criminal who was looking to take over a homegrown racket. Unlike the Italian Mafia, who had learned to work as a cooperative unit, the neighborhood-by-neighborhood nature of the Irish-Americans meant that organized crime was decentralized. The Greenwich area docks might, at any given time, be controlled by three to four different small groups, while the Chelsea area may have had another two to three different gangs in control of that region's docks. This fluid criminal activity usually guaranteed instability and regular violence. This was the dangerous and volatile environment that McGrath would be entering upon his release from prison.

6

The Gang's All Here

MCGRATH WAS RELEASED on parole in September of 1933 on the condition that he would reside at the home of his sister, Anna Connors, who was newly married and already had three young children. Anna welcomed McGrath into her home in Queens, but he often spent more time staying with friends in Manhattan.

McGrath, Dunn, and McCrossin had decided that upon their releases, they would do what they did best to raise money to fund their future criminal ventures—commit robberies. After building up a nest egg, they planned to identify a valuable pier, run by a weaker group of criminals, and move in by force.

The criminal scene on the West Side was noticeably different than anything McGrath had experienced before. At the time of his release from Sing Sing, there was no boss of the West Side like Joey Rao had been to McGrath in East Harlem, but instead, there were small gangs who, at the drop of a hat, could turn from partners to enemies. Through Dunn's friendship with a strong-arm man and hijacker named John "Peck" Hughes, whom he had known since his formative years, the three parolees began to operate in the sphere of a mob of robbers, turned burgeoning racketeers, who operated up and down the West Side.

The gang had no name, but was occasionally referred to by law enforcement as "The West Side Gang" and was one of the larger collections of criminals in the area. Organized into two groups, which were loosely allied with each other, some were led by a charismatic younger gangster named Joseph "Big Joe" Butler and his veteran confidant Robert "Farmer" Sullivan, while the others worked under a former New Jersey-based robber named Charlie "The Jew" Yanowsky.

The Butler and Yanowsky groups first aligned at the tail end of Prohibition, and most of the members were natives of the West Side who had crossed paths for years. Under the leadership of Butler and Yanowsky, it was decided that it would be easier for their respective associates to work together rather than to fight it out. The West Side Gang had no hierarchy, outside of recognized senior members, and the gangsters did not have to answer to each other in any way. Instead, the members of the two groups routinely came together to participate in scores, share potential robbery tips, and help fund one another's illegal escapades. Like McGrath, Dunn, and McCrossin, most of the group were robbers by trade, but a few had already begun to snatch up waterfront territory.

Peck Hughes, the man who made the initial introductions for McGrath, Dunn, and McCrossin, earned his nickname due to his bird-like facial features, which included a beaked nose and a slightly lazy eye. Although not an intimidating physical presence, Hughes had a long rap sheet, including once being charged with murder. The same age as the rest of the group, Hughes mainly preyed on the trucks and warehouses around the Chelsea and West Greenwich piers. While McGrath, Dunn, and McCrossin had been incarcerated, Hughes had been operating as a member of The West Side Gang and had become pals with three notorious brothers who were also members of the group.

The Bell brothers, James "Ding-Dong" Bell, born in 1908; Henry F. "Buster" Bell, born in 1910; and Leslie "Lester" Bell, born in 1914, were raised with three other siblings in an apartment on West 18th Street. As the oldest, Ding-Dong

Bell had helped solidify the family's troublesome reputation in Greenwich Village. Along with his thirteen arrests for various offences, he had served time in the workhouse and the city jail for his crimes, which included striking two pedestrians with his car during a drunken Christmas Eve joyride. Like most West Side criminals, Bell was in the business of robbery, but his career was almost cut short on June 7, 1928, when he was shot twice during a late-night quarrel.

That night, Ding-Dong Bell was witnessed standing in front of the Abingdon Square Hotel in Greenwich, wearing a bath robe, and arguing loudly with two men. The disagreement grew more heated, and one of the men drew a pistol from his pocket and shot Ding-Dong in the face and neck. Bell was taken to the hospital, where a priest was fetched to administer last rites. Police arrived and questioned Bell, as doctors stated he would not live through the night, but Bell pressed his lips together and shook his head when asked to provide the name of the men who shot him. Ding-Dong Bell lingered for the next few days, and then suddenly took a turn for the better, although he still wore the bullet scar on his face.

Henry "Buster" Bell was viewed as the least reckless and the smartest of the Bell brothers. Despite being related to Ding-Dong, he had avoided being both shot and arrested. The third brother, Leslie, was a loose cannon who generally remained on the outskirts of The West Side Gang due to his unruliness. The Bell brothers dabbled in everything they could get their hands on, from gambling to robbery, and loansharking to extortion. Both Ding-Dong and Buster Bell were a well-known presence on the Greenwich Village docks, and they established ties with an up-and-coming union official named George "Georgie" Daggett, who was also part of The West Side Gang.

The blond haired Daggett was a throwback to longshoremen of the past. Born into a large family of legitimate dock workers, he was more likely to be found in a Greenwich Village saloon nearest to the docks than in a union office. Daggett was a talented former southpaw boxer who fought as a lightweight from 1927-1931, and before he quit the fight game, he was one of the top New York prospects in his weight class. Extremely popular among the locals, Daggett's toughness and fighting ability had helped him become a Business Agent of the International Longshoreman's Association Local 1258. According to law enforcement, Daggett was tied to the criminal element on the West Side docks and used his position of influence to help other criminals gain access to the valuable piers.

Peck Hughes, the Bell brothers, and George Daggett were all connected to the Butler faction within The West Side Gang. Their leader, Joseph "Big Joe" Butler, was relatively young but possessed both the charisma and birthright that made had him one of the unofficial bosses of the mob. Butler was born in 1908 and was the son of former local Alderman, and famous dock organizer, Richard "Big Dick" Butler. Big Dick was a nefarious character on the West Side of New York, who had been heavily involved in the early unionizing days on the docks during the turn of the century. So famous were his pugilistic ways that Butler Sr. was immortalized in a 1933 biography titled *Dock Walloper: The Story of Big Dick Butler.* Regarded as one of the toughest men on the waterfront, he was a prominent member of the International Longshoremen's Association (ILA) until being booted from the union in 1919, after becoming a leader of an insurgent faction that caused a strike for several weeks.

The Butler family was a tight-knit clan of ten children, who resided in an apartment on the Upper West Side. Like their father, the Butler boys grew up learning the ins and outs of the docks and terrorizing the neighborhood. Joe's older brother, Willie, was a former member of the Gopher's Gang with Owney Madden, and he had been pegged by local police as the family member most likely to end up in the electric chair. Joe and Willie were partners in crime until 1925 when Willie flipped his car on a country road in Newburgh, New York, and was killed. Big Dick would later describe Willie as " . . a good lad, only a little wild."

Joe Butler was no stranger to trouble himself, as he had already been arrested ten times before 1930. Butler's most publicized run-in with the law occurred in September of 1927, when he and three other bandits attempted to steal $11,000 during a payroll robbery in Brooklyn. On the day of the robbery, Butler's group opened fire on a policeman who was trailing the cash delivery, but a group of off-duty cops heard the shooting and joined the fray. One robber was shot in the leg, and the driver of the getaway car crashed into a nearby pole. As he tried to flee, Butler was cornered in a doorway by one of the policemen. Butler allegedly raised his pistol and pulled the trigger, but the gun jammed. In February of that year, Butler pled guilty to the reduced charge of attempted grand larceny and was packed off to the city prison for two years.

Butler's longtime partner was Robert J. "Farmer" Sullivan, a veteran gangster and one of the most feared men in Greenwich Village. Born in 1896, Sullivan had a permanent smile on his face from a moon-shaped scar that ran from his lip to his upper cheek and a rap sheet that stretched back to the years when he was a crony of Joe Butler's father. Nicknamed Farmer, as he had been brought up in the old part of Greenwich Village, near the old Wouter VanTwiller tobacco farm, Sullivan was a former professional boxer who was renowned for his toe-to-toe fighting style and the unsanctioned smash-ups he participated in on the streets. Sullivan viewed himself as a statesman to the people of Greenwich and could be counted on to settle disputes, or enforce unofficial community laws, with his fists. With established political ties to both the local Democrats and Republicans, Sullivan did good business "persuading" uncertain voters on election days for a fee.

In 1931, Sullivan was convicted of the murder of Paul Zimmer, after the robbery of a local bar went wrong. When a policeman arrived on the scene, a dying Zimmer identified Sullivan as the man who shot him. The following year, Sullivan miraculously had the conviction reversed by the Court of Appeals, which further added to the rumors of his political connections. Sullivan's headquarters was The Farmer Sullivan Bar and Grill on 8th Avenue, where it was long believed that one of Sullivan's ex-friends, "Happy" Ahrens, was shot and buried in the basement. Police dug up the floors, but Happy's remains were never found.

Butler's main enforcer in The West Side Gang was another veteran criminal named Matthew "Mattie" Kane, a man who had spent more time in prison during his life than he had out of it. This was especially strange considering Kane was the son of a police officer and a registered nurse. He obviously didn't follow in his parents' footsteps, and as a teen, he was sent to the Elmira Reformatory. The day he was released from Elmira, he enlisted to fight in World War One and Kane rose to the rank of Corporal with the Motor Transportation Corps, seeing active duty throughout Europe. The Army did little to straighten him out, as, within a year of his discharge, he was convicted of robbing a cigar store at gunpoint and was hit with a sentence of seventeen years in prison.

Mattie Kane had first met McGrath, Dunn, and McCrossin while serving time in Sing Sing, and he also joined up with the gang after his release in March of 1934, despite the fact that he was still on parole for nearly another decade.

Rounding out the Butler-Sullivan group were the following:

Arthur and James Gaynor: Growing up alongside the Butler boys, the Gaynors were part of a large Hell's Kitchen brood. Arthur, known as "Scarface," was first arrested for murder in 1921, after shooting a man during an argument. He was not convicted, and the following year he and his brother James were arrested together after they, and four other men, decided it would be a good idea to shoot their revolvers out of the window of a taxi cab as it drove down Broadway. In 1924, James was also arrested for a murder, but ultimately acquitted, after allegedly shooting a man in the head during a failed robbery and then engaging police in a running gun battle. In 1933, Arthur would be arrested for yet another murder, but again discharged, in relation to a machine gun shooting in a saloon during a fight for the control of a pier in Chelsea.

Leo Tocci alias Massi: Tocci was a nomadic gangster who worked with the Butler Gang, but also had many of his own illegal ventures. Operating in both New York City and Pennsylvania, the boisterous lady's man and compulsive gambler was tied to bootlegging syndicates in both states. After escaping from the New York City Reformatory in 1925, Tocci fled back to Pennsylvania where he was later arrested and served time in Pittsburgh. After serving his sentence, Tocci was arrested in New York City in 1933, along with Joe Butler, while attempting to rob a silk warehouse, after which he again fled to Pennsylvania. Finally, in 1934, Tocci decided to permanently plant roots in The Big Apple after being named as a suspect in a triple gangland slaying in Old Forge.

James "Jimmy" Skinner: Skinner was a friend of Mattie Kane's from Long Island City, Queens. He had no major convictions but had worked as a bootlegger in Upstate New York at the tail-end of Prohibition.

Victor "Vic" Patterson: Patterson, who was originally from Brooklyn, became acquainted with members of the gang while

serving a sentence of twelve years in Sing Sing for burglary.
Underworld trickery won Patterson an early release after a
fellow convict from Brooklyn, named John Maxwell, signed
a sworn affidavit before being executed for an unrelated murder, which stated that he had committed the burglary and
not Patterson. Patterson and Maxwell looked similar and a
judge bought it.

Frank "Sonny" Campbell: Campbell was born in 1911, and
even as one of the youngest members of the Butler group, he
was one of the most active participants in their various robberies. Residing near Central Park, Campbell was a product of
the West Side and had been involved in the business of larceny
since his youth. Campbell was first arrested for theft in 1927 and
sentenced to an indeterminate term in the Elmira Reformatory.
After hooking up with Butler and his friends, Campbell continued to rack up arrests, including one bust with Joe Butler after
the two hoods were caught with a truckload of stolen liquor.

The other group within The West Side Gang was led by Charlie "The Jew" Yanowsky. A shrewd hoodlum, with an aptitude
for generating money, he was regarded as a cagey and ruthless
individual who could also be deeply loyal to those he liked.

Born in New York City on January 31, 1906, Yanowsky
was the son of a pair of Russian Jewish immigrants who
had arrived in the United States four years earlier. In 1908,
the family packed up their belongings and moved across the
Hudson River to Jersey City, New Jersey. The Yanowsky
family prospered in The Garden State, where their patriarch,
Max, opened up three successful furniture stores. The young
Yanowsky was a popular boy in the neighborhood and regularly
collected stray cats and dogs and provided them with food.
Yanowsky finished Grade 8 in Jersey City and planned to study
mechanical dentistry, but instead joined his father in the family

furniture business. By 1926, Yanowsky was starting to show his wild side. He began to distance himself from his family and instead preferred to hang out with young criminals, with whom he was arrested regularly for minor offences.

When The Great Depression hit, the Yanowsky family lost everything. Yanowsky's father struggled to re-establish himself, and on March 28, 1933, he died of a stroke, which the family believed was brought on by the stress of his failed businesses. Perhaps it was seeing his hard-working father die penniless that drove Yanowsky even further into criminality, as following his father's death he committed himself to a life of crime.

Yanowsky rose to prominence as one of the leaders of a Jersey City group known as "The Rope Ladder Gang." Consisting of around twenty individuals, the gang's modus operandi was using rope ladders to scale rail cars and steal from the train's containers. In mid-1933, the New Jersey authorities began cracking down on the gang, and after being hit with a suspended sentence for his Rope Ladder Gang crimes, Yanowsky moved across the river to the West Side of New York City. It was at this time that he began to meet members of The West Side Gang, and, with his moneymaking ability, it did not take long for others to gravitate to him.

On the West Side, Yanowsky ran a growing policy numbers business (an illegal lottery game) with his most powerful ally in his group, George Keeler. Born in 1900, and raised around West 19th Street, Keeler was a longtime figure on the docks. With an arrest record dating back to 1917, Keeler had been convicted in 1927 of the murder of a man named John Millen, but, within the year, Keeler's conviction was tossed out by the Court of Appeals.

After getting away with murder, Keeler's reputation on the West Side grew. Holding a legitimate job as a hiring foreman for a shipping line, he had his headquarters on Pier 59, where he ran one of the most successful loansharking operations on the docks. Keeler and his family had moved to a nice suburban home in the Flatbush section of Brooklyn, and he made the daily commute to Manhattan in an expensive and sporty coupe. The car, which doubled as a mobile loanshark office, could be found motoring up and down the West Side piers as Keeler made his collection rounds and charged hefty interest rates to longshoremen.

Keeler's bodyguard, and constant companion, was a burly young hood named Albert "Acky" Ackalitis. An imposing figure with a broken nose that slanted to the left, Ackalitis was born in 1908 in Philadelphia, Pennsylvania to a pair of Russian immigrants. Ackalitis' family moved to Greenwich Village when he was five years old, while his father remained behind in Pennsylvania to work as a coal miner, where he would later be killed in a workplace accident

In early 1933, Ackalitis began working for Keeler as a bodyguard, and in that year alone racked up seven arrests on charges including receiving stolen goods, possession of a pistol, assault, robbery, and burglary. At the time McGrath became a part of The West Side Gang, Ackalitis had been arrested for an attempted loft burglary and was serving a sentence of a year and a half in prison. Ackalitis would eventually be released on April 2, 1935.

Also part of Yanowsky's group were the following:

Joseph Kress: Born in 1901, Kress, real name Karasik, was a car thief and getaway driver. Originally from Brooklyn, his uncle owned a mechanics shop and Kress was handy with all sorts of automobiles. Arrested often, he had never been convicted of a crime or served a day in jail.

John "Fats" Manning and Bernard "Bennie the Bum" McMahon: An unlikely partnership, Manning and McMahon had joined forces at the end of Prohibition.

Manning, born in 1907, had blond hair, a slight build, and a baby-face. The nickname, "Fats," came from the fact that he was anything but fat. Manning, who was born in Ireland, wore glasses, shied away from nightclubs, talked softly, and could have easily been mistaken for a banker.

His polar opposite partner, McMahon, was born in 1893 and had been operating in criminal circles longer than Manning had been alive. Known as a petty thief, McMahon's claim to fame was that he had once been a part of the same juvenile gang as the famous mobster Jack "Legs" Diamond.

McMahon and Manning had both worked as low-level bootleggers, but once Prohibition ended, the out of work gangsters began to specialize in the hijacking of trucks around the West Side docks. While McMahon dreamed of finding fortune and blowing it in Manhattan's finest bars and seedy Broadway burlesque shows, Manning's ambition was to earn enough money to buy a hobby farm upstate.

John "Joe Portuguese" Silba: Joe Portuguese was a mysterious character, who, within The West Side Gang, was tied to both the Yanowsky and Butler groups. A Portuguese immigrant, his arrest record cannot be officially verified, as he had great success with using various aliases and addresses. Held under his real name, John Silba, in Newark for assault in 1926, Joe Portuguese's police blotter also shows arrests under the name of Manuel Martins, for assault in 1934, and John Rossel, for criminally receiving stolen goods in the same year.

Thomas "Tommy" Adobody and Michael "Mickey" Kane: Two of the younger members of the group, Adobody and Kane were responsible for assisting with Yanowsky's numbers racket.

Adobody, born in 1913, was one of the youngest members of the gang and had become a protégée of Yanowsky. The husky hoodlum in training had a bad temper and a scowl to match.

He had served time as a youth in the Elmira Reformatory, for robbery, and coincidently enough, his accomplice in that crime was Edward Budd, brother of Grace Budd, who, in 1928, was one of the young girls kidnapped and murdered by infamous New York serial killer Albert Fish.

Kane (no relation to Mattie Kane of the Butler group) was Adobody's close friend and partner in crime. Always a dapper dresser, he had only two arrests on his record: one suspended sentence for grand larceny in 1930 and another arrest for possession of a pistol.

By early 1934, McGrath, Dunn, and McCrossin had blended into the gang with ease and were actively taking part in a variety of both small and large scale dock pilfering. Together, The West Side Gang had become a collective of some of the most active hoodlums in the area, and their ascension to becoming one of the main criminal organizations operating around the North River was well underway.

Rubel

MCGRATH AND HIS friends continued to steal their way around the West Side throughout mid-1934, and it ushered in a period when The West Side Gang was participating in an unprecedented number of robberies and hijackings. The two sides, the Butler group and the Yanowksy group, remained friendly, but as their expansions began to overlap, they became cautious about what work they shared with each other.

One of McGrath's bigger scores occurred on June 14, 1934, when he, Dunn, McCrossin, and a fourth accomplice, who police believed was Peck Hughes, pulled off a daring heist of the Rubsam & Horrmann Brewery Company. The payroll deliveryman had just left the main offices of the building and a group of thirty workers waited anxiously in the courtyard for their weekly earnings. One of the robbers idled the car while the other three ran, unnoticed, up the stairs to the building's offices on the second floor. At gunpoint, the bandits filled a sack with $9,500, and then fled into the waiting automobile. The robbery netted a pretty penny, but members of the Yanowsky group would soon top them with their next crime.

On a sunny day in June 1934, Yanowsky gangsters, Fats Manning and Bennie McMahon, were relaxing in Coney Island when they had an epiphany: the two watched intently as an armored truck collected bags of money from the Brooklyn Trust Company bank at Surf Avenue and West 12th Street. The bank, which was situated only a block from the boardwalk, was popular with tourists and did a considerable amount of business, which was evident to Manning and McMahon as they sat in awe as guards moved bag after bag of cash.

Manning and McMahon turned to another West Side character who worked independently but was on such friendly terms with the Yanowsky Gang that many identified him as a member of the group. John "Archie" Stewart, born in 1900, specialized in robbery and only robbery and was a go-to figure on the West Side when extra hands were needed. With Stewart came his partner, Stewart "One Arm" Wallace. Wallace, who was fifty-one, had met Stewart in Sing Sing, and the two had pulled numerous jobs since their releases. Although unusual, Wallace's nickname was as straightforward as it sounded—he only had one hand as a result of an old amputation.

Manning, McMahon, Stewart, and Wallace went to case the bank. The veteran robber, Stewart, believed that at least two more men would be needed for the job and suggested two gangsters from upstate New York, who were currently wanted and on the lam. The recommended gunmen, John Oley and Percy Geary, had been hiding out on the West Side of New York City since orchestrating the kidnapping of John O'Connell Jr., the son of a politically powerful and wealthy family in Albany, for a ransom of $40,000. Geary and Oley requested that Oley's younger brother, Francis, who was also on the run due to the O'Connell kidnapping, be included as well. With more men participating, it was decided that another driver would be needed. Naturally, the favorite wheelman for the Yanowsky group, Joe Kress, was brought into the fold.

For eight weeks the robbers took turns following the armored truck on its long daily route. They found that the truck had no set route, that the order of pickups changed frequently, and the truck itself appeared impenetrable, as it was built with thick steel, had bulletproof glass, and contained three armed guards.

The robbery crew had a breakthrough when they discovered

one vulnerable point. In the Bath Beach section of Brooklyn, and only about two miles from the bank, the armored car always made a stop at The Rubel Ice Corporation at Bay and 19th Street. It was decided that they would ambush the drivers there and then use boats for their getaway, as The Rubel Ice Corporation was located only a block away from Gravesend Bay. The robbers were confident that their unusual escape plan would confuse police during the getaway. For the boats, they hired two out-of-work West Siders, Thomas Quinn and his cousin John Hughes (no relation to Peck Hughes), who had captained rum-running ships during Prohibition.

At 9:00 AM on August 21, 1934, Manning, dressed as an ice peddler, leaned against the loading platform of the Rubel Factory and waited. Inside the cart were two machine guns, that Charlie Yanowsky had provided, and a sawed-off shotgun. Francis Oley and Stewart lay lounging in the sun on a nearby grass hill, while nearby Percy Geary sat on the edge of the loading platform and chatted with some nearby ice peddlers. All of the robbers wore a few days beard growth, which they hoped might hinder identification. Meanwhile, Wallace, Quinn, and Hughes sat docked with two boats in Gravesend Bay, at 35th Street.

Kress, driving a blue Lincoln sedan, and McMahon, at the wheel of a Nash sedan—both cars stolen by Kress—tailed the armored car as it pulled away from the Brooklyn Trust Company Bank. The robbers waited nervously as the truck made its scheduled stops around Brooklyn, and at one point a boy attempted to buy ice from Manning, who chased him away with profanities. At 12:25 PM the armored truck finally rolled up to the Rubel Factory. The robbers all slipped on white cotton gloves and positioned themselves to pounce.

The first guard drew his revolver, exited the cab of the truck, and began walking toward the platform. Upon seeing the guard step out of the truck, Francis Oley and Archie Stewart walked over from the grassy hill, and Percy Geary hopped down from the loading platform. As the second guard opened his door to exit the truck, Manning flung the cover off of his ice cart, grabbed a machine gun and stuck it into the door of the truck, pointing it at the driver. Stewart grabbed the other machine gun, and at gunpoint, disarmed the second guard. Geary sprinted forward, drew a revolver from his pocket, and stuck his gun into the back of the remaining guard. In a matter of seconds, all the guards were disarmed and lying with their noses pressed to the pavement.

Kress and McMahon had pulled the stolen sedans up to the scene and both got out of their cars, hopped into the back of the armored truck, and joined John Oley, who was already starting to remove the loot. The three men deposited the money sacks into the Lincoln automobile, and with all the loot in the car, minus some coins, Kress jumped back into the driver's seat, followed by the Oley brothers and Geary, and sped away.

After the car with the money was gone, Manning and Stewart jumped into the waiting Nash. As Manning was entering the car, McMahon released the clutch pedal too soon, and the car jumped forward before Manning had fully entered the automobile. Manning accidentally dropped his machine gun, but yelled for McMahon to drive on. One guard stood up, grabbed the fallen machine gun, and let loose a burst of gunfire toward the fleeing car. The three then climbed back into the armored truck and attempted to give chase, but the faster Nash sedan sped off.

The hold-up had taken only three minutes, and although the police had flooded the surrounding streets within thirteen minutes, the robbers were already beginning their creative getaway by water to Arverne, Queens, which was located about ten miles away. The plan was to destroy the evidence and throw all the guns overboard during the trip. McMahon started to toss the weapons overboard, but the trigger guard of the sawed-off shotgun had become tangled in the drawstring of one of the canvas money bags. McMahon pulled the shotgun, which unexpectedly caused the gun to fire. A blast exploded out of the barrel of the shotgun and into McMahon's kneecap.

The shot had torn away a sizeable portion of McMahon's leg and he went into shock. The others attempted to assist McMahon, and a makeshift tourniquet was fastened above his knee. Both boats picked up speed with increasing urgency as McMahon continued to bleed out. After arriving in Queens, the robbers disembarked and transported the money sacks into a large black truck. Quinn then scuttled his boat in hopes it would sink any potential evidence.

Hughes remained behind with McMahon, while Kress took a taxi to a friend's house to borrow a car, and Archie Stewart popped into a nearby saloon to purchase a bottle of whiskey to ease his friend's pain. When Kress returned with a car, McMahon was bundled into the automobile by Stewart, and quickly driven away. Hughes then scuttled the second boat and headed home.

The robbers could not risk taking McMahon to a hospital, so instead Kress and Stewart took him to the type of place where a landlord would not ask questions about a critically injured man and potato sacks filled with money. Located at 334 Riverside Drive, Madeline Tully, an aging gangster moll, ran a seedy rooming house that doubled as a brothel and a place where fugitive criminals could lay their heads while on the run. Extremely well-known to gangsters on the West Side, the Yanowsky group had previously used Tully's house as a rendezvous spot.

Once at the rooming house, McMahon was put in a room upstairs, and Madeline Tully arranged for a gangster friend of hers, Michael Piccardo, to fetch a doctor who he knew. Dr. Harry Gilbert had become acquainted with Piccardo while treating him for a sexually transmitted disease, and Piccardo soon realized he was dealing with a frequently drunk physician who was willing to work for the underworld if the price was right. Dr. Gilbert briefly examined the now conscious, but fading, McMahon, and noticed that even though the wound was no longer bleeding, what was remaining of McMahon's knee had become bloated and discolored. Without telling McMahon, the doctor informed Archie Stewart, and the now present Stewart Wallace and Fats Manning, that McMahon's leg would have to be amputated above the knee. Payment was agreed upon and Stewart and Dr. Gilbert left with Piccardo to gather surgical instruments and painkillers to perform the gruesome task. By the time Dr. Gilbert arrived back at the house, McMahon was already dead.

The robbers located a large black clothing trunk in Madeline Tully's house and asked if it could be used to transport McMahon's body; however, when they attempted to stuff McMahon into the case, they found that he was too tall to fit. Instead of coming up with other options, they decided to pay the still available Dr. Gilbert to amputate the dead man's legs. With Wallace using his good hand to assist the shady physician, Dr. Gilbert removed McMahon's legs at the knees. McMahon was then placed into the trunk with his missing appendages tucked carefully beside him. Dr. Gilbert was paid $2,500 for performing the operation and arranging for a fake death certificate to be issued by a cooperative undertaker that the doctor claimed to know.

The following day, the men met at another Queen's apartment, and the robbery money was counted and divided. Although the robbers initially believed that they had taken close to a million dollars, they were still happy to find that they had stolen $427,950, which made it the largest cash robbery in American history at the time. Their bounty was split into nine full shares of $47,000 and two half shares $23,500 for Quinn and Hughes. McMahon's share was taken by Manning to give to the dead man's family. The group knew that the robbery would attract attention from law enforcement, and they left the apartment that day with no plans to ever work together again.

Much to Manning, Stewart, and Wallace's chagrin, McMahon's body was found five days later in front of a house at 154 West 74th Street. Apparently unable to complete the burial task he had promised, Dr. Gilbert, with the assistance of his gangster medical-broker Michael Piccardo, decided to ditch the increasingly smelly corpse-filled trunk.

The streets were abuzz about the crime, and informants were talking. Within a week, the police had tentatively identified all of the participants in the hold-up, and the sunken boats were found and linked back to Hughes and Quinn. Even though the police believed that they knew who had perpetrated the crime, they were unsure of the specific roles played, and other members of The West Side Gang such as Yanowsky, Sonny Campbell, Joe Butler, Peck Hughes, Joe Portuguese, and George Keeler would all, at one time or another, be tied to the theft by law enforcement.

Deputy Chief Inspector Ryan, who was the head of detectives in Brooklyn, was given charge of the investigation, and the case was made a priority for the department. Despite his best efforts, he was unable to find any concrete evidence to tie any of the robbers to the crime. Eyewitness statements were weak, evidence had been destroyed, and no one directly involved with the heist was talking to police.

The Rubel robbers stayed apart, as they knew that any contact with each other could jeopardize their freedom. Francis Oley moved to Denver, while John Oley and Percy Geary began to live under assumed names in Brooklyn. The three were all eventually arrested in 1937, for the O'Connell kidnapping, and transferred to upstate New York to stand trial. Both John Oley and Geary were found guilty and sentenced to seventy-five years in Alcatraz, while Francis Oley hung himself before the trial.

Boat captain John Hughes fled New York and was never heard from again. Some police officers believed that he was killed in an effort to silence witnesses, but this was never proven. Thomas Quinn remained in Manhattan and submitted to intense questioning by police regarding his sunken boat. After being held as a material witness for more than a month, he was released without charge. Police pressure remained, but the duo of Archie Stewart and Stewart Wallace ignored it. The pair could instead be found in Broadway cabarets, bars, and hotels, blowing their earnings on booze, gambling, and women. Manning and Kress continued to work closely with the Yanowsky Gang, and besides enjoying their take, they also began funneling some of their stolen money into the gang's operations on the West Side piers.

With success comes envy, and although no one in the Butler group said it outright, there was resentment and jealousy following the heist. The others could not comprehend how a score that big was not shared with them, and instead performed with outsiders from Albany. The Butler group was already growing weary of Yanowsky's expanding reach on the West Side waterfront; however, after the robbery, the negative feelings were more apparent than ever.

8

The West Side Wars:
The Trouble with Red and Tommy

WHILE MCGRATH AND Dunn were growing closer with Joe Butler, their partner Red McCrossin was also meeting new friends. By late 1934, McCrossin had been spending more time with Yanowsky's young apprentice, Thomas Adobody. While in Sing Sing, McCrossin, McGrath, and Dunn's names used to be synonymous with one another, but it was now more common to hear about the duo of McGrath and Dunn with no mention of McCrossin.

As both the Butler and the Yanowsky groups' waterfront operations continued to expand, the two began to occupy many of the same territories and rackets. With only so many areas to control, it was inevitable that tensions would spill over.

The tipping point came on October 11, 1934, when Joe Butler, Charlie Yanowsky, and Sonny Campbell were arrested in Linden, New Jersey, in connection with hijacking of a truck that contained $10,000 worth of expensive imported cheese. Two days prior, a driver for a truck company in Philadelphia had been pulled over by the three men who commandeered his load. There was a disagreement regarding whether they should drive the cheese back to New York City or leave it overnight and return the following morning and transport the goods back in a clean truck. That night, police in Linden found the abandoned truck, and instead of seizing it, left the vehicle and waited to see if the hijackers would return for it.

The next morning, Yanowsky, Butler, and Campbell returned to scout the location. The police watched a car containing the trio slowly pass by the stolen truck. After a second drive-by, the cops pulled out of their hiding places with sirens blaring. A short chase began before the gangsters pulled over and were arrested. After providing false information, the group was released with a promise to appear, but Butler, Yanowsky, and Campbell left the area with no plans to ever return for their court dates. Butler and Yanowsky held each other responsible for the arrest and hijacking failure. Although it was not important enough to murder over, the two groups grew even more distant.

The gangs remained in a cold war situation for the next two months. Remaining in the middle was McGrath and Dunn's friend, Red McCrossin. McCrossin was living with his family at 204 West 14th Street, and he had become so close with Tommy Adobody that Adobody moved his wife and newborn baby to an apartment just down the street at 356 West 14th Street. McCrossin had introduced Adobody to Dunn and McGrath, and at McCrossin's encouragement, the four began to commit crimes together. In early December of 1934, McGrath and Dunn, who had become increasingly dissatisfied with McCrossin, discovered that he had shorted them from the proceeds of a theft. To further incite the situation, the word was that McCrossin had been assisted by his new friend Tommy Adobody when ripping off McGrath and Dunn. Adobody and McCrossin had been brazen with their actions, and the two were becoming increasingly out of control. Adobody's seventeen-year-old wife had even left him in November of 1934, as Adobody was regularly drunk and abusive.

On December 16, 1934, Red McCrossin, who was unaware that the Butler group knew about his unfair profit split, picked up Dunn and McGrath for a night on the town. That evening, the three were spotted in various watering holes along 2nd Avenue, and they appeared to be the best of friends. At around 2:00 AM, the trio piled back into McCrossin's car, which was parked at 462 2nd Avenue, near 25th Street. Either McGrath or Dunn jumped into the front seat, and the other sat in the back directly behind McCrossin. The passenger turned up the radio dial to full blast as McCrossin started the car. Before McCrossin realized what was happening, two .38 caliber bullets struck his skull in rapid succession. One bullet entered the back of his head while the other penetrated behind his right ear and exited through the right side of his face.

The next morning, a taxi cab driver noticed a running car, with the radio still blaring, and a man slumped over the steering wheel. The taxi driver, who assumed McCrossin was sick, flagged down a nearby policeman who discovered the dead body. The area was canvassed, but no witnesses remembered hearing any shots.

On the night of December 21, 1934, only six days after the murder of Red McCrossin, Tommy Adobody stepped out from an automobile at Washington and West Houston Street. The area was bustling with Christmas shoppers who were on their way home after the shops had closed.

As Adobody closed the door to his automobile, another car, that police theorized contained McGrath, Dunn, Joe Butler, and Ding-Dong Bell, roared up alongside him at a high rate of speed. Two revolvers and a short barreled repeater rifle poked out of the car's windows and twelve shots were fired at Adobody, with most striking him in the body after he had collapsed. As pedestrians ducked for cover, Adobody lay dead in a large pool of blood.

The hit car, which had been stolen a month prior, sped away, and within an hour of the killing, it was located only three blocks from the scene. Inside the abandoned stolen car, two .38 caliber revolvers and a rifle were found. Testing was done on the guns, and it was determined that one of the pistols had also been used in the murder of Red McCrossin.

The day after Adobody's murder, NYPD detectives decided that it would be a good idea to check in on Mickey Kane, Adobody's partner in crime. They believed that Kane would either know something about the killing or would already be planning his own revenge on the Butler Gang.

Two detectives, disguised as workmen, conducted a surprise raid on Kane's apartment at 354 Cathedral Parkway. After a brief search, the officers found two pistols hidden under blankets inside a baby stroller. Kane was charged and released on bail, with a trial scheduled for February of 1935.

The West Side Gang was no more and, like Mickey Kane, everyone began to arm themselves for the violence that was sure to come.

The West Side Wars: Returning Fire

THE NEXT CASUALITY of the developing war on the West Side was an indirect target, and although the victim had no ties to problems on the waterfront, it was an example of what can happen when gangsters ready themselves for war.

Thomas Sheridan (no relation to McGrath's former partner Andrew "Squint" Sheridan), who was known as "The Harp," had a checkered past that included being a one-time member of the Legs Diamond Gang, a murder charge following a nightclub stabbing, and being shot and wounded in 1931. After being released from prison on a robbery charge, Sheridan found work as a bartender at a watering hole known as The Lowery Tavern, at 40-16 Queens Blvd.

On January 9, 1935, Mattie Kane and James Skinner had started drinking at The Lowery, which was close to Kane's home. Just before 3:00 AM, Kane offered to buy everyone in the bar a round of drinks. Sheridan, who was preparing to close, told Kane no. After exchanging heated words, Sheridan, who was no stranger to conflict, physically removed the inebriated Kane and Skinner from the bar. Sheridan had obviously underestimated what an agitated gangster with a bellyful of whiskey was capable of. Moments later, Kane reappeared at the front door, raised his gun, and called Sheridan's name. As Sheridan looked up, a volley of shots echoed through the tavern, and Sheridan slumped dead behind the bar.

Police arrived, but most customers had already fled the scene, and the remaining ones were not the type of clientele who talked to police. Within hours, the whispers on the street told police that Kane and Skinner were responsible for the shooting, but the police had no evidence with which to charge them.

Back on the West Side, and less than a month after the murder of Adobody, Charlie Yanowsky found someone to answer for the crime. On January 16, 1935, Yanowsky and Joe Kress were searching all of the Butler group's usual hangouts when they stumbled across Ding Dong Bell in the Market Diner at Christopher and Washington Streets, in Greenwich Village. The eldest Bell brother had just ordered his meal and was sitting alone at a table in the middle of the diner.

As a waitress would later put it, "The Fourth of July cut loose and everybody ducked." Yanowsky took a few steps inside the door of the diner, drew a revolver, and emptied it toward Bell. As Bell dove for cover, he was struck on the right side of the head, the left shoulder, and left arm. Also shot was an innocent bystander, who was grazed on the left side of his neck by a stray bullet. After Yanowsky had fired all six shots from his revolver, he dropped the gun, and ran out of the door.

Yanowsky jumped back into the passenger seat of the car driven by Kress, while two nearby motorcycle policemen, who had heard the shots, sped toward the scene. The policemen gave chase, with Kress leading them on a wild pursuit around the streets of Greenwich. As they approached Abingdon Square, near Hudson and Bleecker Streets, Kress suddenly stopped the car and both he and Yanowsky jumped out to make a run for it. Before they could even start to flee, the motorcycle patrolman pulled up beside them with his gun drawn. The two put their hands above their heads and kneeled on the ground.

The officer conducted a search and found a loaded revolver on each of them, another .45 caliber revolver in the car, and a sawed-off automatic rifle lying across the backseat. Before backup could arrive, Yanowsky offered the arresting officer a

$500 bribe if he was willing to let them free. The officer refused and instead charged him with attempted bribery. Yanowsky provided his usual alias, Harry Alberts, and Joe Kress stated that his name was Joseph Jacobs. In addition to bribery, the two were charged with felonious assault, a Sullivan Law charge for the illegal guns, possession of a machine gun, and, since the car they were driving was stolen, an additional charge of grand larceny.

Meanwhile at St. Vincent's Hospital, Ding-Dong Bell's condition was found to be stable. The bullet that struck him in the head had only grazed his skull, and the left shoulder and left arm wounds were minor. For the second time in his criminal career, he had been shot at close range and lived to tell about it.

Yanowsky and Kress had a bail hearing on January 25, 1935, and each was released on a $10,000 bond with a court date set for February of 1935. Not liking the odds of beating the case, and with a war for the West Side now underway, Yanowsky and Kress jumped bail and fled New York City to the nearest area that Yanowsky knew best—New Jersey. Joining them were Joe Portuguese, who had jumped bail on an assault charge; Albert Ackalitis, who was already wanted for parole violation following his recent release from prison; and Rubel robber Fats Manning. Yanowsky's decision to hide out in New Jersey led law enforcement to begin calling Yanowsky's group "The Jersey Mob" and the Butler group "The New York Mob."

Mickey Kane initially stayed in New York City, but he too would make a spur-of-the-moment decision to join the group in New Jersey. On February 5, 1935, Kane was at the court-house for his trial for the gun charge he received following Thomas Adobody's murder. Kane realized that a conviction was in the cards for him, and during a recess in the trial, he left through the front doors of the courthouse, hailed a car, and fled the state.

While Yanowsky and his group traveled around New Jersey discreetly, the Butler group grew comfortable operating openly on West Side piers. The guns remained quiet for the next two months, but even while in hiding, Yanowsky was planning to even the score with the Butler gangsters.

On March 23, 1935, James Gaynor was walking down Jefferson Street, near 5th Street in Hoboken, after the bars had closed. As he passed 600 Jefferson, a car pulled up behind him and a man slowly climbed out of the passenger seat. At a quick pace, the man then ran up to Gaynor and fired three shots into his upper body. Gaynor was taken by ambulance to St. Mary's Hospital where he died from his wounds thirty minutes later. The detectives who later investigated the shooting were extremely confident that the shooter that night had been Yanowsky himself.

From Yanowsky's gang, only George Keeler remained in New York City, as his youngest daughter was recovering from pneumonia and his wife had been frequently ill. Despite staying in the war zone, Keeler attempted to remain low-key, and his sporty automobile could no longer be found cruising up and down the West Side highway. With the rest of his gang in New Jersey, including his bodyguard Albert Ackalitis, Keeler needed reinforcements, which he found with some old friends who had recently been released from prison.

Keeler turned to an up-and-coming and murderous West Side gangster named Thomas "Tough Tommy" Protheroe. Born in 1908 to Irish immigrants, his first adult arrest took place in 1923, when Protheroe was sixteen years of age. Despite his youthful looks, he wore his battle wounds proudly and had a crooked nose and a large scar on the back of his head.

Protheroe's escapades were famous on the West Side. In 1927, he was on a train to Great Meadows prison when he slipped out of his handcuffs and jumped head first out of a window. By the time the train stopped, the only sign of

Protheroe was his gray prison jacket, although he would later be re-arrested after he was found back in his old haunts. On October 27, 1933, Protheroe was charged with homicide following a dispute for control over a pier in the Chelsea section of Manhattan. The murder took place on October 18, 1933, when Protheroe and two others, including Arthur Gaynor, the brother of the recently murdered James Gaynor, invaded a beer garden at 10th Avenue and West 33rd Street. The target of the attack was seventeen-year-old John Kelly, a substitute pier boss for his uncle, William Costello, who was recovering after being shot in the head only weeks earlier. Kelly had been sitting at a table with a group of men when Protheroe entered, machine gun in hand, and opened fire on the group. Kelly was hit in the arm, the owner of the bar was shot in the side, and a friend of Kelly's was hit three times in the chest and killed. Gaynor and Protheroe had worked together at the time of the murder, but the two would end up on opposite sides of the warring West Side when Protheroe went to prison for a period and Gaynor became closer with the Butler group.

Protheroe was arrested for the slaying, and ballistic tests discovered that the gun was the same one that had been used to murder the infamous Vincent "Mad Dog" Coll. Protheroe has occasionally been credited with the famous hit, but he likely later received the gun from underworld friends, as, according to records, it appears that he was incarcerated at the time Coll was shot in 1932.

On April 29, 1934, Protheroe was again charged with homicide, this time after he ran over a man with a car after a drunken quarrel. Like the machine gun killing, the charge could not be proven, but Protheroe was sent back to prison for being intoxicated and violating his parole. He would not be released until January 1935, when the West Side War was just beginning.

With Protheroe came his two friends, Francis "Buster"

Smith and John Harvey, who had also just been released from prison. Harvey had been an acquaintance of Protheroe for years and had recently been released from Sing Sing after serving a long prison term, while Smith had been incarcerated for nearly a decade for a robbery charge, at which time he had met Protheroe in Clinton Penitentiary.

The trio of recently released gangsters had their eyes on the waterfront rackets, and Keeler enticed the ex-cons to join his cause by offering them a partnership in the rackets on Pier 59. Keeler had been sharing this pier with a pair of West Siders known as the Dillon brothers. Although one of the brothers, John Dillon, had been charged with the murder of another longshoreman in the 1920s, he had shown no interest in becoming involved in the current violence, and Keeler had little use for him.

Keeler, Protheroe, Smith, and Harvey went down to Pier 59 in late March of 1935 and informed the Dillon brothers that they were no longer welcome on the docks. The Dillons were tough customers, but they knew they were dealing with a different class of criminals and left without argument. Keeler picked a veteran longshoreman and loanshark named Eddie O'Connell to oversee the rackets on Pier 59, and to be responsible for passing on the largest cut to Keeler, Protheroe, Smith, and Harvey.

Not content with only having Pier 59, the group looked directly north to Pier 60, which was controlled by a friend of the Butler Gang named Thomas "Red" Burke. Burke, who was a gangster with an arrest record two pages long, often paid the Butler Gang a small tribute, which made him an appealing target. Before Keeler could make a move on Pier 60, Buster Smith spoke to another Clinton Penitentiary alumni named Phil "Philsie" Sheridan (no relation to McGrath's old partner Andrew "Squint" Sheridan or Thomas "Harp" Sheridan), who informed them that with the assistance of Yanowsky gang member Fats Manning, he had already planned to chase Red Burke off the pier. Keeler told Sheridan that Pier 60 could be his as long as he continued to only claim territory that belonged to the Butler group. Keeler was making new friends quickly, and the Butler Gang's list of enemies was growing.

Keeler again began to make his presence known on the West Side since finding support from Tommy Protheroe and his friends. On April 10, 1935, Keeler, Protheroe, Smith, and Harvey were cruising around in Keeler's car when they noticed a truck on a pier being loaded with what appeared to be furs. Keeler recognized the driver and knew that the man might be willing to let them steal the truck for a cut of the profit. After speaking to the driver, the group learned that the truck contained $100,000 worth of furs from Russia, which the driver would allow them to take during a staged hijacking later in the day. The group was ecstatic about the potential massive payday.

The four would-be robbers sat waiting, when, much to their surprise, they watched another car containing Joe Butler, Peck Hughes, Sonny Campbell, and James Skinner roar up. At gunpoint, the Butler gangsters commandeered the waiting fur truck and drove away. The Butler mobsters had already been made aware of the incoming furs, and although they would not have known it, they had just scooped their rivals.

Keeler, Protheroe, Smith, and Harvey were furious and decided to try to get the truck back. Keeler knew the area where Sonny Campbell lived, and the next morning went searching for him. After spotting his parked car, he got in touch with Protheroe and Smith, who then headed to the location to wait for Campbell to appear. The plan was to stick him up, force him to tell them the location of the furs, and then bump him off.

Later in the day, Campbell exited his apartment and entered his car. As Campbell sat down in the driver's seat, Protheroe and Smith sprang from their hiding places and jumped in behind him with guns drawn. When questioned by Smith and Protheroe, Campbell professed that he did not know where the furs were, and in an unexpected betrayal that likely saved his life, he admitted that after the robbery he had been in touch with Charlie Yanowsky and told him where the truck containing the stolen furs had been hidden. Campbell said he was friends with Albert Ackalitis and that he had planned to join up with the Yanowsky group. Protheroe and Smith did not know what to make of the situation and called Keeler, who informed them that he would contact Yanowsky.

Protheroe and Smith took Campbell to Protheroe's apartment, and when night fell, the trio got in a trailer-truck and drove about thirty miles north of New York City, to the location where Campbell said the furs had been stashed. Upon their arrival at a secluded farm, they found the furs were already gone. Protheroe and Smith got back in touch with Keeler who confirmed that Campbell was not lying and that he had betrayed the Butler Gang and given up the location of the unguarded furs to Yanowsky. Keeler informed them that Yanowsky was near Marlboro, New York and that they should meet him at the Brass Rail in Newburg the following night.

The next day, Smith, Protheroe, and Campbell met Yanowsky, Ackalitis, Mickey Kane, Fats Manning, Joe Portuguese, and Joe Kress at the bar. Yanowsky told Protheroe and Smith that Campbell was now with them. In a show of friendship, Yanowsky offered to cut Protheroe and Smith in on the profits once the furs had been fenced, but the duo reciprocated by politely refusing. They let Yanowsky know that they were with him in the war and that they were okay to not take a cut as long as they knew that the Butler Gang did not have the furs.

Yanowsky told Protheroe and Smith that he and his gang were hiding out in Cliffside, New Jersey, as Frank Borelli, the corrupt Chief of Police in the small community, was allowing Yanowsky to stay there as long as he did not cause any trouble in the city. Protheroe and Smith thanked Yanowsky for the offer to stay with them but declined as they planned to go back to New York City. Campbell also returned with them, as at this point the Butler Gang was unaware of his duplicity.

Protheroe, Smith, and Harvey, who were late in joining the gang warfare, may not have recognized how dangerous the Butler Gang was, as upon their return to the city they made no effort to hide themselves. With the shooting of Ding-Dong Bell, the murder of James Gaynor, and the unexpected theft of $100,000 worth of furs, the Butler Gang was foaming at the mouth.

One week after the theft of the furs, Protheroe, Smith, and Harvey were sitting in Keeler's car at the base of Pier 72. As the three relaxed, another automobile containing John Dunn, George Daggett, Ding-Dong Bell, and Peck Hughes pulled up next to them. Two pistols and a shotgun were thrust out the windows, and the gangsters cut loose at the newcomers to Yanowsky's group. Protheroe and Harvey, who were in the front, managed to duck, but Smith was hit in the stomach with a pistol bullet. As Smith fell to the floor of the car, Peck Hughes leaned out of the window of his own automobile and fired a shotgun blast directly at his prone body. Smith's leg took the brunt of the buckshot and was hit in eight places. Dunn, Daggett, Bell, and Hughes sped away, as a midday shooting on a busy dock was sure to attract attention.

Keeler's expensive car, and Smith himself, had a handful of new holes in them courtesy of the Butlers. Keeler and Protheroe decided to drive the maimed Smith to the Yanowsky Gang in Cliffside, where a local doctor was paid to perform surgery on his stomach and remove the shotgun pellets from his leg. The surgery was a success, and Smith decided to stay on with the group in Cliffside while he recovered from his wounds. Keeler and Protheroe again returned to New York City with plans to avenge the attack on them while, after his near death experience, John Harvey did not participate any further in the West Side War.

At around 1:00 AM on April 21, 1935, Protheroe and Keeler were driving around Midtown Manhattan in Protheroe's automobile and hunting for members of the Butler Gang. As they cruised through the crowded streets, which were lined with the late-night Broadway crowd, they spotted Ding-Dong Bell and a second man, who police speculated may have been John Dunn, standing near an automobile near the Hotel Edison and the 46th Street Theatre.

Protheroe and Keeler passed by their targets slowly and began firing shots from the window of their car in the direction of Bell and Dunn. Ding-Dong Bell was hit in the shoulder with one of the bullets and was now the unlucky recipient of three gangland shootings. Bell and the second man were able to react, draw their own guns, and return fire. Protheroe and Keeler stopped the car and jumped out with guns blazing, and what followed was a wild shootout that sent bystanders fleeing in all directions. Police found that about a dozen shots were exchanged and that both pairs of men used their respective cars as cover. Sirens were heard moments later, and all four men took off running in different directions.

Police began to try to identify the cars, but they found that neither were registered. A minor breakthrough occurred a week later, when it was discovered that Protheroe had been arrested for possession of a pistol, in early January of 1935, while driving a car with the same description and license plate number as one of the bullet-ridden cars left behind after the shooting. Police around Manhattan and Long Island City, where they believed Protheroe was staying, were advised to arrest him on sight.

The West Side Wars:
Reputations Are Made

POLICE WERE HOT on the waterfront gangsters' trails following the four months of shootings that had shaken the West Side underworld. The attention of the NYPD turned to the Butler associates in New York City, and the Federal Bureau of Investigation took up the hunt for the members of the Yanowsky group in New Jersey. The FBI had found that Yanowsky was hiding in Cliffside, but when the gangster-friendly Police Chief Borelli became aware of the G-Men's presence in his town, he tipped off Yanowsky that the authorities were closing in.

Yanowsky and the rest of his gang fled to a farmhouse in Marlboro, which was located along the Hudson River about an hour and a half north of New York City. The area had been a hideout spot for the gang in the past, and they had previously used it to store the $100,000 worth of furs that they had ripped off from the Butler Gang. Once the Yanowsky group arrived in Marlboro, the remaining New York City holdouts, Tommy Protheroe, George Keeler, and Sonny Campbell, made the trip north on May 14, 1935, to visit them.

Upon arriving back in New York City, Protheroe, who obviously missed the nightlife while visiting quiet upstate New York, headed out for a night on the town. His choice of companion for the evening was a woman from Hoboken named Grace Owens Moore. Moore had been married at seventeen, had a child who died in infancy, and was divorced a short time later. In 1931, she was arrested under the name Elizabeth Connors after striking a man with a sugar bowl during a brawl at an 8th Avenue restaurant. Moore had left her family the week prior and had been staying with friends in New York City before hooking up with Protheroe. Protheroe and Moore went to a bar located at 39-33 Queens Blvd, Long Island City, which, oddly enough, also happened to be a tavern that he was once convicted of robbing at gunpoint.

The pair departed at 4:30 AM on May 16, 1935, and Protheroe maneuvered his new blue car to the front curb of a walk-up apartment he was using at 42-39th Avenue, Long Island City. As Protheroe and Moore began to walk toward the apartment's front entrance, a car roared up behind them and stopped inches from where they were standing. Protheroe attempted to draw his own revolver from his pocket as a gunman leaned out the window and fired four bullets into his body. A fifth bullet hit Grace Moore in the arm and spun her to the ground. The shooter quickly exited the car and fired two more bullets at close range into Protheroe's head. The shooter then turned toward Moore, who was now sitting on the ground, placed a gun to the top of her head, and fired a bullet directly downwards. The police believe that the hit team that found Protheroe consisted of Eddie McGrath, John Dunn, Joe Butler, and Mattie Kane. FBI sources later identified Dunn as the shooter that night, but given the reputation of the four men allegedly involved, it seems possible that the triggerman could have been any of them.

As the car containing the killers peeled off down the street, a neighbor who had heard the shots rushed to the scene. He found Protheroe dead and Moore still breathing but slipping in and out of consciousness. Despite living through part of the morning, the doctors were unable to remove the bullet from her brain and she died at 10:40 AM. Tales of Moore's death quickly became exaggerated in the barrooms on the

West Side, and the story told was that the Butler Gang shot Moore in the head while she was holding a Bible and praying on her knees for mercy.

With the Yanowksy group still hiding in Marlboro, George Keeler and Sonny Campbell did not plan to make the same fatal mistake as Protheroe, and again started to avoid their usual hangouts. Keeler remained at home for the most part and always carried a gun when he needed to leave his house in Brooklyn. On May 23, 1935, only days after the Protheroe murder, Keeler left his three young children with his mother-in-law and took his wife, Elsie, to watch a gangster movie at the Albee Theatre. Elsie had not been well, and the two had not enjoyed an evening together in some time. After taking in the picture show, the Keelers returned home at around 2:00 AM. The house was quiet when the couple entered, as Keeler's two boys were sound asleep in one bedroom, Keeler's mother-in-law slept in a room next to the couple's, and the youngest was already fast asleep in a separate bed in their room. Keeler, who had left his loaded revolver in his car, likely felt secure in his own home as he and his wife went to bed.

Outside the house, in a waiting car with McGrath at the wheel, sat Dunn, Joe Butler, Mattie Kane, and Ding-Dong Bell. Determined to purge New York City of the remaining members of the Yanowsky Gang, the group had been searching for Keeler around his home. At 4:00 AM, when the would-be killers knew everyone in the house was sleeping, Butler and Dunn crept up to the side of the vine-covered brick residence. The two were able to remove a screen from a first-floor window, jimmy it out of the frame, and climb into the front room. Moving slowly through the dark house, Dunn and Butler found the phone on the first floor and cut the cord, after which they drew their pistols and headed upstairs.

Butler and Dunn found Keeler's room and gently pushed the door open. The two approached the side of the slumbering

Keeler and leveled their guns only inches from his prone body. Two loud booms pierced the silent house. Elsie sprang up and let out a scream as blood splattered around her. She would later tell police that, in that dizzying moment, she believed she was still watching the gangster film that she had seen earlier with her husband. The first two shots struck Keeler in the head and chest. More shots rang out—two bullets hit Keeler in the stomach, three targeted bullets struck him in the groin, and another three shots wildly hit the wall as Dunn and Butler ran from the room.

The hysterical Elsie ran downstairs to call for help but found that the phone line had been cut. A neighbor rushed into the home and stated that he had seen two men enter a black automobile that sped away. Police arrived, secured the scene, and began their investigation. They were surprised that no one in the house had heard the killers breaking in, but at that point, they did not know that they were dealing with an experienced thief like Joe Butler. The next morning, as Keeler's son rode his tricycle in front of the house, blissfully unaware of the horrible violence that had taken place, Elsie Keeler told police that Keeler "[. . .] was a loving family man who never brought work home with him."

If the murder of Tommy Protheroe had helped build McGrath and Dunn's reputation in the underworld, the brazen killing of a sleeping man at home took it to a new level. The Butler Gang was starting to be considered untouchable, while the Yanowksy gang appeared to be out of the picture due to the efforts of law enforcement. However, everyone on the streets knew who was responsible for the two recent murders, and the mandate came down from senior police officials to do everything in their power to lock up members of the Butler Gang.

On May 28, 1935, McGrath and Dunn felt comfortable enough to go out and celebrate their recent gangland triumphs.

The two, who were both avid boxing fans, had tickets to the Polo Grounds in New York City to watch Jimmy McLarnin defend his Welterweight World Title against Barney Ross. McGrath and Dunn, along with thirty-thousand other fight fans, were lined up to enter the arena when two New York City homicide detectives approached the duo and charged them with the murder of their old partner, John "Red" McCrossin.

Prior to the arrests, the NYPD knew that they did not have enough evidence to win a conviction in court, but they went ahead with the charges, as they had come up with their own novel way to curb both McGrath and Dunn. Along with Mattie Kane, McGrath and Dunn were the members of the Butler Gang who were still on parole as a result of their recent stays in Sing Sing, and the police believed that they could use this as a way to get them off the street.

On June 6, 1935, the murder charges against McGrath and Dunn were withdrawn, but the two, who were still being held in jail, were charged with violating the terms of their release. It was found by the Parole Board that they had violated their parole by frequently socializing with known felons—each other. The two were sentenced to serve an additional year in prison and both were shipped back to Sing Sing.

11

The West Side Wars: On the Offensive

FOLLOWING THE PROTHEROE and Keeler murders, the streets were quiet for once. Back in the city, Butler and his group had been snapping up waterfront territory that used to belong to Yanowksy and Keeler, while Butler's partner, Farmer Sullivan, focused on his own local rackets in Greenwich Village. The gangsters received almost no pushback as, after the recent killings, independent waterfront hoodlums were quick to cooperate with the fearsome group.

The Butler Gang was unaware, but in June of 1935 Francis "Buster" Smith, who had been a regular thorn in their side before being shot and injured, decided to leave the Yanowsky group in Marlboro and head back to New York City. He had recuperated from his wounds, and despite the warnings from Yanowsky, he decided that he was going to resume the war in New York City on his own. Smith's first stop was Pier 59 where he, along with Keeler, Protheroe, and John Harvey, used to control the rackets through Eddie O'Connell. When Smith arrived at the pier, he was informed that Butler, Mattie Kane, and James Skinner now collected the weekly profits from O'Connell.

Smith called upon an old friend who had been in Clinton Penitentiary with him named Ralph "Lulu" Clements. Clements, who was from Brooklyn, had been part of the Legs Diamond Gang along with his partner Edward "The Snake" Kenny. The two Brooklyn gunman were members of

Diamond's gang during the time it was dissolving, and both were suspects in a series of murders including that of Legs Diamond's ex-wife, Alice, following Diamond's own murder. With the demise of the Diamond Gang, the two Brooklyn hoods were looking for new opportunities and had recently been hanging around the West Side Waterfront.

Smith and Clements scouted out Pier 59 and approached Eddie O'Connell on a day when no members of the Butler Gang were around. Without having to even draw their guns, they told O'Connell to turn over all of his money to them. Smith declared it was his pier again and that he would be back next week to collect his share of the take.

The brash Smith headed back to Pier 59 the same time the following week, but upon entering the pier, he was met by a security guard. The guard asked to search him, but Smith was reluctant as he had a loaded pistol in his coat pocket. Instead of complying, Smith punched the guard in the face and ran toward his car, which was parked on 18th Street. As he turned onto the street, he saw Joe Butler and Mattie Kane crouched next to his vehicle. Smith went for his gun and both Butler and Kane ran back to their own car, where Butler gangsters James Skinner and Vic Patterson were already waiting. Butler, Kane, Skinner, and Patterson then accelerated their automobile toward Smith.

Smith sprinted down the street, but the Butler Gang was able to catch up to him at a parking lot on 17th Street. Butler began to shoot from the moving car and Smith returned fire at the automobile. Smith took off running again, but Butler was able to lean out the window and fire another volley at the fleeing gangster, this time hitting Smith in the upper thigh.

The bleeding Smith limped back to his car and began to drive away, but despite trying to leave the scene quickly, the car clunked slowly down the road. Smith leaned out of the window and found that his tires had been slashed, which was the reason that Joe Butler and Mattie Kane had been lurking around his vehicle when he discovered them — it had been a trap. Smith hailed a cab and was taken back to the doctor in New Jersey, who was able to remove the bullet from his leg.

Smith hid out for a few months, and when he eventually returned to New York City, he was arrested on December 21, 1935, for the assault on the pier security guard. Smith, who was still on parole, was held without bail and would later be convicted. Given his lengthy record, he was given a sentence that would keep him out of the mix for the next five years.

With Farmer Sullivan focusing on Greenwich Village and Eddie McGrath and John Dunn in prison, Joe Butler was left to make important gang decisions on his own. Butler had received a tip through the underworld grapevine that provided him with the whereabouts of the Yanowsky Gang's hideout in Marlboro, and he began to plan his violent offensive. Arthur Gaynor, who was still seeking revenge for the murder of his brother James; Ding-Dong Bell, who was still sour about being shot twice; and Peck Hughes all agreed to join Butler on the seek and destroy mission. Additionally, Eddie McGrath's old friend and robbing buddy, Eddie Gaffney, agreed to participate in the plan after he had become connected to the Butler Gang through his friendship with McGrath.

Also recruited for the trip were some new gangsters who hoped to make a name for themselves on the West Side. Joining the Butler Gang members were Frank Foy, a recent Sing Sing alumni from Brooklyn who previously had been convicted of a kidnapping; his partner Joseph McCarthy; and a hired gun who had arrived from Detroit named Louis Balner. Balner, who had been chased out of Brooklyn after being on the losing side of a gang war, had been offering his services as a killer for hire, but contract work must have been slow, as he had recently been sleeping on a park bench.

The eight gangsters borrowed a cottage in the Pompton Lakes area of New Jersey from George Maiwald, a petty criminal the gang knew. The choice was strategic, as the Pompton Lakes area was a well-known vacation spot that was located only an hour directly south of Marlboro, New York. The crusading gangsters brought a cache of weapons with them to New Jersey that included a bottle of nitroglycerine, a gas kit used to create explosives, six hand grenades that were charged with T.N.T., and a barrage of weapons, including two handguns with the engravings "I Will Right All Wrong" and "Be Not Afraid Of Any Man." The group settled into the small cottage with the owner, Maiwald, staying in a neighboring property with his wife. The plan was that after Butler confirmed the actual location of the Yanowsky Gang's hideout, they would blow up their rivals with T.N.T. while they slept soundly.

Butler would come and go from the Pompton cottage while the others waited patiently for further instructions. The gangsters would spend the day playing cards, barbecuing, and swimming but would often leave at night. Nearby cottagers soon took notice of the group of suspiciously polite young men, and one neighbor called the police. An officer arrived, and after noticing a handful of cars hidden among the trees, he recorded their license plate numbers. When New Jersey authorities ran the plates, they found that all of the vehicles were stolen. The next day, police began to conduct surveillance from a distance, and after confirming the identities of some of the men, they decided to raid the cottage on June 23, 1935. More than twenty state troopers and a handful of detectives from New York City, who were familiar with the Butler Gang, surrounded the property at 5:00 AM.

The officers quietly entered the front door and found Louis Balner, who was supposed to be the lookout, asleep in a chair with a half-finished game of solitaire in front of him. As a detective grabbed the sleeping Balner, the other officers poured through the cottage door into the sleeping area. The police shouted for everyone to freeze, and the gangsters awoke yelling, "Don't shoot! Don't shoot!" The prisoners were lined up against the wall of the cabin and guns were found under each of their pillows. The only one missing from the group was Joe Butler, who police would be unable to tie to the cottage raid, as although New York City detectives had reported seeing him earlier in the day with the others, he had left for the night. After the bust, police went to the neighboring cottage and seized George Maiwald and his wife, and the whole group was transported to jail in Paterson, New Jersey.

Labeled as a "Murder Mob," the media jumped upon the arrests of the gangsters with wild speculation. Only one or two papers briefly mentioned any type of connection to the waterfront, although most identified the group as the possible murderers of Keeler and Protheroe. Most news outlets wrote that the gangsters were suspected in dozens of other killings; the Rubel robbery; and a planned kidnapping of boxer Joe Louis, who was training for an upcoming fight nearby.

Justice was swift in the small community, and Bell, Gaynor, Foy, and Maiwald were all charged under New Jersey's new Public Enemy Law, which allowed lengthy sentences for criminals with previous convictions. On July 12, 1935, Bell, Gaynor, and Foy were sentenced to ten to twenty years in prison, while Maiwald was ordered to stand trial with the others. The judge stated that the firearms found were meant to "mete out death" and "this gangster business must stop; it will not be tolerated in this county; sentence is imposed as a lesson to you and a warning to others." The rest of the gang quickly pleaded guilty. Balner and Hughes received three years for possession of the explosives, Gaffney received two to three years for possessing the gas kit, McCarthy had a minor record and was sentenced to a term in the New Jersey Reformatory, and George Maiwald was sentenced to five to ten years.

Two days after the Butler gangsters were convicted, another interesting development in the West Side War unfolded when a body was found floating in the Hudson River near Marlboro. Police fished out the remains and discovered that the decaying corpse had likely been in the water for close to two weeks. The victim had been wrapped in a curtain, trussed up in a tarp, and then had eighty pounds of weights attached to him before being tossed into the river. Despite the attempts to sink the corpse, the body had become bloated and began bobbing along the surface of the water. The unidentified dead man had numerous head wounds, and it appeared that he had been beaten to death.

Fingerprints were taken, and it was determined that the deceased was Yanowsky gangster John "Joe Portuguese" Silba. The police first believed that the recently arrested Butler gangsters had gotten to Silba, but following an interview with his on-again, off-again girlfriend, Mary Figueria, they decided that his own gang, and specifically Charlie Yanowsky, had been responsible for his death. Figueria told police that prior to Joe Portuguese fleeing from New York City, he would not even walk with her as he feared that Butler gunmen would find him at any moment. He had visited New York City from Marlboro shortly before the raid on the Butler gangsters in Pompton, and he had let Figueria know that he and Yanowsky had recently had a heated argument.

Police came to the conclusion that the Yanowsky Gang suspected that Joe Portuguese had informed the Butler Gang of their location in Marlboro during his short trip to New York City, which occurred prior to the Pompton Lakes raid. The discovery of Joe Portuguese's body alerted the FBI to the general location of the Yanowsky Gang, and the search for them became focused on the North Hudson region. As local police closed in, the gang disguised themselves as berry pickers and left the area.

The Yanowsky group temporarily found refuge an hour further north in Phoenicia, a very small community in the mountainous Catskills area of New York. Tensions were high amongst the gang, as they had now been on the run for the better part of a year and were nearly broke.

The solution to their problem came in the form of two robbers who were also on the lam. Frank "The Polack" Peraski was originally from upstate New York but moved to Michigan and later Pennsylvania, where he served terms for robbery in both states. On the run with Peraski was his partner, a significantly older ex-con from New York City named John Ryan. The two had recently been identified as participants in a jewelry store heist at the Ritz-Carlton in Boston and had fled to New York City in August. After they arrived, they found refuge in a boarding house run by Rubel robbery accomplice, and Yanowsky Gang friend, Madeline Tully. The wanted duo had been referred to Tully by Rubel robbery accessory Michael Piccardo, with whom Peraski had previously been convicted of a robbery in Pennsylvania. Through Tully's connection to the Yanowsky Gang, Peraski and Ryan joined the rest of the group and offered to help them commit some robberies.

After some careful planning, the gang hit their first target, a bank in Prospect Park, New Jersey. On November 8, 1935, the bank had just opened, and about twenty customers were waiting in line, when six gunmen burst through the doors. All of the robbers were wearing caps or fedoras, and some wore sunglasses. One gunman stayed at the door while the lead robber, who carried a machine gun, shouted, "This is a stickup. Keep quiet and stay where you are!" A third robber, armed with a shotgun, lined up all the customers, while the other two vaulted the counter into the cashier's cage and proceeded to empty all of the money into sacks.

While the robbers were on the ground floor of the bank, a manager in a second-floor office heard what was going on, jumped out of his window onto a lowered roof, and triggered the bank alarm. Another robber, who was parked in a waiting getaway car, saw the commotion on the roof and began to sound his horn frantically. The robbers inside the bank heard the warning and ran into the waiting car. Following on their heels was an armed employee of the bank, who emptied his revolver at the gangsters as they sped away. The bullets smashed into the back window but hit no one inside. The gang had been in the bank for only three minutes but had managed to steal $18,000 in currency.

Witnesses stated that there had been one getaway driver and six armed robbers, who were all in their late twenties and early thirties, minus one who appeared to be in his fifties. Some customers also noted that another suspicious car was idling near the bank at the time of the robbery, which police came to believe was a backup or switch car. FBI agents who were on the trail of the Yanowsky gang theorized that the perpetrators were Yanowsky, Albert Ackalitis, Mickey Kane, Fats Manning, Sonny Campbell, Joe Kress, and their new friends Frank Peraski and John Ryan.

While FBI agents and police in New Jersey were pursuing the Yanowksy gang, the NYPD in New York City were still interested in the remaining members of the Butler Gang. After successfully violating McGrath and Dunn's parole, they turned their attention to Mattie Kane, who had his own restrictions after being released early from his old robbery sentence.

On November 27, 1935, detectives in Queens, who had been trying to solve the murder of Thomas "The Harp" Sheridan, arrested Kane alongside James Skinner as the two exited Kane's mother's apartment. Kane and Skinner were searched, and police found a key in Skinner's pocket for a room at The Hotel President. The two were taken to a station house where they were questioned at length about the Harp Sheridan homicide. While being questioned, one of the gangsters provided an address, 57 Vermilyea Avenue, New York City, where they reported that Skinner had a room. The Queens detectives left Kane and Skinner at the station house and went to search Skinner's address and the hotel room for which they now had a key.

When the police arrived at the hotel, they found a man named Samuel Altman. Altman admitted to police that he was a friend of Skinner's and that Skinner had given him a key so that he could visit. Altman said that he did have a criminal record and until recently had operated as a bootlegger in upstate New York. The room was searched, and police found a loaded revolver in Altman's coat pocket. Altman was arrested and taken to join Skinner and Kane at the station house in Queens.

When another group of officers arrived at Skinner's apartment, they were surprised with the scene that awaited them. Jumping up and down on the sidewalk and yelling "Joe! Come on down! Joe!" were Butler gangsters, George Daggett and Vic Patterson. The two were placed under arrest for suspicion of burglary. The officers sprinted up the stairs and found Joe Butler lounging comfortably in Skinner's apartment. Butler played dumb and informed them that he was waiting for his friend James Skinner to arrive home.

Police began their search of Skinner's apartment, and it didn't take them long to realize they had stumbled on the location that the Butler Gang used to store their arsenal. In a suitcase under the bed and in a dresser drawer the police found a submachine gun, two sawed-off shotguns, and six handguns.

Butler, Daggett, and Patterson were taken to a nearby station house, and Skinner, Kane, and Altman were driven over from Queens to join them. When asked about the weapons cache, Skinner stated that two friends had asked him to pick them up the guns, and that they had been given to him by a guy he met on the 42nd Street Ferry only a week before. In an attempt to turn the blame to his rivals, he said the two friends that asked him to collect the weapons were Harry Alberts and Joseph Jacobs, who police knew were the aliases of Charlie Yanowsky and Joe Kress.

Skinner, Kane, and Altman were charged with the murder of Thomas "The Harp" Sheridan, as police hoped that one of the guns found could be linked to the shooting, and Skinner was also charged with possession of a machine gun. Butler, Daggett, and Patterson could not be tied to the gang's arsenal and were released when Skinner took responsibility for the weapons.

After testing confirmed that none of the guns were used in the Harp Sheridan slaying, the murder charges were dropped. Mattie Kane would be shipped to prison to serve out the remainder of his old robbery sentence, as authorities deemed that he had violated his parole for not having a legitimate income and for consorting with known felons. Kane would not be eligible for release for nearly two years. In early 1936, Skinner would plead guilty to the machine gun charge and would be sentenced to five to seven years in Sing Sing. With another two Butler gangsters off the street, the participants in the West Side War were rapidly thinning.

Back in New Jersey, the Yanowsky Gang were preparing for their second robbery, and no doubt hoping that it would go smoother than the first. Using the same motif as the last theft, the gangsters hit the First National Bank in Fort Lee, New Jersey, on December 20, 1935. Just after 10:00 AM, a car pulled up to the front doors of the bank and five bandits, who were all dressed the same as the last robbery, rushed inside. The leader, brandishing a machine gun, shouted commands while two robbers lined up employees and another two vaulted behind the tellers' desk.

The cashier's cage was locked, so one of the robbers forced the manager to open it at gunpoint. When the manager took too long, the robber snarled at him, "Quit stalling or we will plug you." The bandits made off with $16,000 worth of old bills that were waiting to be shipped to the Treasury for new ones.

The police had no immediate leads, but three months later they arrested a nineteen-year-old youth from Cliffside, New Jersey, named Ralph Sorrentino. He told police that a gang led by Yanowsky had paid him to steal a car for the heist and to act as a lookout. Sorrentino said that he did not know the names of all of the robbers, but tentatively identified Yanowsky, Ackalitis, Mickey Kane, Campbell, and Peraski as participants.

Authorities found that the Yanowsky Gang was still funneling money back to New York City, to fund what remained of their rackets, after some of the proceeds of the robbery turned up on January 10, 1936, during the arrest of a familiar face — Rubel robber John "Archie" Stewart.

The police had been watching an apartment at 109 West 88th Street, as they believed that the dwelling was being used as an office to run an illegal numbers game. At around 1:00 AM, the NYPD officers watched as Archie Stewart exited the building. Once inside the office, police found a group of men who were in the process of throwing two policy slip making machines out of the window. The arrested individuals included well-known local numbers operators, the Kelly brothers — James, Peter, Thomas, and Joseph. Police found $500 worth of policies slips, $1,100 in cash and, curiously, a $245 bundle that was identified as money that had been taken from the Fort Lee bank. Stewart was later released without charge.

Any ambitions that Charlie "The Jew" Yanowsky had of triumphantly returning to New York City, to seize control of the waterfront, were violently thwarted by FBI agents on January 30, 1936. That day, the FBI had received a tip that the gangster would be waiting for a ride on 9th Avenue in Hoboken. The tipster was obviously someone who was intimate with

Yanowsky's movements. Although it has never been established who dropped the dime, odds are that the person was part of Yanowsky's inner circle and that they had grown tired of his leadership or the law enforcement attention he was generating.

Two carloads of armed FBI agents quietly drove around the area where Yanowsky was supposed to arrive. At 10:30 PM, Yanowsky appeared carrying a large suitcase. Two FBI agents approached him, drew their weapons, and identified themselves. Yanowsky took one look, dropped his belongings, and sprinted away. The FBI agents later reported that, as he was running, Yanowsky reached into his jacket and removed a pistol from a shoulder holster that he was wearing. The two FBI agents, who were armed with a machine gun and a sawed-off shotgun, both fired a burst of bullets at Yanowsky. The shotgun blast hit Yanowsky in the side and some of the pellets pierced his lung. Two machine gun bullets struck him in the side of the head, one hitting his neck and the other hitting him in the head. The bullet wounds ended Yanowsky's short run, and he fell forward to the ground.

The next morning, many papers read "Yanowsky Shot Dead" along with captions such as "One of the most dangerous criminals in the country shot by FBI agents." One paper reported that Yanowsky was taken to St. Mary's Hospital in Hoboken, where he lingered until the morning in a delirious state while babbling to police about his past crimes.

By the late edition, the newspapers that had reported that Yanowksy was dead began to post correction notices. Miraculously, Yanowsky had not only lived through the night, but also he was stabilizing. An FBI report taken at his bedside confirms that Yanowsky was completely lucid and that he displayed the truculence that you would expect from the hardened gangster. Any words that came out of his mouth were recorded as being profanity-laced tirades against the FBI. Earlier in the night, when it appeared that Yanowsky was sure to die, a priest was brought to his bedside to administer last rites. The priest asked Yanowsky to repeat the words, "Jesus, Mary, and Joseph, help me in this hour of need." The semi-conscious Yanowsky replied, "Jesus, Mary, and Joseph, help me so that I'll be able to kill a couple of those fucking G-men."

Over the next few days, Yanowsky continued his rants against the FBI. He said that the FBI's story about the shooting was wrong and that he did not draw his gun. Instead, he said he was running away when he was hit by the shotgun blast. He claimed that, while laying prone on the ground, the agent with the machine gun walked up and attempted to let off a burst of machine gun fire at his head. The machine gun allegedly jammed after two bullets.

On February 7, 1936, Yanowsky was carried into the courthouse in Hoboken while still lying on a stretcher. He was sentenced to serve two years in federal custody for the suspended sentence that he had originally received as part of the Rope Ladder Gang. A warrant was also lodged for his arrest in the James "Ding-Dong" Bell shooting, and, after completing his federal sentence, he was informed that he would be sent back to New York to serve further prison time.

Given Yanowksy's high profile, he was transferred to Alcatraz in California. The infamous island prison was known as the toughest facility in all of America, and it housed the worst offenders in the country. Yanowsky settled into his new surroundings and could be found hanging out in the yard with other famous residents of Alcatraz, such as Alvin Karpis and members of The Barker Gang.

Joe Butler, Farmer Sullivan, and the other remaining members of the Butler Gang, which, courtesy of law enforcement had now been diminished to George Daggett, Victor Patterson, Buster Bell, Leslie Bell, and Leo Tocci (who had missed almost the entire West Side War after being returned to Pennsylvania to serve a year in prison for violating his parole in that state), were likely in a celebratory mood since the homicidal figurehead of their rival gang was now locked in one of the most secure buildings in the United States.

The Butler Gang had managed to take control of the more lucrative West Side piers, while Joe Butler's partner Farmer Sullivan had been making his own inroads establishing rackets in Greenwich Village. Joe Butler began to move out in the open again, as the war for the waterfront had been won, and his gang was now recognized as the main criminal force on the West Side. Capitalizing on the notorious reputation that he had established during the West Side War, he started to socialize with other prominent figures who worked on the waterfront, such as union leaders, business owners, and a variety of the remaining independent West Side criminals. Although Butler was busy enjoying his newfound status, he may have underestimated the capabilities of the leaderless Yanowsky Gang, as one final bloody curtain call was still to come.

The West Side Wars: The End and The Beginning

EVEN AS YANOWSKY was on a one-way journey through the penal system, the remaining members of his gang were busy making contingency plans, with both Frank Peraski and Albert Ackalitis filling the leadership void. The remaining members of the group decided that they were done hiding in the sticks and planned to return to New York City. For a hideout, they began to use Madeline Tully's latest boarding house, which was located at 322 West 19th Street.

With Madeline Tully occupying one of the apartments in the boarding house, Mickey Kane, Frank Peraski, and John Ryan rented rooms in the home, while Ackalitis, Campbell, Kress, and Manning came and went. Also staying with the bloodthirsty group, and usually acting as cooks, were Peraski's wife and a friend of hers named Jean Martin. Upon their return to the city, the on the run gangsters called in some reinforcements. Joining them was a good friend of Ackalitis' named Joseph "Heels" Murphy, who had been his co-accused during his arrest for burglary in 1934, and another career criminal named Joseph McKenna alias Joseph Devine, who had just been released from prison after completing a sentence for manslaughter.

The remnants of the Yanowsky Gang heard that members of the Butler Gang would be in attendance at a testimonial dinner at Cavanagh's Restaurant on West 33rd Street, which was being held for John "Ike" Gannon, a West Side resident and a senior member of the International Longshoremen's Association. The powerful International Longshoremen's Association, which was commonly known as the ILA, had been around since the early 1900s and was the union responsible for representing the dock workers in New York City. Given the Butler Gang's new stranglehold on the waterfront, most of the gang had integrated themselves into the union and become card carrying members.

Butler attended the dinner in the company of his partner Farmer Sullivan and Sullivan's new bodyguard, Robert "Barney" Baker. The hulking Baker was born in Brooklyn in 1911 and had come into Sullivan's employment while he was being trained as a heavyweight boxer. Mostly used as an undercard prizefighter, he amassed an 11-11 record during his unsuccessful boxing career, which spanned from 1929-1934. No saint before meeting Sullivan, Baker was a small-time thug who was known for his almost comedic ability to talk himself in and out of trouble. Prior to meeting Sullivan, he spent a year in prison after being convicted twice of throwing stink bombs in theaters while acting as a union goon during a theater workers strike.

At around 12:30 AM on March 15, 1936, the trio of Butler, Sullivan, and Baker departed the dinner along with an emerging labor leader named John O'Rourke. O'Rourke, who was friendly with Butler, was an official in the Teamsters Union. His territory encompassed the trucking industry on the West Side, so naturally, he was heavily involved in the waterfront.

Butler, O'Rourke, and Baker walked slightly ahead of Sullivan as they neared their car, which was parked in a large lot on West 34th, next to the Hotel New Yorker. As the four walked down the sidewalk, a covered automobile containing four men approached from behind and pulled up next to Butler. Two sawed-off shotguns peaked out of the car, and what happened next was described by one witness as "the sound of a fireworks factory exploding."

The shooters simultaneously cut loose with both barrels of their shotguns. Butler, who was the target of the shooting, was hit in the side of the face and the abdomen. Baker and O'Rourke attempted to turn away from the blasts, but they were also struck, Baker in the hip and left arm and O'Rourke in the back and right hand. Sullivan, who was slightly removed from the group, was not shot. A shocked Butler stumbled forward briefly, then fell to the pavement alongside Baker and O'Rourke. The gunmen's car sped away and disappeared in traffic down 9th Avenue.

Pedestrians ran to help the injured men, and when police arrived, they found a crowded and chaotic scene. The three shooting victims were rushed by ambulance to St. Vincent's Hospital while Farmer Sullivan, who had been pointed out by witnesses in the crowd as the fourth member of the group, was arrested and taken in for questioning. Sullivan was questioned for hours but remained tight-lipped. The frustrated police gave up when the thug would not even confirm his address.

At the hospital, Baker and O'Rourke's conditions were found to be not life-threatening, but Butler seemed to be deteriorating. Police were brought to his bedside to see if he would provide any information about the shooting, but Butler would not cooperate. At 2:00 AM, he died from his wounds.

The next morning, police provided a statement saying that Richard Butler had been killed, as the police were likely confusing Joe Butler as being the namesake of his father Richard "Big Dick" Butler. The mix-up was problematic for the elder West Side patriarch, as one of Joe's brothers happened to be named Richard; as a result, their father did not know which one of his sons had actually been killed.

New York Times reporter Meyer Berger caught up with

Big Dick Butler at the Avon Bar while he was trying to write a follow-up piece on the murder. When the newsman arrived, Big Dick Butler appeared calm and nonchalant while sitting in a booth alone and drinking. The once powerfully built Butler had aged considerably and relied on a cane to walk. Butler, who never shied away from media attention, allowed the reporter to remain with him while he tried to find out which one of his sons had been killed the night before.

Butler arrived at the morgue, and the reporter noted that the elderly man knew his way around the building too well. He approached the clerks at the front desk and asked which one of his boys lay dead in the back. The clerk fumbled through the cards on his desk and said, "It was Joe. We changed it after we found a union card in his jacket." Big Dick Butler did not flinch. With cane in hand, he hobbled up to the room where the detectives were working on his son's murder.

"So it was Joe," he announced as he entered the office. The detective responded, "It was Joe alright. That doesn't leave many more for you to identify then, does it?" Big Dick Butler's jaw tightened and, without a hint of bitterness, he listed off the names of his five remaining children. He then turned and walked down the stairs.

Back at the bar, Big Dick lamented to the reporter that when he ran the docks it was different. He stated that he did it with finesse, while his son Joe was rougher around the edges. Big Dick then reflected on the divide that led to his son's murder, "I always taught him, and all the rest, to stick together in one family. I kept them covered with my wings, like the old mother hen. They were alright. They were good lads."

The old man made one last attempt to rationalize the situation and asked, "Little things like this happen in any family and there's nothing I could have done to stop it, was there?" Butler let out a sigh as he could no longer keep up the tough façade. Sitting in the nearly empty bar, he stared ahead blankly as tears welled up in his red eyes and slowly streamed down his weathered face.

Within days of the Butler murder, police received an anonymous tip informing them that Butler's killers could be found in an apartment at 322 West 19th Street. Shortly after midnight on March 17, 1935, a large group of armed officers surrounded the building. A lone detective made his way up the stairs to the front gate of Madeline Tully's apartment and buzzed for her. Tully appeared and was questioned about her tenants. She cleverly provided false names, but the detective was not satisfied, and, at gunpoint, he forced her to open the gate.

The rest of the officers filed into the hallway behind Tully as she approached Peraski's apartment door. Tully knocked once and a voice asked who was there; Tully responded, and the door creaked open. The detectives pushed Tully through the door first and then crashed into the small front room with guns drawn. Peraski was caught standing at the door, and seated in the front room, eating ham and eggs, were Albert Ackalitis, Sonny Campbell, Heels Murphy, and Joseph McKenna. In the kitchen, police found Peraski's wife and Jean Martin cooking more food for the gangsters, while in the bedrooms Mickey Kane and John Ryan were sound asleep.

As detectives moved the group into the main room, Peraski made a move for an open window, but a detective drew a blackjack and struck him on the head. The apartment, which was sparsely furnished with wicker seating and large colorful curtains, contained no personal effects other than a number of expensive suits. However, when police began to search under the beds and inside the dressers, they found a plethora of incriminating evidence.

Scattered around the apartment were eight guns and a variety of burglary tools. In the garage, the police located two stolen cars. A large safe was also discovered in the closet, and after using blow torches, the police managed to crack it. Inside were two machine guns, two submachine guns, a repeating rifle, a hand grenade, two automatic pistols, assorted gun parts, and over 10,000 rounds of ammunition. Also, an unmailed letter addressed to Joe Butler was discovered in a drawer. The unsigned correspondence was filled with profanity and death threats directed at Butler and his friends. It had obviously been composed before the gangsters had followed through on their promises.

The press coined the men as "The Arsenal Mob" due to the number of weapons found in the apartment. Very few reporters actually connected them to the imprisoned Charlie Yanowsky, but, instead, preferred to write about them in more salacious ways, making them appear to be a roving band of murderers and robbers.

Detectives at the station house, who were more realistic about the group than their media counterparts, began to bring in witnesses from the bank robberies that had taken place in New Jersey. Peraski and Kane were charged with the Fort Lee and Prospect Park bank robbery, based on witness identifications, while Ackalitis and Campbell were identified as possible participants in the latter.

Additionally, Campbell, Peraski, and Heels Murphy were charged with the murder of Joe Butler. The detective in charge of the investigation stated that he was "morally certain" that the three had been at the scene, but he did not disclose what led him to that conclusion. The murder charges against the three were eventually dropped due to a lack of evidence, but the men still faced significant charges in relation to their other crimes.

The police also put out a notice to arrest Joe Kress on sight. Although Kress, who was still wanted for jumping bail as a result of the Ding-Dong Bell shooting, was not at the apartment at the time of the arrests, police believed he had been there only the day before the raid. The only member of the

Yanowksy group who was not arrested, or even mentioned by police, was John "Fats" Manning.

On May 1, 1936, after only fifteen minutes of jury deliberation, the entire gang was found guilty of being in the possession of an illegal machine gun. The conviction not only allowed the judge to pass a sentence of between seven to fourteen years, but also contained a special stipulation that a minimum term of fourteen years would be given if the guilty parties were found to be second-time felony offenders. On May 14, 1936, while chewing gum and not making eye contact, Ackalitis, Campbell, Peraski, Ryan, Murphy, and McKenna were all sentenced to fourteen years in prison, while McKenna was advised that he would likely also serve a remaining twelve years for his old manslaughter conviction. Kane, who had no previous felony convictions, received a three to seven-year sentence, along with the three women arrested with the gang.

Later, in 1941, Sonny Campbell would cop a plea to the Fort Lee bank robbery, Frank Peraski to the Prospect Park robbery, and Mickey Kane to both. They were all given ten-year sentences to run concurrently with their current prison terms. Peraski would be hit hardest, as Massachusetts would pursue the old jewelry store robbery, which was the charge that had originally led him to flee to New York City, and he received an additional ten years in that state.

In June of 1936, Joseph Kress, one of the last Yanowsky stalwarts, was finally caught by police. Kress was sentenced to five years in prison for possession of a machine gun, as a result of the James "Ding-Dong" Bell shooting.

Although there was essentially nothing left of the Yanowsky Gang, they suffered another setback only three days before the majority of the group was sentenced. On May 11, 1936, two of the last remaining friends of the gang, Archie Stewart and Stewart Wallace, were also arrested. The two former Rubel robbers had attempted to rob a bank in Pine Bush, New York, with three other ex-cons. The robbery was a success, as the group managed to steal more than $10,000, but the getaway was a complete failure. As state troopers converged, two of them managed to escape to the city and were caught at a later date; Stewart Wallace was arrested while walking on the side of a country road; Archie Stewart was wounded during a brief gun battle with the police; and another robber shot himself in the head moments before he could be arrested by pursuing law enforcement. Caught in the act, both Stewart and Wallace were given prison terms of thirty to sixty years, which was essentially a life sentence for men their age.

The Yanowsky Gang had officially gone the way of the dinosaur, and the timing could not have been better for both Eddie McGrath and John Dunn, as the two were scheduled to be released from prison within weeks of their rivals being packed off to the penitentiary. The West Side War was over, and by virtue of who was not dead or in prison, the Butler Gang had triumphed. Using the reputation that the group had established during the violent war, the path was now clear for the surviving members to attempt to solidify themselves as the top gangsters on the West Side waterfront.

13

Loose Ends

IN MAY OF 1936, McGrath and Dunn were both released from Sing Sing again, and along with George Daggett, they immediately vaulted themselves into leadership positions within their gang. Although McGrath and Dunn had only been gone for a year, a great deal had changed. Only George Daggett, Henry "Buster" Bell, Leslie Bell, Victor Patterson, Robert "Farmer" Sullivan, Robert "Barney" Baker, and Leo Tocci were left on the streets. In prison were John "Peck" Hughes and Edward Gaffney, who were serving short sentences, while Matthew Kane, James Skinner, Arthur Gaynor, and James "Ding-Dong" Bell would be gone for the next three to twenty years.

Following the death of Butler, the police began to refer to the gang as the Dunn-McGrath Mob due to the duo's senior standing on the waterfront. While Farmer Sullivan, with the assistance of his bodyguard Barney Baker, continued to focus his attention on the criminal operations within Greenwich Village, the rest of the gang had taken over the docks in McGrath and Dunn's absence. Shortly after their release, McGrath and Dunn got jobs as unionized loaders on Pier 59 and became card carrying members of ILA Local 895.

The two did no actual work and came and went as they pleased. An investigator from the parole office was frequently sent down to the pier to check on McGrath, but the docks were a busy labyrinth of workers, ships, trucks, and offices, and it proved difficult for him to find McGrath. On one occasion, the parole investigator believed, but could not prove, that McGrath pulled up to Pier 59 in a red convertible with a good-looking blonde beside him. McGrath reportedly ran into the offices, changed into work clothes, splashed water under his arms and on his face, and arrived, looking exhausted, to meet the investigator.

Everything was going smoothly for the Dunn-McGrath Mob, but there was still one loose end left from the Yanowsky Gang. The night of July 9, 1936, was a scorcher in the city, and the front stoops, roofs, and fire escapes in Harlem were lined with people trying to escape the heat of their apartments. Fats Manning, who was wearing an undershirt and dress pants, was out strolling. At 9:20 PM, he passed 336 East 108th Street, when a waiting gunman, who had been lurking in an alley, stepped out behind him. The shooter drew a pistol and fired four bullets into him. The triggerman, who police believed was John Dunn, fled from the crowded street. A small group of pedestrians ran to help Manning, but he was already dead. The rumor was that the lucky cops who arrived on the scene first found more than $2,000 in Manning's pocket, which was his remaining cut of Rubel profits. If the officers did actually find it, it never made it to the evidence room.

On July 25, 1936, another interesting body was discovered by police. At 1:00 AM, a semi-conscious minor criminal named Joseph Potter was found dumped on a lonely road in Whitestone, Queens. Potter had a record of arrests that mainly occurred in Pennsylvania, but he had also been recently held on charges in Brooklyn. It was evident that Potter had been beaten around the head before he was shot in the face and numerous times in the body.

Potter was taken to Flushing Hospital. The bullet that struck him in the face had shattered his jaw, and he was unable to communicate with police. While a gangland shooting of an out-of-town criminal was hardly a rare occurrence in New York City, the police were interested in a business card that they found in his pocket. Scrawled on the back of a lawyer's card was the prison mailing address for Frank Peraski's wife. Given that Peraski had operated, for a time, as a robber in Pennsylvania, they hypothesized that Potter was his associate. The theory was soon proven correct.

The police returned to Potter's bedside with a number of mug shots of people that they knew were tied to Peraski and the Yanowsky Gang. As police flipped through the images, Potter nodded up and down when shown a photograph of Frank Peraski's longtime friend, and fellow Madeline Tully acquaintance, Michael Piccardo. Before police could take a written statement from Potter, he died.

Homicide investigators found that Piccardo, who was also originally from Pennsylvania, had been a close associate of Potter, and that both men were aware that the remaining members of the Yanowsky Gang had been hiding with Madeline Tully. Although they did not confirm it to the media, it was suggested that Potter was actually the informant who provided the location of the gang to police. Detectives believed that when Piccardo found out, Potter was taken for a one-way ride. Piccardo was charged with first-degree murder, but Potter's deathbed statement was not admissible in court, and Piccardo was subsequently freed.

14

Loading

AS THE SUMMER of 1936 began, McGrath and Dunn were likely unaware that their criminal behavior on the waterfront would soon be welcomed by the very union that was supposed to be responsible for protecting the dock workers. Instead, the two, who had no ambition of becoming labor leaders, were focused on the task of taking control of the entire loading racket in West Greenwich and Chelsea.

Loaders, or "public loaders" as they were officially known, were groups of men who, through what was essentially squatters rights, controlled the loading and unloading of trucks at the piers. Public loading had started shortly after World War One and involved groups of men who banded together and assisted trucking companies with loading goods at the pier for a small fee, which would be based on the overall weight of the goods. Over the next ten to twenty years, the practice evolved to more organized groups, who were members of the International Longshoremen's Association, who worked at their own particular dock every day. The stevedoring companies who leased the piers, and should have been responsible for the job, were happy to allow the unaffiliated men to perform the task, as it reduced labor costs.

The ports in New York City had the unsavory honor of being one of the only locations in the United States where public loading was an accepted practice. The truck drivers, who were often affiliated with other unions, such as the Teamsters, either supported their fellow workers or were not interested in the hassle they would receive if they refused the service. Ultimately, the truck drivers passed the costs onto the trucking companies who, in turn, passed it on to the businesses who were receiving the product, which finally meant the increase was charged to the unknowing consumer.

The loading racket had always been ripe for gangster exploitation given its chaotic nature and the fact it generated over $25 million dollars in profits annually in New York. Each gang had a "boss loader" who was responsible for collecting the loading fees and distributing the final earnings to the rest of the loaders (who were paid at the set union rate). The remainder of the profits were kept by the boss loader, who often did no actual work other than assigning the men. The boss loader needed no certification, the business was not regulated, and the shipping companies had no say as to whom was acting as a loader on their docks. If the shipping companies attempted to fire a loading boss, then they risked a work stoppage from the other union members who worked on the pier.

By the 1920s, local gangsters realized how lucrative the business could be, and they began to bully themselves into the boss loader positions around the port. Under mob management, shady practices became the new norm; often, truckers were forced to do the loading themselves, loaders were using stevedoring company equipment to complete their own work, and in some cases, non-unionized employees were used. When shipping company executives or union officials were queried on the issue, everyone always agreed that it was just the cost of doing business in the busiest port in the world. Criminals flourished under the quasi-legal loading system. What began as charging a .5 cent per 100lbs loading fee in the early 1930s, quickly jumped to more than .11 cents per 100lbs within five years (or $1.75 in today's currency). Given the thousands upon thousands of pounds of freight that was moved through the piers each day, the revenue was considerable.

The few members of law enforcement that investigated the questionable system were never able to lay any charges against the gangsters due to the lack of cooperation they received. Everyone knew that the truckers had no choice if they wanted their goods moved or did not want to be intimidated by local gangsters, but proving it was another story. All over the docks, the longshoremen spoke of truckers who had been assaulted or thrown in the North River after refusing the use of loaders, but no one dared step forward with the information.

Once they had returned home from prison, McGrath and Dunn asked some of their most notorious friends to take over boss loader positions on piers up and down the West Side. McGrath and Dunn met no resistance to the changes, as any of the remaining independent operators were quick to vacate their piers after seeing what happened to those murdered during the West Side War. By spreading out their gangster friends, the Dunn-McGrath Mob hoped to take a cut of the loading from each dock and solidify their presence along the North River.

The men who were placed on the piers were all seasoned veterans of crime, and most seemed to have at least one arrest for murder on their police records. A sampling of their key enforcers on the docks during their early takeover of the loading racket included the following:

Tony Deliss, Pier 32: Deliss was an older gangster and close friend of Farmer Sullivan who was born in the late 1800s. Originally from Greenwich Village, Deliss led his own youthful gang of toughs until 1915, when he was convicted of murder when the hitman who he had used to kill a rival ratted on him. Deliss served nearly twenty years in prison, and when he was released, he began hanging around with his old friend Farmer Sullivan. When the Dunn-McGrath Mob started taking control of the piers, Sullivan arranged for Deliss to assume the position of boss loader on Pier 32, which was one of the most profitable spots on the North River.

Frank "U-Boat" Kelly, Pier 25: Kelly, born in 1898, was another older gangster who was fresh out of the penitentiary. Originally from Brooklyn, Kelly was convicted of murder in 1915, after shooting a robbery victim during an attempted mugging. Kelly met Tony Deliss in Auburn Penitentiary and became friends with famous gangster Owney Madden and a number of Madden's lieutenants, such as Arthur Biehler and Terry Reilly. After his release, Tony Deliss referred Kelly to George Daggett, who assisted him in obtaining a job on Pier 25. Kelly got along well with the members of the Dunn-McGrath Mob, and he became a trusted member of the gang. Kelly would later move to Pier 32, and join Deliss as co-boss loader, when Pier 25 closed in the early 1940s.

John "Chopsie" Plattner, Pier 34: A veteran of the ILA, Plattner had a long arrest record but no serious convictions. Popular with other ILA members and close to George Daggett, the well-connected waterfront veteran was a respected figure on the waterfront.

John "Mickey" McLoughlin, Pier 57 and Pier 58: McLoughlin was another career criminal who was born and raised on the West Side and knew the docks well. With over eight arrests, including one for homicide, McLoughlin had recently been released from Sing Sing after serving a long sentence for armed robbery. While in Sing Sing, he had become friendly with members of the Dunn-McGrath Mob and was rewarded with a boss loader job upon his release in the mid-1930s.

Edward O'Connell, Pier 59: The youngest of the Dunn-McGrath boss loaders, O'Connell was the overseer of Pier

59 during the West Side War. O'Connell had worked on the docks from a young age and also ran his own loansharking operation. He had served time in Elmira Reformatory when he was sixteen years old, but following that had been successful with staying out of prison.

Thomas "Red" Burke, Pier 60: Already the boss loader on Pier 60 during the West Side War, Burke had remained a Butler loyalist, and like O'Connell, he was left in the position following the demise of the Yanowsky Gang. A veteran of the West Side crime scene, Burke had a long arrest record and was close friends with Dunn-McGrath Mob member Leo Tocci.

Nicholas "The Bull" Tanzella, Pier 45: Tanzella, who was McGrath's original partner in crime before Dunn, was immediately welcomed back into the fold when he was released from prison in 1938. McGrath provided his old friend with a boss loader position on Pier 45, which was regarded as one of the most favorable docks on which to work.

For the first time in the history of the West Side, a singular gang was recognized as the rulers of the Greenwich and lower Chelsea piers. It hadn't taken long after the West Side War, but McGrath, Dunn and the rest of the gang were suddenly important people on the docks. Money was rolling in, courtesy of the loading racket; opportunities were opening up to them; and the gang was gaining access to powerful friends.

One such friend happened to be a longtime acquaintance of both George Daggett and the current International Longshoremen's Association (ILA) President, Joe Ryan. Thomas "Teddy" Gleason had grown up in Greenwich Village and had been the union delegate of Local 1258, which was the local branch that originally sponsored Daggett for membership in the ILA. Born in 1900 to Irish immigrants, Gleason was the first of twelve children. Teddy's father worked on the docks, and when Gleason's mother died, the then thirteen-year-old joined him on the piers.

The intelligent Gleason was known to speak his mind and possessed natural leadership abilities. His feisty attitude got him into trouble in 1932, when he was blacklisted by the shipping companies for arguing against what he felt were unfair working conditions. When the New Deal Legislation was passed, which gave union men the ability to elect their own officials, Gleason was able to triumphantly return to the docks after being elected as an ILA delegate in 1934. By 1936, Gleason was still only managing union affairs on a local level, but he had already been pegged by many as a future leader within the ILA.

Gleason recognized the hard nature of the docks, and he had grown up dealing with the criminals who operated on them. Recognizing that the gangsters were as much part of life on the piers as the ships themselves, the ambitious Gleason did not shy away from friendships with men like Daggett. Through Daggett, Gleason became acquainted with other members of the Dunn-McGrath Mob, which provided the group with another connection to the ILA.

It did not take long for McGrath and Dunn to realize that, as the leaders of the West Side loading racket, the largest longshoremen's union in North America would be even more welcoming to their gang's presence than they could have ever imagined.

Boss Joe and The Boys

LONG BEFORE THE Dunn-McGrath Mob became waterfront powers and the leaders of the Irish Mob, they recognized that to access the docks they would need to be members of the union that had jurisdiction over them — the ILA. What the gangsters did not realize was that the political winds on the waterfront were changing, and were blowing in their direction. While Eddie McGrath and John Dunn's underworld clout was growing, a perfect storm was brewing in the form of a shifting labor movement, increasing profits associated with New York City's shipping industry, and the greed of an overly ambitious ILA President.

The ILA itself first came to prominence in 1892 in the Great Lakes area. At the turn of the century, maritime shipping was one of the primary sources for moving goods and people, and a massive number of American men relied on the ports for work. The majority of these workers were recent immigrants who lacked the ability to advocate for themselves, so by joining the ILA, they gained bargaining power in numbers. The union found immediate success organizing and providing support to the dock workers, who were often subjected to irregular work and dangerous employment for low wages. During its early years, the ILA also became affiliated with the American Federation of Labor, an extremely powerful umbrella association that regulated unions across America.

The union negotiated better contracts for dock workers and membership swelled to over one hundred thousand men by 1905. To be eligible to work, the ILA members would pay regular dues to fund the union's operating costs. Although gains were being made, the working conditions that long-shoremen were subjected to were still harsh and unstable due to the nature of the work and the absence of workers' rights laws. Injury, and even death, was commonplace, and the pay was barely enough for someone to live on.

At the time of McGrath and Dunn's ascension on the waterfront, the current ILA President was Joseph "Joe the Boss" Ryan. Ryan was born on May 11, 1884 in Babylon, Long Island. Both of his parents were Irish immigrants who would die within months of each other, when Ryan was still in grade school, and he would eventually be adopted by a woman who resided near the docks, on West 19th Street in the Chelsea section of Manhattan. In 1912, he joined the ILA, but within his first year on the job, he was left unable to work after being hurt while unloading a ship. Ryan, who would become the prototype everyman politician, was not going to let his inability to work stop his social-climbing ways. The thickset and reddish-haired Irishman used his gift of the gab and his barroom manners to become popular with other union members. Within the year, he was appointed Secretary of ILA Local 791, which, at the time, was a relatively small union local within the ILA. The position opened doors for Ryan, who began to interact with ILA leaders, including Joe Butler's father Richard "Big Dick" Butler.

Using his public speaking ability and charisma, Ryan began to play a big part in the growth of the ILA in the New York City region, and he successfully led numerous membership drives. With shipping moving away from the Great Lakes region to New York City, and Ryan becoming the face of the organization, he was elected International President, the highest position in the union, in 1927.

The timing could not have been better for Ryan. When the

Great Depression swept over the country, masses of unemployed workers flooded the market with cheap labor. With a surplus of available workers, ILA membership flourished, and it soon became one of the largest unions in operation. Ryan was able to use this momentum to plant ILA flags across other port cities in the United States, including the entire West Coast. The success that Ryan obtained caused him to gradually lose touch with his members, and he began to turn the union into his own personal playground.

Ryan maintained a lavish office in the Lawyers Trust Building, at 265 West 14th Street, where he courted the rich and fabulous of New York City. Although Ryan appeared to be the spokesperson for the working class, he played both ends of the spectrum and was also friendly with some of New York City's most elite businessmen and politicians. Ryan created the Joseph P. Ryan Association and would host annual black tie dinners to celebrate himself. In 1931, the guest list included future President, and then labor-friendly governor of New York, Franklin D. Roosevelt; Jimmy Walker, the corrupt Mayor of New York City; New Jersey political boss Frank Hague; shipping tycoons such as William "Big Bill" McCormack; and the President of the American Federation of Labor, William Green. Long gone were the days of sweating it on the docks.

Ryan was able to keep the longshoremen of the ILA in line through a simple method of control known as the shape-up system, which was a basic way to hire men and guarantee that he would continue to provide the shipping companies with an endless supply of low-cost labor. All able-bodied union men would turn up every morning at their local pier for work. A hiring boss, who had been designated by the stevedoring companies, usually at the recommendation of an ILA official, would then select the longshoremen that he wanted to work on the pier that day. If you wanted to be picked often, it was best to keep your mouth shut and support Ryan. The system itself divided the union membership deeply, as the men who were receiving regular work were in favor of it, while those who did not, resented it. Regardless of how the men felt about the practice, the decision to give the hiring boss complete control over the work of hundreds of longshoremen often led to further corruption. On some piers, hiring bosses were even known to collect a financial tribute, or "pass the hat," before granting men the right to work.

Under Ryan's leadership, the union had grown all over the United States, and although Ryan's ultimate goal was to control all of the dock workers in the country, he was meeting resistance. Dissention was brewing amongst the ranks, and in 1934, Harry Bridges, a leftist union leader from San Francisco who was a longtime Ryan rival, organized a strike of the entire West Coast ILA in response to a contract that Ryan had negotiated. The West Coast ILA felt that the contract was unfair, and they also demanded that Ryan abolish the shape-up in favor of a hiring hall system based on seniority. Ryan outright refused. ILA membership on the West Coast rejected the recommended contract, and against Ryan's orders, went off the job. The result was a violent eighty-two day strike that paralyzed ports from California to Washington.

Ryan was livid and embarked on a West Coast speaking tour. His efforts were a complete failure, and at each stop, he was met with hostility and anger. At one point, strikebreakers violently clashed with the West Coast longshoreman and the mini riot was only quelled after the National Guard was called to intervene. Using the new legislation that allowed union members to elect their own leaders, Bridges, and other striker leaders, replaced Ryan loyalists in union elections up and down the West Coast. Ryan's rivals then broke away from the ILA, and in 1937 they established their own West Coast longshoremen's union known as International Longshore and Warehouse Union (ILWU). With the creation of the ILWU, the ILA ceased to exist on the West Coast and Ryan's dreams of controlling waterfront shipping across North America were over.

Ryan knew that if he was going to remain in power, he had to stop the spread of change. He was desperate to maintain the lifestyle he had worked so hard for, and he decided that to enforce his control over the rank and file members in New York City, he would need backup. Ryan needed men who could intimidate, enforce his rule, and crush dissidents. Ryan needed men like McGrath and Dunn.

The answer to Joe Ryan's predicament was to fully embrace the criminal element, even though he once was appointed to a term as the head of the New York State Parole Board. In the rough world of the waterfront, he was perfectly aware of who the players were on the piers. Rather than make an attempt to expel these men, or put a stop to the spread of criminality in his union, Ryan invited them to his office and courted them.

All along the New York City waterfront, Ryan was embracing, or completely dismissing, the fact that gangsters were taking over. In Brooklyn, Tony Anastasio and his brothers controlled docks; however, their power lay in the fact that one of the brood was Albert "The Mad Hatter" Anastasia, a future boss of the later named Gambino family. Also from the Gambino family was Alex "The Ox" DiBrizzi, a criminal with a two-page-long criminal record who had muscled his way into power on the Staten Island docks with the assistance of his nephews. The remaining piers in Manhattan, which were not located in the Dunn-McGrath Mob's West Side territory, were controlled by members of the Genovese family. Soldier Michael Clemente was in charge of the East River piers, while his mentor, Joseph "Socks" Lanza, ran the docks at the Fulton Fish Market.

Ryan became friendly with various hoodlums, as he knew

that by having these men in his pocket, he could enforce his will through old-school terror tactics. No West Coast ILA man, who Ryan denounced as communists, would dare try to incite revolution if a gangster was present to threaten him, give him beating, and throw him in the Hudson.

Criminals had long infiltrated the ILA ranks, and many already held leadership positions in the union, but in a number of goodwill gestures, Ryan played favorites with some of the most dangerous men operating in his world. With Teddy Gleason acting as an intermediary, Ryan met with McGrath, Dunn, and Daggett. Ryan knew that the men sitting in front of him were the de facto leaders of his own home base on the West Side, and that was just fine with him as long as they were waving his flag. The Dunn-McGrath Mob would become Ryan's go-to men, as, although Italians controlled many sections of the waterfront, these men were fellow Irish West Siders.

To legitimatize the rough-and-tumble criminals, and to give them the power that they needed to keep control over their territory, Ryan granted them their own local charter within the ILA. There would be no election or consultation with other ILA representatives, and in later years, Ryan would swear that his own union members had chosen these men as their leaders. In November 1936, Eddie McGrath, Johnny Dunn, Teddy Gleason, George Daggett, Leo Tocci, and a new partner named Cornelius "Connie" Noonan formed a "Worker's Committee" that led to the creation of a new ILA Local known as ILA Local 1346-2: Terminal Checkers and Platform Men. The addition of Noonan in the venture was as a frontman who would provide legitimacy to the new union local.

Noonan was born in 1896 in Jersey City, New Jersey, to an impoverished family. When he was young, his family was taken in by a local politician and saloon owner named Nat

Kenny. Noonan and his brothers grew up alongside Nat's own son, John V. Kenny, who, like his father, would become a powerful politician in New Jersey. With the connection to the Kenny family, the Noonan boys did well for themselves, the pinnacle being when Connie's brother, Edward, was promoted to Commissioner of the Jersey City Police Department. Connie Noonan would drop out of law school after one year and become an auditor with United States Shipping Board. It was during his time with the Shipping Board that he first became acquainted with a number of ILA leaders.

Noonan did not shy away from the seedier side of waterfront business. Notoriously greedy, he gravitated to men like McGrath and Dunn, and he would turn out to be the perfect organizer for their new union venture. Noonan had an employment history, no criminal record, and actually knew a bit about managing a business. Daggett sponsored him into the ILA shortly before the creation of ILA Local 1364-2, and he was placed in the role of President of the new charter. Dunn became the Vice-President, Gleason became the Secretary-Treasurer, and Leo Tocci was given the title of Business Agent. Keeping their hands in every pot, Daggett also maintained his position as Business Agent with ILA Local 1258. Since McGrath and Dunn had already once violated their parole for associating with each other, it was decided that McGrath would remain, at least on paper, a loader on Pier 59.

Jurisdictionally, the new charter would allow the gang to organize the platform men who worked at the largely non-unionized freight terminals, warehouses, and shipping centers that were located near the docks. With the assistance of Joe Ryan, men like John Dunn, a veteran of Sing Sing who had been charged with one murder and was suspected in many others, were now drawing a salary as officials for one of the largest unions in the United States. The Dunn-McGrath Mob had been given their own charter for personal pilferage and official access to the waterfront. Overnight the gang had become labor leaders.

A brief union drive netted about two thousand terminal workers. No elections were held, and the terminal workers who were already part of existing ILA unions, but now fell under the control of ILA Local 1346-2, were sent a letter informing them that due to jurisdictional issues they were being absorbed into the new charter.

An account of one longshoremen's dealing with Ryan's new goons was documented in an anonymous letter to a labor newspaper. The ILA member stated that he attended a union meeting with about one hundred others concerning a particular grievance that they felt Joe Ryan was doing nothing about. Also in attendance were John Dunn, Peck Hughes, and Barney Baker. The longshoremen, who were all West Siders, knew of the gangsters' reputations, and their presence was enough to silence the room. However, one member decided to bravely take the podium and publicly address his concerns. During a break in the meeting, the outspoken longshoreman was roughed up by the three gangsters and reminded that he should keep his mouth shut. The anonymous writer of the letter claimed that this public intimidation occurred in the presence of a police officer who was on friendly terms with the gang and ignored everything.

For the handful of ILA men who did not heed the gang's warnings, they could expect the same treatment that ILA member George Donahue received. Donahue, who was college educated, but had taken a job on the waterfront as a checker during the Great Depression, began to actively speak out against the growing criminal element in the union. One day while he was working, George Daggett, Barney Baker, and two other men who Donahue did not recognize, approached him. Daggett informed Donahue that he should keep his opinions to himself or they would "shoot him in the head and throw him off the pier." Donahue told the group that he had no intention of shutting up, so Baker and the other two men with Daggett took turns using him as a punching bag.

Donahue did the unthinkable and actually went to the police and filed charges against Baker and Daggett. Daggett disappeared off the waterfront for a time and Baker was found and arrested on April 1, 1937. When Baker's trial started, a longshoreman, who was friendly with the gang, testified that Donahue had initiated the fight. Baker was acquitted and Daggett returned to the docks.

After Baker's acquittal, Donahue could no longer find any work on the waterfront. His checking job was gone, and the hiring bosses would not select him for other longshoremen work. Donahue was an example of the treatment that long-shoremen who were anti-Ryan received, and although many shared the same distaste for their leader, they did so quietly, as they knew that the next step after a beating was likely a bullet.

16

Spaghetti Dinners

WHILE MCGRATH AND Dunn had been focused on taking over the West Side docks, Farmer Sullivan had become somewhat of a thorn in the side of a number of powerful gangsters. Though the docks were an institution for the West Side Irish, Sullivan's Greenwich Village neighborhood had begun to become increasingly multicultural. Different ethnic groups were active in the area, the most prominent being the Greenwich Village crew of the then Luciano (and later Genovese) crime family. McGrath had always gotten along well with the Italians, but Sullivan frequently butted heads with the Luciano family's acting boss, Vito Genovese, and his right-hand man Anthony "Tony Bender" Strollo.

Farmer Sullivan despised Italian gangsters, as he felt that they were nothing but pimps and low-class criminals, and he took their expansion as a personal affront. Not only did it negatively impact his rackets, but also Sullivan had a unique perception that it was his role to protect the original residents of Greenwich from the growing number of immigrants. The stubborn old fighter had no quit, and with his own group of men, including his key enforcer Robert "Barney" Baker, he began to wage an antagonistic guerilla war.

Sullivan began to threaten, beat, and rob the runners who sold tickets for Genovese's Italian lottery in Greenwich. Next, he wrecked a prostitution operation and roughed up two pimps who paid tribute to Strollo. A staunch Catholic,

Sullivan looked down upon the pimping business and hated the idea of "white women" working for Italians.

The situation was sure to become more violent, so McGrath attempted to intercede with his good friend, and now Luciano crime family captain, Jimmy Alo. Although the diplomatic McGrath was looking for a solution to the problem, he also had his own self-serving motivations. McGrath was finally making headway onto the piers, and he wanted to make it clear that he was not behind any of the recent troubles. Alo, who had recently been spending time in Florida with Lucky Luciano's best friend Meyer Lansky, as part of their new plans to open a string of casinos in the state, informed McGrath that he would approach other members of the family about the situation.

The response back from the Italians was that they would stay away from the actual piers in Greenwich, since McGrath was friends with Alo; however, it was made clear that Sullivan should stop his expansion and retain what he had in Greenwich. The compromise suited both groups, as the Dunn-McGrath Mob was solely interested in the piers, and Genovese and Strollo were tired of the problems that Sullivan was causing.

The hard-headed Sullivan told the rest of the gang that he would handle his own problems, and he continued to terrorize Strollo's rackets until word came down that the Italians wanted to set up a meeting, to negotiate peace in Greenwich and allocate territory. The late-night rendezvous was to be held on September 20, 1936, at a new restaurant named Joe Martini's in Matawan Township, New Jersey. The Italians informed Sullivan that they would all sit down to a spaghetti dinner and sort out their problems like men.

Late that evening, Sullivan, who was wearing an expensive suit, flashy tie pin, and diamond ring, arrived with four other men at the tavern, which was located on a lonely country road.

The owner, Joe Martini, later told police that a large man, who was likely Barney Baker, shadowed Sullivan closely. The group placed a big food order and then began to talk in hushed tones.

One staff member later told police that he heard what sounded to be a powerful automobile pull up to the bar shortly after Sullivan's arrival. The automobile remained running and two men approached the window of the tavern, where Sullivan was sitting with his back turned. The two then drew revolvers, and in succession, fired eight shots through the glass at Sullivan. Seven bullets missed their mark and wildly smashed into the walls around the bar, including one that went through a bathroom wall and hit an innocent customer in the hip. A single bullet found its mark and traveled through Sullivan's back and into his heart.

By the time that the innocent bystanders came out from their hiding spots, all they found were overturned chairs, an open door, and Sullivan lying face down on the floor. Sullivan's party, who had arrived in two automobiles, had fled the scene in one of the cars and left behind Sullivan's own sedan. Police arrived and searched Sullivan's pockets. They found $80 cash, a number of business cards that identified him as a member of the ILA, and a curious hand-written list that outlined particular pay-offs to upcoming Democratic and Republican campaigns.

Detectives, who suspected that Sullivan had participated in up to ten murders during his criminal career, climbed the stairs to his apartment to notify his wife of the news. Ella Sullivan, with dry eyes, sent her eighteen-year-old son Robert Jr. to the morgue to identify Sullivan, while the gangster's beloved pet parrot chirped at the exiting detectives, "Good-bye! Good-bye! Good-bye papa!"

Years later, Barney Baker's future wife informed police that Baker confessed to her he had been shot twice during his criminal career, once at the Joe Butler murder scene in

1936 and then the following year "at a spaghetti dinner in New Jersey." According to her, he said that he and his group were invited out as a peace offering and that when they got there the other group just, "opened up on them." Baker said he was superficially wounded in the shoulder by one of the bullets that night. The police were unable to confirm if Baker had been present, and he always denied any knowledge of the incident. Following the murder of his mentor, Baker was given work on the docks and taken in as a full-time member of the Dunn-McGrath Mob.

The murder of Farmer Sullivan was not the only excitement to take place on the night of September 20, 1936. At nearly the exact same time that Sullivan was being murdered, John Dunn's brother, Peter, and John "Chopsie" Plattner, the boss loader of Pier 34, were drinking at Hymie's Bar at 55 Christopher Street, in the heart of the Greenwich Village bar district, with a tavern owner named Harold Sullivan (no relation to Farmer Sullivan) and Richard Maher, a neighborhood cop who was friendly with the gangsters.

As the group was standing in front of the bar, at around 4:00 AM, they got into an argument with two off-duty policemen named John Buckley and John Bell (no relation to the Bell brothers). The argument became more heated, and Chopsie Plattner punched Bell in the face. The other police officer, Buckley, steamed in to assist Bell, but he was beaten and thrown down a set of stairs next to the bar by Peter Dunn and Harold Sullivan. As the inebriated Buckley lay at the bottom of the stairs, he drew his gun and fired two shots upward at Dunn and Sullivan. Dunn was struck in the thigh and Sullivan in the abdomen. Hearing the shots, Maher, the police officer who was friendly with the members of the Dunn-McGrath Mob, ran over and returned fire at Buckley from his own service revolver. Buckley was hit in the shoulder and thigh. The drunken battle royale only ended when the group heard sirens approaching. Dunn, Sullivan, and Buckley were all taken to St. Vincent's Hospital, where Sullivan died from his wound. The media covered the embarrassing shootout, but the charges against the officers were quietly dropped.

Varick

WITH THEIR CONTROL over the loading on the West Greenwich and Lower Chelsea piers, the Dunn-McGrath Mob was receiving a considerable income, and with their own union and support from the leader of the ILA, they now had the credentials to back up their claim.

Besides McGrath and Dunn, the gang's inner circle in 1937 included George Daggett, who was essentially the third part of the gang's leadership, Connie Noonan, Henry "Buster" Bell, Leo Tocci, boss loaders Nick "The Bull" Tanzella and Frank "U-Boat" Kelly, Thomas "Red" Burke, Robert "Barney" Baker, and the pair of John "Peck" Hughes and Edward Gaffney, who had both been recently released from prison in New Jersey.

Also joining the core of the gang were two friends of McGrath's named John "Jackie" Adams and Daniel "Danny Brooks" Gentile. Adams was a gambler and occasional businessman who fit in well with the gang's plans to find less notorious associates to represent their new growing portfolio. Gentile had known McGrath and Nick Tanzella since boyhood, and he gravitated towards his old friends once he found out about the success they were having. A stout man, who had an unsuccessful career as a prizefighter, Gentile had begun operating as a minor criminal along the West Side docks after washing out of the ring.

Shortly after being granted their union charter, the Dunn-McGrath Mob set up a waterfront office, in the heart of ILA territory near Christopher Street, at the union hall at 10th

Avenue and Waverly in West Greenwich. Once settled into the
ILA offices, most of the gang who were not already employed
on the docks were also given plum jobs within the new union.
The gangsters would come and go from the union offices as
they pleased, and they could usually be found socializing in
the nearby bars and restaurants.

One remaining nuisance to the gang was Philip "Philsie"
Sheridan (of no relation to McGrath's old prohibition partner
Andrew "Squint" Sheridan), a hardened con who had served
over ten years for rape. Sheridan had been the gangster who,
along with Fats Manning, had attempted to take over the
loading on Pier 60 from Tommy Burke during the West Side
War. Following Manning's murder, he had been playing a
dangerous game, as he had begun to bully a handful of ILA
officials in an attempt to get hired into a lucrative position in
the union.

On the night of December 29, 1936, boss loaders Eddie
O'Connell and Frank Kelly, who Sheridan had previously been
friendly with in prison, acted as intermediaries and brought
Sheridan to the gang's union office, where they were to discuss
how they could accommodate him on the waterfront. Kelly
and O'Connell led Sheridan into an empty room, where he
was seated across a desk from McGrath and Dunn. According to a confidential police report, a friendly talk commenced
until Frank Kelly drew a gun, and without warning, fired
three bullets into Sheridan's head and upper back. The murder
of Sheridan would serve as another reminder to those who
thought of crossing the gang.

Sheridan's body was loaded into a car while the murder
weapon and another pistol were left in John Dunn's car, which
was parked near the union hall. The gang had left to make
the short drive to the North River so that they could dump
Sheridan's body into the freezing water, when a pedestrian
walked by Dunn's car and noticed the two guns partially

covered in the backseat. The pedestrian then flagged down a nearby patrolman who also looked in the car and saw the guns. The patrolman immediately left to call the station and speak to a detective. By the time more officers returned to the scene, both the car and the guns were gone. The license plate, which the patrolman had recorded, was checked and came back as belonging to a John M. Dunn. The police, who were unaware that a murder had taken place only hours earlier, decided not to pursue charges since they had not successfully seized the guns, which would make it difficult to prove a case.

In April of 1937, the decomposed body of Sheridan, which could only be identified through fingerprint records, floated to the surface near a Brooklyn pier. Since four months had passed, no connection was made to the guns that were spotted in Dunn's car, and the case went cold.

The gang's next venture was a natural progression that tied their new union charter to their control over the loading operations on the West Side. The business was a wild brainstorm by the gang's union accountant, Charlie Miller, and it would eventually make the members of the gang significantly wealthier. In the loading business, bills were often provided to the truckers, who would then return the information to their employer. Many times the employers would neglect to pay these loading fees. Miller rightly theorized that the gang could buy other loading businesses' bad debt at a cut rate, and given their fearsome reputation, collect the full bill themselves. The gang's well-honed intimidation skills would make them the perfect operators of a collection agency.

In May 1937, Varick Enterprises was officially incorporated. On paper, Connie Noonan was again President of the corporation, McGrath's friend John "Jackie" Adams was Vice-President, and an additional frontman, named Benjamin "Benny" Estreicher, was listed as an Officer. Charles Miller was also hired to manage Varick's finances in conjunction with his role as their union accountant. An office at 99 Hudson Street was rented, which was conveniently located within five minutes of the ILA head office. Two women were hired to work as secretaries, names were put on the doors, and from the outside, it looked like just another small business. In reality, the venture's main financial backers, along with Noonan and Adams, were Eddie McGrath, Johnny Dunn, George Daggett, Leo Tocci, and McGrath's Mafia connection, Jimmy Alo. To an outsider, the business appeared to be a moderately busy collection agency, although the office became conspicuous to building staff and tenants due to a steady stream of visitors from the rougher parts of town.

Varick was so successful in their collections that they became a clearinghouse for companies' red ink. Loaders who did not possess the considerable clout that the Dunn-McGrath Mob had on the waterfront, and who were having problems collecting payments, would sell their entire receivable accounts to Varick at discount price. At any given time, Varick only had a handful of strong-arm men on the payroll, as within months of the business' conception the name of the company alone was usually enough to encourage unpaid debts to be honored. Barney Baker, Leo Tocci, and Tommy Burke were three of the main collectors, but essentially all members of the gang could be relied upon for their "services" at a moment's notice. Experts in extortion, when the gangsters came for the cash they often left with even more money than what was originally owed. Investigators later believed that within half a year Varick had over one thousand active accounts throughout the Port of New York. The business even grew to include other shipping companies who weren't involved in loading, but were still looking to offload their overdue accounts.

The real business was not actually taking place at the Varick offices, but instead in watering holes where waterfront criminals gathered. Every morning the gang's loaders and collectors would meet in the West Shore Bar and Grill, which was located across the street from Pier 45, and owned by gang associate Raymond "Sonny" Thompson. Connie Noonan would be on hand to delegate the day's orders and cash pickups. The bar, along with the union office and the Varick offices, would then be used as a drop-off point after the day's profits had been collected.

Miller, the gang's accountant, cooked the books and hid the company's illicit profit. The success of Varick can best be illustrated in a comical interaction that took place between Miller and Connie Noonan, which was witnessed by an investigator assigned from the district attorney. From afar, the investigator watched as Miller met Noonan in a cigar shop and gave him one day of "unofficial earnings," which was in the form of two large rolls of banded cash. The rolls were so large that Noonan could not fit them into his pant pockets and had to strategically squeeze and maneuver them into his waistband. Life was good for the gang.

18

Let the Good Times Roll

THE BEGINNING OF 1937 kicked off with a literal bang as one of the last minor players in the West Side War, who had been aligned with the Yanowsky Gang, would meet an end similar to a good number of his contemporaries. On January 30, 1937, Ralph "Lulu" Clements, who had accompanied Francis "Buster" Smith to Pier 59 when he robbed boss loader Eddie O'Connell, was sitting in the back seat of his friend James Lavin's car. Lavin and Clements got into what appeared to be a meaningless argument until Lavin pulled out a gun and shot Clements four times in the body. After a brief but wild escape attempt, Lavin was arrested, and Clements' body fell tumbling to the pavement when the police opened the rear passenger door. Lavin, who had already served nearly fifteen years for a manslaughter charge in 1923, was tried for the murder. Any information about the reason for Clements' slaying died with Lavin, as, only hours after he was convicted, he hung himself in his prison cell.

Another Dunn-McGrath Mob related murder occurred during the early morning hours of July 4, 1937, and like the previous ones that members of the group had committed, it would help cement their reputation as stone cold killers. That night, Leslie Bell, the younger sibling of Ding Dong Bell and Buster Bell, was enjoying a night out on the town with two women and four other men. Part of Bell's touring company that evening was a fellow ex-convict named John Kirby.

Numerous witnesses later stated that they saw a sudden

argument break out between Bell and Kirby in front of a bar and grill at 823 Greenwich Street. Bell stepped away from the group, drew a pistol, and yelled a threat at Kirby. Oddly enough, one of the females in the party broke out in laughter at the sight of Bell with the gun drawn. Kirby took a small step forward as Bell yelled, "Here it is!" Bell then fired four shots into Kirby's chest. The laughing girl continued to shriek with delight as Kirby lay dead on the sidewalk.

Bell admitted to being one of the people in the touring party, but he stated that he was not present during the shooting and that he did not know Kirby. On August 16, 1937, homicide charges against him were dismissed due to a lack of evidence. Although there were numerous witnesses to the shooting, no one was willing to positively identify the killer. Bell was not off the hook though, as during his brief incarceration, he had reportedly acted erratically. A psychologist assessed him and, under New York State's strict mental health laws, it was deemed that Bell was a "mental defective" who would need to be committed. He was then shipped off to an institution for the next seven years.

With the past year having been a hugely successful one for the Dunn–McGrath Mob, some of its members decided to invest their profits into one last new venture — the numbers racket. The numbers game was a long-standing tradition on the docks and operated under a relatively simple system. A "controller" would be responsible for certain piers, warehouses, or terminals, and would have anywhere from six to twelve "runners" working for them, who were usually union men or neighborhood kids looking to make an extra buck. The runners would comb their turf and sell tickets to the longshoremen who were interested in playing. The winning number of the day would then be derived from the last number before the decimal in the handle at a particular daily racetrack.

McGrath, Dunn, George Daggett, Connie Noonan, Varick

Vice-President Jackie Adams, boss loader Tony Deliss, and original Butler gang member Victor Patterson all bought into the start-up, with McGrath, Dunn and Daggett contributing the lion's share. With Eddie Gaffney assisting in coordinating the entire operation, the gang appointed Johnny Dunn's brother Peter, Danny Gentile, Tommy Burke, and another ILA official named Joe Franklin, who was already involved in the numbers racket in Staten Island on behalf of local dock overlord Alex DiBrizzi, as controllers.

Like the gang's other recent expansions, the numbers game also prospered. With no other competition on the Lower West Side piers, their numbers game had so many players that it would take Noonan, Gentile, and Gaffney nearly three hours to count the money and sort the winnings every day. On occasion, other members of the gang, including McGrath, would come along to help due to the sheer volume of tickets sold. Once the winning players were identified, Noonan would handle the payoff.

Since the gang was making good money in the numbers racket, they would not tolerate any potential competition. One of the last big independent hoods on the waterfront was John "Kiki" Costello. The Costello family had been involved in the rackets on the Chelsea piers since the late 1920s and were part of the feud with Tommy Protheroe that led Protheroe to try to machine gun one of the Costellos in 1933. The older Costello brother, William, had been a notorious character in the area until he was killed in a shootout with a policeman during an escape from a robbery. Kiki, who still controlled a numbers game around Pier 51, was no angel either and had two murder charges on his police record.

On June 15, 1937, Costello, who lived at 98 9th Avenue, took his one-year-old son out in his stroller. At 10:00 PM, his wife came out of their home and met Costello, who was talking to a group of neighborhood men. She collected the child and left Costello lounging on a stoop. Within five minutes of Costello's wife leaving, a dark sedan pulled up to the curb. Before Costello had time to notice, two men stepped out of the car and moved toward him. In front of a large crowd, both men pointed revolvers at Costello and fired four bullets into his head. The two gunmen, who were later described as young and well-dressed, calmly got back into the car and sped away.

A reverend from the nearby St. Bernard's Church raced to the scene and administered last rites to the dead man. His wife was interviewed and stated, "They were after him, but I don't know why."

The rest of 1937 was the beginning of a new dawn for the Dunn-McGrath Mob. For the first time in the gang's history, they had significant money flowing in, they had established the political and criminal connections to continue to create opportunities for themselves and, most importantly, they had successfully eradicated almost all of their direct competition.

The always dapper McGrath embraced his new role as a gang boss. Unlike Dunn, who had the reputation for being the hands-on partner, McGrath assumed the role of the problem solver. Always the more presentable of the two, McGrath represented the gang in their interactions with politicians, senior ILA members, businessman, and the revolving door of faces on the New York City social scene.

Still a bachelor who had no plans of settling down, McGrath rented a posh hotel suite at the Shoreham Hotel at West 55th Street. McGrath, who had a taste for the finer things in life, was a regular at Curtis Custom Tailors Inc., on 5th Avenue, where he would often spend thousands of dollars a year. McGrath was not only generous with himself, but also he would regularly shower his parade of girlfriends with expensive gifts and clothing. Known as a serial dater, his taste in women tended towards well-built showgirls and Broadway dancers.

Some of the gang's favorite haunts were Dinty Moore's Restaurant, on West 46th Street, Gallagher's Steak House, on West 52nd Street, and the Copacabana after it opened in 1940. The Dunn-McGrath Mob, which included many ex-West Side boxers, could usually be found in attendance at the big fights. In later years, when questioned by police about their association with other members of the gang, the usual response was, "Yeah I know him, I think I ran into him at one of the fights," or "I may have seen him having dinner once at Moore's."

Other gang favorites included Pappa's Restaurant and Pool Room, on the South Side of 14th Street, which was a regular hangout for the ILA crowd; Eddie Maxwell's Bar on Christopher and West Street; the Washington Diner on Christopher and Greenwich, which was also used as a cheque cashing establishment for the gang; and Duffy's Tavern, on West 48th Street, which was owned by William "Broadway Bill" Duffy, the famous boxing manager and former lieutenant of Owney Madden.

When McGrath wasn't spending time with his gang, he could be found with other well-known organized crime figures. McGrath and his old friend Jimmy Alo often met to play cards, and through Alo, McGrath became acquainted with influential gangsters such as Meyer Lansky, Bugsy Siegel, and a variety of other mobsters who belonged to the Luciano (later named Genovese) crime family. Alo had continued to explore expansion into Florida, and by the late 1930s, he had moved to the sunshine state after opening a number of quasi-legal, and incredibly lucrative, casinos with Meyer Lansky, which included the lavish Colonial Inn in Hallandale. To protect his waterfront investments while in Florida, Alo introduced McGrath to a friend, and an equally powerful player in the Luciano family, named Joe Adonis.

Giuseppe Antonio Doto, who went by Joe Adonis, was born in 1902 and was a close confidant of Lucky Luciano. When

Luciano was convicted and sentenced to thirty to fifty years in 1936, Adonis remained one of the most powerful individuals in the Genovese crime family, with rackets from Brooklyn to New Jersey, as well as being an investor in Alo and Lansky's Florida casinos. Like his relationship with Jimmy Alo, McGrath also grew close with Joe Adonis, as well as then Genovese boss Frank Costello, and he was regularly spotted with various high-ranking Mafia members.

While McGrath was socializing with the underworld elite, Dunn was pursuing a relationship that would permanently tie he and McGrath together. A frequent visitor to McGrath's sister Anna's home during the time McGrath had been living there, Dunn had fallen hard for the good-looking housewife. After Anna's marriage ended, Dunn, with the approval of McGrath, began to court her. The two fell for each other and married. Moving to the suburbs with Anna and her children from her previous marriage, Dunn purchased a nice home in Corona, Queens, and in time the couple would add another child of their own.

McGrath and Dunn presented themselves as legitimate but still thrived on the vicious reputations that they had created for themselves. One trucking executive stated to investigators, "I have known John Dunn for years. He is cold-blooded and efficient. He makes a good impression until you notice his eyes. His eyes are a cold steel blue, and when you notice them you know you are dealing with a dangerous man," while an ex-con who provided information to the cops described McGrath as "[. . .] very pleasant to meet and very jovial; but he will kill you in a minute."

Even though the two gangsters were enjoying their personal pursuits, they were in no way neglecting their business interests, and what had started out as a problem for the group in early 1938 would later transform itself into a new opportunity.

The American Federation of Labor (AFL), to which the

ILA belonged, was the first federation of unions in the United States and the largest in the first half the twentieth century. The group had organized unions in the country under one umbrella with the goal of expanding the labor movement in the United States.

While ILA president Joe Ryan was attending the 1937 AFL Annual Convention in Miami, a complaint was brought forward about the Dunn-McGrath Mob's new ILA union charter, ILA 1346-2. The AFL Brotherhood of Railway, Steamship Clerks, and Freight Handlers argued to longtime AFL President William Green that ILA 1346-2 had been encroaching on their union's jurisdiction when handling freight at the inland terminals.

When Ryan brought the concern back to the Dunn-McGrath Mob, it was decided that a show of diplomacy was the best way to handle the situation. Joe Ryan, John Dunn, Connie Noonan, and Teddy Gleason packed their bags and traveled to Washington to meet with the President of the AFL himself. The group explained to Green the great work that they had done in organizing the inland freight terminals, negotiating new contracts, and growing their membership numbers. Offering an olive branch, the officers of ILA Local 1346-2 suggested that with President Joe Ryan's permission, they could leave the ILA and join the AFL to avoid any jurisdictional problems. Green, who was unaware of Dunn's past criminal history, later explained that he had no second thoughts about the men that Ryan was vouching for.

Green granted the Dunn-McGrath Mob three new AFL charters: AFL Local 21510 New York, AFL Local 21512 New Jersey, and AFL Local 21511 Pennsylvania. The new union was now known as the AFL Motor and Bus Terminal Checkers, Platform and Office Workers. ILA Local 1346-2 was immediately replaced by AFL Local 21510, and the group also activated AFL Local 21512, as they had plans to expand to New Jersey. Noonan succeeded himself as President of the new charter, Gleason remained the Secretary-Treasurer, and Dunn stayed on as Vice-President, while also making himself the Business Agent of the new charter.

While the Dunn-McGrath Mob members associated with ILA 1346-2 transferred their allegiances over to AFL 21510, most of the gang also kept dual membership in various ILA unions, and Teddy Gleason remained an officer in a number of ILA charters. The group moved their offices from the ILA union hall to the Bankers' Trust Company, which is coincidentally where Joe Ryan had his own offices on the 19th floor of the building.

Although the Dunn-McGrath union charter had officially separated from the ILA, the connection between the two groups remained unchanged. Ryan had fended off the rebel ILA members from expanding into New York City and had become more comfortable openly associating with his questionable companions. In one famous quote from Ryan, which was reportedly heard by a reporter while Ryan was discussing the presence of men with criminal records in his union, he stated, "Some of the boys from the old ladies' home up the river [prison] came down to the waterfront and made good. I'm proud to have them as members of this union. I'm proud to have my picture taken with them and proud to be in their company."

With the moral and physical support of the criminal element, Ryan began to attack any naysayers, and he freely labeled the groups that opposed his leadership as communists or reds. Some of Ryan's favorite catch phrases were "[. . .] if you are an enemy of me then you are an enemy of labor," and that the ILA did not just stand for the International Longshoremen's Association, it also stood for "I Love America."

In September of 1937, McGrath, who did not hold an official position in AFL 21510, was promoted by Joe Ryan to the esteemed position of ILA International Organizer. The job, which Ryan later stated was given to McGrath at the recommendation of Teddy Gleason, made McGrath responsible for organizing the men in the ILA and making sure that enough bodies were available for work on the piers during any given day. McGrath, the murderous ex-con, was now one of the best paid officers in one of the most powerful unions in New York City.

It was not only Joe Ryan and Eddie McGrath's stock that was on the rise within the ILA, but also on the up was the current Secretary-Treasurer of AFL 21510, Teddy Gleason. Ryan treated the fiery and stubborn young union leader as one of his protégées, and the two were often side by side at various ILA rallies and events.

In the mold of Ryan's own Joseph P. Ryan Association, Gleason took the initiative to start his own group, known as the Teddy Gleason Association. The black tie dinner and dance event would help support Gleason's rise in the ILA and tickets were sold to other ILA officials, politicians, and businessmen associated with the waterfront and the gangsters. The event would be held at fancy locations such as the Palm Garden Restaurant or the Hotel Commodore, and most of the Dunn-McGrath Mob would be in attendance. For the dinner in 1938, the program listed the Committeemen, and organizers for the event, as John Dunn, Cornelius Noonan, Jackie Adams, Barney Baker, Thomas Burke, and a James Bagley, who at that time was employed by Varick as a collector. In one keepsake picture from the 1939 dinner at the Palm Restaurant, Joe Ryan is photographed watching the band play alongside Dunn, Barney Baker, Jackie Adams, Leo Tocci, Buster Bell, Danny Gentile, and Tommy Burke. The Dunn-McGrath Mob members smiling in the picture, with one of the most powerful labor leaders in the country, shared nearly thirty arrests amongst them, including three for murder.

Besides the gang's new friends in high places, they were receiving additional help from some old hands on the docks.

The Dunn-McGrath Mob had been attempting to manage a large area of the waterfront and did not have control over many of the northern piers in the Chelsea neighborhood. Working alongside a well-liked former bootlegger named Timothy O'Mara, the gang quickly took control of the region without any violence. The seasoned O'Mara had an arrest record dating back to 1910 and had been a member of the original Gopher's gang, along with West Side prohibition boss Owney Madden and Joe Butler's deceased brother, Willie. Following Prohibition, O'Mara obtained an interest in a number of legitimate breweries, including West End Beer Distribution, where he kept his prized racing pigeons in a coop on the roof. A true Fagen character, O'Mara was viewed as an underworld emissary by younger hoodlums, and he regularly staked criminal ventures and acted as a fence for their stolen goods.

O'Mara had remained friendly with a number of former Owney Madden gang members, with whom the Dunn-McGrath Mob were also on good terms, such as Artie Biehler and Terry Reilly. Through these connections, O'Mara and his gang, which included his brother John and Charles "Whitey" Munson, began to work closely with the Dunn-McGrath Mob; by the late 1930s, he eventually took control of the loading on Piers 61 to 74.

The Dunn-McGrath Mob also welcomed McGrath's old bootlegging partner back into the fold. Andrew "Squint" Sheridan was released from prison in early 1937. After reconnecting with McGrath, Sheridan began hanging around with the gang and was provided with no-show waterfront jobs. Sheridan was grateful to McGrath, and with his newfound stability, he was soon living comfortably with his wife and daughter in Jersey City. Sheridan would be promoted to Business Agent of the newly established AFL Local 21512 (which was the New Jersey branch of the Dunn-McGrath Mob's AFL Local 21510), while his brother Frank was appointed President of the local.

19

Ghosts From the Past

EVEN THOUGH THE Dunn-McGrath gang had risen above the small-time street level rackets, they did not shy away from the violence that propelled them to the upper echelons of the underworld.

One example of the gang's no-nonsense rule over the docks was the murder of Edward "The Snake" Kenny. Kenny, who resided in Brooklyn, had been close friends with the murdered Ralph "Lulu" Clements. Kenny himself was identified as a person of interest in six open murder cases and he had twice been charged with homicide, including the murder of a West Side bartender named James Comerford, who was hit by a bullet that was shot through the window of a tavern. After the murder of Clements, Kenny, who had a fearsome reputation on the waterfront, was hired by the Dunn-McGrath Mob to work as a collector for Varick. All was initially fine with Kenny, but word started to get around the docks that he had been skimming from his Varick collections and pocketing some of the money for himself.

At around 10:00 PM on June 13, 1938, Kenny arrived at Callahan's Bar and Grill, at 260 Tenth Avenue and 26th Street, and headed to a table in the back area of the bar. Soon after his arrival, a man described as "young and dapperly dressed" jogged in through a side door of the bar, stepped into the back area, and fired six shots at the seated Kenny. The customers at the bar saw the young man slowly jog back out the door and climb into an automobile that sped past the watering hole. The customers ran to the back area to check on Kenny but found him lying on the floor with four bullets in his head.

In the criminal world, few things ever stay buried. In 1938, a crime, which only some members of the Dunn–McGrath Mob were loosely tied to, would once again rear its ugly head, make the front page of every evening paper, and set off a chain of events that would almost destroy the gang.

Inspector John Ryan of the NYPD had been the man in charge of the Rubel robbery investigation. Although no charges were ever laid, Ryan had continued to pursue the case. During the summer of 1938, a tip led Ryan to Auburn prison to interview Dunn–McGrath Mob member Matthew "Mattie" Kane, who had been in prison since his parole violation arrest in 1935. Kane had been transferred to Auburn from Sing Sing the year prior, and Inspector Ryan believed that, while in Sing Sing, Kane may have been friendly with someone who had knowledge of the robbery (which could have been Stewart Wallace or Joseph Kress, as both were serving time in Sing Sing during the time Kane was there).

It is unclear what happened during the interview with Kane, but the events that followed did not paint him in a positive light to his underworld friends. Although it was not confirmed if Kane ever provided information to Inspector Ryan, it was rumored that he had been seeking an early release, as his beloved mother had fallen ill. Whether Kane did or did not squeal, the damage was done. Within days of Kane's interview, the police were suddenly following up on new leads, and there was more activity on the Rubel case than there had been in the past two years combined.

Inspector Ryan headed to Clinton Penitentiary to visit the incarcerated Rubel robbery principal, John "Archie" Stewart. It was evident that Inspector Ryan had a nearly perfect picture of the robbery, but Stewart would still not crack. The police were not deterred by his silence and instead produced a surprise to deal with his lack of cooperation. Inspector Ryan had found out that Stewart had a younger brother named Robert, who had recently become a probationary police officer on the West Side. Patrolman Robert Stewart agreed to help with the case and was sent to Clinton in an attempt to get a confession from his older brother. After three days of conversation, Stewart agreed to turn stool pigeon with the agreement that he may get to see the light of day again if he testified about the robbery.

The police proudly announced that the case had been cracked. On November 4, 1938, police charged Stewart Wallace and Joseph Kress, who were already in prison serving sentences, and one of the boatmen Thomas Quinn, who was the only gang member who was free and could be found. Cases against John Oley and Percy Geary would not be pursued, as the two were already serving life sentences for kidnapping. Bennie McMahon, Fats Manning, and Francis Oley were already dead, and the other boatman, John Hughes, was never located. Charged as accessories after the fact were Madeline Tully and Dr. Harry Gilbert.

Although not involved in the Rubel heist, the Dunn-McGrath Mob had been hearing a lot of troubling stories through the underworld grapevine. Why did the police have such a clear picture of the crime after their interview with Mattie Kane?

McGrath and Dunn had the most reason to be concerned, as they had together committed multiple murders with Kane. If Kane had squealed to Inspector Ryan once, then who knew what else he could be leveraged into? To further the gang's suspicions, they also heard that Kane was being released on parole from Auburn on November 18, 1938. The timing was troublesome. Kane was a repeat offender with one year left on his sentence, and now his sudden release was occurring only two weeks after the break in the Rubel case.

On November 18, 1938, Kane was paroled from Auburn

with the condition that he return immediately to his mother's house. He boarded a train with $707 that had been in his commissary account. Kane, who had previously been remanded for lending money to a guard, had earned the cash through loansharking in prison.

At 6:00 PM, Kane's mother, Theresa, waited anxiously for her son at her apartment at 48-19 44th Street, Woodside, Queens. The night was a relatively clear one, but it had been getting darker earlier and only a few children played in a nearby courtyard. Kane made his way under the arch of the building's entrance. Lurking in the darkness, in a small alley between the buildings, two figures in long coats appeared and snuck up to Kane from his left side. Four shots echoed through the night air. Two hit Kane in his left side and one struck him the head. The other missed, deflected off the wall of the building and struck the elbow of one of the children who was playing in the courtyard. Each of the hitmen then fired an additional bullet into the downed Kane's head. The two shooters, followed by a third man who police believe was acting a lookout, jumped into an idling car at the building's entrance, which contained another two men.

Hearing gunshots, the father of the injured boy, who happened to be a police patrolman, ran out of the hallway and fired three shots from his service revolver at the fleeing car. Kane's mother heard the commotion from her apartment and fainted. An ambulance arrived and transported the injured boy to the hospital, where it was found that his elbow wound was relatively minor. Police began to process the crime scene and a sheet was placed over Kane's body. All that could be seen was the dead gangster's feet and a few small trails of blood that ran from under the cover.

When a local detective who knew Kane arrived and looked under the sheet to identify the dead gangster, he was shocked. The dead man was not Mattie Kane.

The body lying in front of the apartment was actually John F. O'Hara, a hardworking twenty-seven-year-old credit analyst who shared a vague resemblance. O'Hara was a recent graduate of Syracuse University who, along with his widowed mother, sister, and brother, lived in the same apartment complex as Kane's mother. O'Hara, who helped support his family, was described by his employer as an, "unusually bright and a very estimable young man."

Over time, police would develop the theory that one of the shooters that night was actually new gang gunman Andrew "Squint" Sheridan. Living up to his nickname, they believed that Sheridan, who had poor vision and was not familiar with Kane, mistook him for O'Hara and was the first to open fire. Police put Sheridan under surveillance, shortly after the murder, and found him frequently in the company of a young thug named Charles T. Brady. During a routine stop of Brady, the police discovered an unlicensed revolver and arrested him. The revolver did not match the one used in the O'Hara slaying, and even if Brady was the other shooter that night, his rise in the Dunn-McGrath Mob was short-lived as he was murdered by fellow gang member, Joseph Powell, the following year.

Kane, who was oblivious to what had occurred the night before, arrived at his mother's the next morning and was detained by police. Kane explained to the homicide detectives that he had already broken the conditions of his parole, as he had gotten off the train at Syracuse, got on another train, and then exited on 125th Street. He would not provide an explanation for his indirect route, and police thought it may have been because he was trying to avoid being followed. If that was the case, Kane did not show much concern as he called some friends, met them at an uptown hotel, and spent $110 on booze.

Kane admitted to officers that the killers likely meant to get him. He told them, "They got O'Hara by mistake instead

of me" and that "[. . .] his friends would take care of them."
He added regretfully that the O'Hara murder was "[. . .] the
one thing I am sorry for." When officers asked him for an
explanation as to why he did not return home as planned, he
replied that he was superstitious, "A Friday visit means a short
stay." Detectives told Kane that he was a dead man walking
without their help, but after hours of pressure declared that
"[. . .] he lost his tongue." Kane was arrested, put in protective
custody, and scheduled for a new parole violation hearing.

On November 27, 1938, Kane had his hearing with the
Parole Commission, and it was found that since he had, in fact,
violated the conditions of his release, he would be transferred
back to Sing Sing to serve the remainder of his sentence. Police,
gangsters, and media alike knew that the move was as much
for Kane's protection as anything else.

John Dunn and Eddie McGrath now had a big problem.
When Sheridan shot the innocent O'Hara, the gang had
tipped their hand and had lost the element of surprise against
Kane who, before the shooting, believed that he was still on
good terms with his old gang. If Kane had been an informer,
he would have no reason to protect his old friends. It was only
a matter of time before Inspector Ryan would be trying to turn
Kane into his next star witness. Feeling a sense of urgency,
the Dunn-McGrath Mob turned to an old enemy who had
his own ax to grind with Mattie Kane.

On April 19, 1938, Charles "Charlie the Jew" Yanowsky
finished serving his federal sentence at Alcatraz and was
transferred back to New York to face charges in relation to
the 1935 shooting of James "Ding-Dong" Bell. Yanowsky
accepted a plea bargain for the attempted bribery of the police
officer, following the shooting, and was sentenced to two to
four years in Sing Sing.

In desperation, McGrath and Dunn reached out through
prison channels to the incarcerated Yanowsky. The longtime

rivals shared an enemy in Kane, as his potential squealing had compromised both the Dunn-McGrath Mob and the remaining members of the Yanowsky Gang, who could not be sure what other information Archie Stewart would be providing about them as a direct consequence of someone ratting about the Rubel robbery.

Yanowsky's criminal career on the waterfront had been cut short, his entire gang was dead or serving long prison sentences, and he was due to be released in a year and a half to an uncertain future on the outside.

The always forward-thinking Yanowsky recognized the opportunity that was presenting itself, and he asked for certain guarantees from the Dunn-McGrath Mob if he was going to handle their problem. The offer was made to Yanowsky that, upon his release from Sing Sing, there would be no attempts to kill him as long as he remained in his native New Jersey. Yanowsky would be allowed to make attempts to take over the increasingly growing waterfront in his hometown of Jersey City and the neighboring city of Hoboken, as long as he stayed in line.

Yanowsky accepted the offer and quickly went to work on a plan to kill Mattie Kane. According to a waterfront gangster, who was familiar with one of the parties involved in the murder plot and later cooperated with police in the mid-1950s, Yanowsky recruited two thugs from the West Side to assist him: John Peters and another man only known to the informant as "Tommy the Greek."

For his part in the murder plot, Peters, who was a former prizefighter, agreed to participate for a promised job as a hiring boss when he was released from Sing Sing in the next two years. Although never confirmed, "Tommy the Greek" was likely Thomas "Tommy the Greek" Kapatos, a young thug who had only arrived in Sing Sing at the end of November. Kapatos had worked as a leg breaker along the Hell's Kitchen docks until he was convicted of the murder of another gangster, Albert "The Ape" Dillulio, and sentenced to twenty-five years.

Kane had been released from the intake segregation and, adhering to the underworld code of conduct, he refused protective custody. On December 11, 1938, he finished lunch and then headed out into the yard for leisure time. When the weather was bad, the inmates would often gather under a covered corridor in the old section of the prison, and Kane headed there and mingled with a large group of prisoners.

While the unsuspecting Kane was standing near a staircase, Yanowsky's underlings put their simple plan into place. John Peters approached Kane from the side and sucker punched him in the jaw. Kane slumped to the ground as Tommy the Greek ran over and rapidly stabbed at Kane's neck with a sharpened four-inch butter knife. Although the stabbing had been witnessed by a dozen inmates, everyone dispersed from the scene and would claim that they had seen nothing.

Kane regained consciousness, stood up, pressed his hand to his neck, and calmly walked over to the nearest guard. Without saying a word he pointed to his bloody wounds. Kane was able to walk himself to the prison hospital where it was found he had suffered three cuts to the back of his neck and a deep stab wound to the side of his throat. Luckily for Kane, the wounds appeared to have caused little damage, and he was admitted to the hospital unit for observation. Kane once again refused to cooperate in the investigation and told prison officials that he did not see his attacker and that he was unsure who would want to cause him harm.

On December 12, 1938, the day after the stabbing, the prison doctor noticed that Kane appeared unwell and that he seemed to be rapidly deteriorating. Emergency surgery was ordered on the wound, and the doctor was surprised to find that the rusty tip of the kitchen knife had broken off inside of Kane's neck.

The piece of metal was removed, but the infection had already spread. The following day, December 13, 1938, Kane died.

One curious aspect, which may add to the mystery of whether Kane did indeed provide information to Inspector Ryan about the Rubel robbery, was that after Kane's death Inspector Ryan phoned Sing Sing's Warden and made the unusual offer of sending two detectives to help him investigate the killing. The Warden did not feel it was necessary but stated that he would keep in touch with Inspector Ryan about the investigation. The resulting search for the killers proved fruitless and it would not be until more than a decade later that further information about the slaying would be brought forward.

Kane's funeral was held on December 16, 1938, and was a reflection of how far his stature had fallen in the underworld. Only fourteen people attended, along with four detectives who had been assigned for added protection. Kane's long-suffering mother was too ill to enter the church and could barely contain her grief at his gravesite.

Kane's murder had tied the Dunn-McGrath Mob to their former enemy Yanowsky and, even though Yanowsky was not scheduled to be released for another year and a half, the Dunn-McGrath Mob knew that he would be cashing in his favors as soon as he was free.

20

The Best of the West

WITH NO NEW investigative leads after the murder of Mattie Kane, detectives turned to one of the few cooperating sources who had knowledge of the Dunn-McGrath Mob's activities: future star witness in the Rubel robbery trial, Archie Stewart. Police questioned Stewart in detail about all of the other previous crimes he had committed, and given his association with the former Yanowsky Gang, he was able to provide some relevant tidbits about crimes that had occurred during the mid-1930s.

On January 27, 1939, both McGrath and Dunn were picked up by NYPD detectives on charges that they had taken part in the Rubsam and Hormann Brewing Company armed robbery in 1934. A police report stated the two had been identified as the culprits by a cooperating informant who was currently housed in the New York prison system. Given the timing of Stewart becoming an informant, there is no doubt that he was the one who provided the information. Dunn and McGrath were held until January 30, 1939, when they were finally brought before a judge. Flanked by expensive lawyers, the two argued that all of the evidence against them was circumstantial. The judge agreed and dismissed the charges.

McGrath was still on parole for another year and was transferred to the Tombs Prison to await a hearing with the Parole Board. Prosecutors argued that McGrath had continued to hang around criminals and that he was heavily involved in waterfront crime. McGrath's lawyer countered that his client was now cleaner than a pair of Sunday dress shoes—McGrath had not been arrested once since his release, and he was currently employed in a stable and lucrative position as an ILA International Organizer. The Parole Board concluded that there were no signs that McGrath was a delinquent. One curious fact, concerning the review by the Parole Board, is that the member in charge of McGrath's hearing would later become employed as an attorney for none other than the ILA.

As for Archie Stewart, he ended up taking the stand against the remaining members of the Rubel robbery gang: Joe Kress, Stewart Wallace, Thomas Quinn, Madeline Tully, and Dr. Gilbert. Also joining Stewart as a witness was Madeline Tully and Dr. Gilbert's friend, and likely killer of Joseph Potter, Michael Piccardo. Both Stewart and Piccardo came across as what they were—hardened criminals with no remorse or interest in testifying. Regardless of the star witnesses' demeanors, the three Rubel robbers were convicted on June 13, 1939. Since Stewart and Piccardo had been less than stellar as witnesses, the cases against Dr. Gilbert and Madeline Tully were dropped, though Dr. Gilbert would lose his medical license.

The case would end up being appealed based on the quality of Stewart's testimony, and in 1941 the court overturned the convictions. Stewart would not testify again and would quietly serve almost another decade in prison before being released early. Wallace remained in prison to serve out the lengthy sentence he had received for the Pine Bush robbery, and Quinn would find work on the docks as a hiring boss in Hell's Kitchen after his release. Joe Kress lasted only six weeks on the streets after his successful appeal, as he had become involved in a plan to rob Frank Erickson, a very close friend of Genovese crime family boss Frank Costello and one of the largest bookmakers in the country. On the day of the robbery, Erickson's maid stopped the robbers and alerted police. As police closed in, one of the robbers killed himself rather than be caught, while the others, including Kress, surrendered. Kress would be resentenced for the new robbery and would not be a factor on the West Side again.

Besides the failure of law enforcement to send McGrath and Dunn back to prison, the gang received more good news courtesy of the state of New Jersey. On March 27, 1939, New Jersey found that the harsh Anti-Gangster Act, which James "Ding-Dong" Bell, Arthur "Scarface" Gaynor, and Frank Foy had been convicted of, following the raid on their cabin in the Pompton Lakes in 1935, was unconstitutional. The law was overturned and the men, who were serving twenty-year sentences, were freed. Gaynor and Foy did not fall back in with the Dunn-McGrath Mob, but Ding-Dong Bell wasted no time in assuming a prominent position in the gang alongside his brother, Buster Bell.

In 1940, the boys in the Dunn-McGrath Mob would be asked by the ILA to use their underworld clout to help Joe Ryan solve a problem that was emerging north of their empire. Unlike the piers in Greenwich and Chelsea, where there was no dispute over who ran the rackets, the remaining West Side waterfront in the Hell's Kitchen district was in a constant state of flux. The piers, which were organized under ILA Local 824 and included Pier 80 to Pier 97, had long been controlled by local gangsters in the extremely tight-knit community. However, unlike other neighborhoods on the West Side, Hell's Kitchen had always failed to produce a gang that could keep control of the docks.

By the late 1930s, the trio of David "The Beetle" Beadle, Richard "The Bandit" Gregory, and Tommy Gleason (no relation to ILA official Teddy Gleason) had cemented themselves as the rulers of the Hell's Kitchen waterfront. Beadle, who had beaten a double murder charge in the early 1930s after shooting a pair of brothers, was a Joe Ryan loyalist, and similar to the Dunn-McGrath Mob, he ensured that the neighborhood longshoremen were kept in line for the ILA. Beadle and Gleason, along with a third friend named John Potter, had even created their own stevedoring company that controlled the loading concessions on the piers. With the younger Bandit Gregory acting as an enforcer, as despite his youth he had three prior murder charges on his police blotter, it finally appeared that Hell's Kitchen had been stabilized.

Peace did not last long, and the usual Hell's Kitchen bloodshed again reared its ugly head in 1939. On December 9, 1939, Beadle was put on the spot in front of a bar and filled with bullets fired by two gunmen. Police believed that the killing was done by a rival mob who wanted to take control of the loading racket, but, like most Hell's Kitchen murders, they had more suspects than answers. Police waited for the next act of revenge, and sure enough, the trail of bodies led them to the likely suspects. On April 23, 1940, two brothers, James and Vincent Doherty, who had recently been throwing their weight around the waterfront, were both shot by a single gunman while they were standing inside a cafe. James was shot in the head and died, while Vincent, who was hit in the chest, lived.

The new leader of the Hell's Kitchen waterfront became Bandit Gregory, who was also local detectives' favorite bet as the shooter of the Doherty brothers. Gregory, with Beadle's old partner Gleason in support, continued where his predecessor left off and became the Business Agent of ILA Local 824. However, Gregory's reign was short-lived; on November 17, 1940, he was standing at the bar of The Hudson Hofbrau when a lone gunman entered and shot him numerous times in the chest and stomach. As the shooter escaped, Gregory leaned against the bar, pulled out his ILA membership card, handed it to the bartender and then slowly sunk to the ground. He would die later that day in the hospital.

Due to the number of untimely deaths within ILA Local 824, it became openly known as "The Pistol Local." Tommy

Gleason, the remaining member of the original Beadle group, did not fill the leadership void well, and the Hell's Kitchen piers became an open market. In the months following Gregory's murder, the regional ILA coffers dried up, as there was no one with enough influence to successfully collect union dues from the local longshoremen. Joe Ryan attempted to send one of his own men, John "Ike" Gannon, to collect the fees, but the tough longshoreman in the area knew that they were dealing with a paper pusher and ignored Gannon's requests. ILA Local 824 was in disarray, and everyone was working for free in Hell's Kitchen.

The Dunn-McGrath Mob and Joe Ryan both knew that the chaos in Hell's Kitchen was bad for business and that a cohesive West Side was needed. With the help of Timothy O'Mara, the veteran gangster who ran the Upper Chelsea piers, the group came up with a solution. O'Mara, who was familiar with the Hell's Kitchen neighborhood, suggested that they approach a group known as the Bowers Mob, who were a collection of hold-up men that he regularly bankrolled or provided tips to, and ask them if they would be willing to take over the waterfront and ILA Local 824. O'Mara felt that, with a little guidance, the Bowers Mob was the perfect choice for the job, as they were from Hell's Kitchen, were well respected in the local underworld, and, most importantly, they had also been on good terms with other criminals from the Beadle-Gleason-Gregory group.

The Bowers Mob was led by Michael "Mickey" Bowers, a wiry thug who established his stand-up reputation in the underworld after being shot in the neck by police during an arrest for a payroll robbery, and then later taking a ten-year prison rap for the rest of his gang. While the slightly built Mickey was unassuming, the gang's mouthpiece was his much larger and more boisterous cousin, Harold Bowers. The rest of the gang, who had been stealing together since the late 1920s, consisted of John "Keefie" Keefe, Bowers' closest associate, whom he had met while serving his robbery sentence in New Jersey; John "Apples" Applegate, a Hell's Kitchen native who on one occasion had been arrested alongside Joe Butler and Leo Tocci during a burglary in 1933; and a portly local hood named John "Big John" Ward.

O'Mara set up a meeting with the Bowers Mob at a restaurant on 50th Street and West Avenue. Attending were Mickey Bowers, John Keefe, John Applegate, and another minor gang member named Dominick Genova. O'Mara told Mickey Bowers outright that Eddie McGrath and John Dunn, along with other waterfront powers, felt that the group should take over the Hell's Kitchen piers and ILA Local 824. Mickey Bowers' first response to O'Mara was that running the Hell's Kitchen piers was a good way to get killed. O'Mara explained that the Bowers group would have full control over rackets like gambling, their own hiring bosses, no-show jobs, and the lucrative loading operations. Mickey Bowers raised the concern with O'Mara that remaining Beadle leader, Tommy Gleason, would be sour about their takeover, but O'Mara assured them that Gleason would stay away as long as he received a regular cut of the profits.

The offer to be promoted from robbers to racketeers was too good to turn down, even though there was a running joke among the group about who would become Business Agent of ILA Local 824, as that person was most likely to get shot first. In the end, it was decided that Harold Bowers would take the job. Within the week, he was on the docks and successfully collecting union dues from the local longshoremen. The neighborhood dock workers knew of the Bowers Mob's reputation and immediately fell back in line, after their short-lived grace period. The Bowers Mob would later install John Keefe as Vice-President of ILA Local 824 and Patrick "Packy" Connolly, a staunch Joe Ryan ally, as local President. Connolly, who would later become Vice-President of the entire ILA, had been on the docks for years and was able to provide the new group advice on the ins and outs of waterfront politics.

The group also expanded into the loading racket by opening a company named Allied Stevedoring. Run by veteran loader John Potter, who had operated the same business with David Beadle and Tommy Gleason, the company had exclusive rights to operate the loading concessions on Bowers controlled piers. Gang member John Ward became President of the company, Potter the Vice-President and Mickey Bowers the Secretary-Treasurer. The gang also moved in on the neighborhoods' most powerful loanshark, Edmund Leahy. Leahy, who was formerly affiliated with the Beadle group, had a visit from Mickey Bowers and was told he had a new partner. Leahy was happy to have the new muscle and did not argue.

The new leaders of the Hell's Kitchen waterfront still had some unfinished business before they could rule in peace. On January 25, 1941, Thomas Cunniff, a local hoodlum, was shot to death while getting a shoe shine, and his companion, Emil "The Polack" Nizich, was hit in the shoulder. The targets, who had also been previously shot and wounded while sitting in a car together in 1937, also happened to be the main suspects in the slaying of the well-liked Bandit Gregory. The killer, who was obviously unhappy that he did not kill Nizich too, caught up with him only weeks later while Nizich was walking to a neighborhood basketball game. The gunman pumped a few bullets into Nizich's back, who then collapsed in the road and was struck by an oncoming car. After the shooter was sure Nizich was dead, he jumped onto the running board of a taxi cab and yelled for the driver to "Drive like hell!"

Under the guidance of O'Mara and the Dunn-McGrath Mob, the Bowers Mob conquered the Hell's Kitchen piers. They replaced most of the hiring bosses in their territory with associates, such as Daniel "Danny" St. John, a former friend of Bandit Gregory, who also happened to be the prime suspect in the Cunniff and Nizich murders. St. John and his brother, John, had a notorious reputation in the Hell's Kitchen neighborhood, but Danny was by far the standout. With a two-page arrest sheet that included three entries for murder, one of which was the slaying of a policeman, St. John was given Pier 84 to run as his own domain.

The only bump in the road was the last of the old guard, Tommy Gleason. The Bowers Mob was flourishing and had grown tired of paying Tommy Gleason his share of the profits while he did nothing. Gleason's stipend began to shrink and the neighborhood knew he was being treated like a patsy. Gleason may have been aging, but with multiple murder charges on his record, he was still a dangerous character. One day in 1944, Gleason came to the Viaduct Bar and Grill on 10th Avenue, which the Bowers Mob used as their headquarters, and asked to speak to Mickey. Mickey came out of the bar and it appeared that Gleason was about to give him a hug. As Gleason outstretched his arms, Mickey jumped back and blood began to stream down his face. Gleason had hidden a straight razor in his hand and had attempted to cut Mickey's throat. The elder gangster then jumped into a waiting cab, which sped away.

Revenge was swift, and on December 14, 1944, Gleason turned up dead with a handful of bullets in his brain. Gleason owned a piece of a local funeral parlor and had apparently been sleeping inside when a gunman managed to creep up on him. In one last macabre detail, the window of the funeral parlor overlooked the same spot where Gleason's longtime partner, David Beadle, had been killed five years earlier.

With the growth of the Bowers' criminal ventures, the murder of Tommy Gleason, and the support of the Dunn-McGrath Mob, the fight for control of Hell's Kitchen piers had finally ended and, for the first time, the West Side waterfront was a united front.

Eddie McGrath outside the New York State Crime Commission hearings, 1953.

Andrew "Squint" Sheridan, 1948.

Joe Ryan meeting with the New York Shipping Association.

Eddie McGrath, 1938.

John "Peck" Hughes, 1934.

ILA President Joe Ryan, 1948.

Matthew Kane.

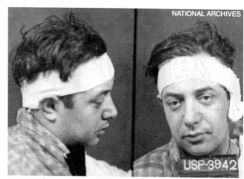

USP-3942

Charles Yanowsky after his arrest in 1938.

Vincent
"Jimmy Blue Eyes"
Alo.

Longshoremen shaping-up.

N.Y.C. POLICE
77415

John "Cockeye"
Dunn, 1939.

Robert "Farmer" Sullivan, 1936.

Michael "Mickey" Bowers, 1957.

The Arsenal Gang's hideout

Butler Gang members arrested in 1935. Pictured are (standing left to right) George Maiwald, James "Ding Dong" Bell, Joseph McCarthy, Louis Balner, Edward Gaffney, (sitting left to right) Frank Foy, John "Peck" Hughes, and Arthur "Scarface" Gaynor.

Longshoremen unloading a ship.

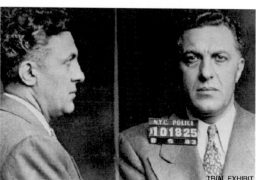

Frank "Frank Mario" Bonfiglio, 1943.

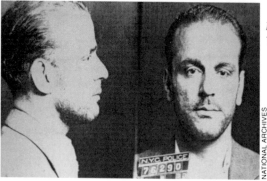

Nicholas "The Bull" Tanzella, 1933.

Albert Ackalitis, 1935.

John "Red" McCrossin, 1924.

Longshoremen arrested in Brooklyn following the New York State Crime Commission hearings.

Timothy O'Mara, 1922.

NATIONAL ARCHIVES

A view of the West Side piers in the early 1900s.

LIBRARY OF CONGRESS

Daniel Gentile, 1947.

N.Y.C. POLICE
251856

TRIAL EXHIBIT

Pier 45, 1951.

Frank "Sonny" Campbell, 1933.

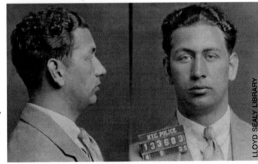

Robert "Barney" Baker, 1935.

Still frame from a surveillance video of Albert Ackalitis outside the ILA-AFL polling stations on December 23, 1953.

Map of the West Side Piers.

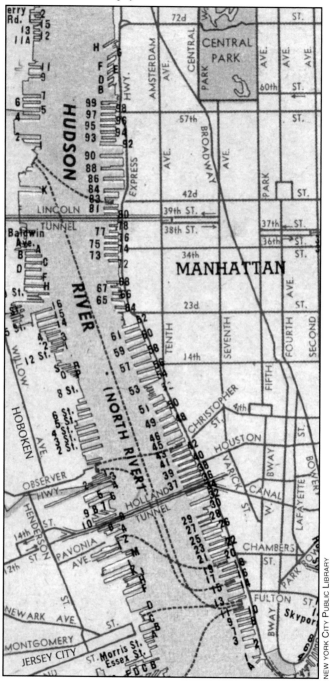

1940

ON THE NIGHT of July 13, 1940, McGrath and fellow senior gang member, George Daggett, decided to drive about an hour and a half outside of the city and go to dinner in the trendy Greenwood Lake area. Joining McGrath and Daggett were Lillian Ganley, McGrath's current showgirl girlfriend, and Daggett's wife, Helen. The twenty-three-year-old Ganley, a dancer at the trendy Club 18, was nothing short of a bombshell and performed under the stage name of Leila Gaynes. The foursome ate at a local restaurant and were reported to have drunk heavily throughout the night. The group departed very late with McGrath at the wheel of the car, Ganley in the passenger seat, and the Daggetts in the back.

Shortly before 4:00 AM, New York State Police received a call that there had been an accident just outside of Greenwood Lake on Route 210. When the officer arrived on the scene, he found McGrath standing on the side of the road next to a wrecked car and Lillian Ganley doubled over nearby. The officer then found the bodies of George and Helen Daggett, who were deceased by the time that he arrived on the scene. The officer approached McGrath, who had only suffered minor injuries, including cuts to his face from the broken glass, and asked what had taken place. McGrath refused to answer any of the officer's questions. When questioned by the officer, Lillian Ganley became hysterical, as she too had suffered cuts to her face, and between tears, Ganley explained how important her face was to her career.

The officer on the scene became angry with McGrath who continued to be uncooperative. McGrath was placed under arrest while Ganley was taken to the hospital where she was diagnosed with multiple broken ribs. The still hysterical Ganley provided a statement to the police that they had all been drinking that night and that McGrath had been driving down the highway when he struck a curb, which caused the car to veer into a stone wall. Based on Ganley's statement, the charge of criminal negligence was filed against McGrath.

McGrath and the rest of the gang were saddened by the death of Daggett and his wife. No expense was spared on the double funeral for the Daggetts, which was held in the heart of the gang's territory. Friends and strangers alike lined the streets to pay their last respects. Later, a local watering hole named "Georgie Daggett's" opened at West and Christopher Street in honor of the deceased Dunn-McGrath Mob member.

Although McGrath was reportedly distraught about what had occurred with George Daggett, he had the immediate problem of criminal charges as a result of Lillian Ganley's statement to police. One prominent socialite gossip columnist even reported that shortly after the accident McGrath and Ganley were married in a secret ceremony so that she could not be compelled to testify against him in court. The writer had it wrong about the marriage, but whether it was loyalty, intimidation, or a payoff, McGrath did get what he wanted. When re-interviewed by investigators, Ganley said that due to the accident she could not remember providing her last statement. She let them know that she now had a clearer head and that she remembered the accident well, telling investigators that it was, in fact, George Daggett driving that night. With no other witnesses, and McGrath not cooperating, the criminal negligence charges had been sunk.

In the always changing world of organized crime, where

easy money or a bullet lay waiting around every corner, McGrath's next problem would turn out to be an unwelcome distraction from the loss of George Daggett.

Leo Tocci, one of the founders of the Dunn-McGrath Mob, had recently been branching out beyond the group's usual rackets while acting as a liaison for the gang and a group of Italian gangsters. Tocci, who was associated with both AFL Local 21510 and the lucrative Varick Enterprises, had a reputation as a womanizer, gambler, and heavy drinker; he was the type of criminal who embraced his role as a crook. In early 1939, through his underworld travels, Tocci had become friends with a bloodthirsty gang that the press would dub "Murder Inc." Based in the Brownsville section of Brooklyn, Murder Inc. consisted of both Jewish and Italian members who had earned a reputation as vicious killers. The murderous gang was so successful in their trade that they became hired guns for heavyweight gangsters such as Louis "Lepke" Buchalter and Albert Anastasia.

It appears that Tocci shared a taste for the brutality that the members of Murder Inc. regularly doled out. On August 23, 1939, Tocci, along with Murder Inc. members Frank "The Dasher" Abbadando, Harry "Happy" Maione, and Vito "Chickenhead" Gurino, reportedly snatched a seventeen-year-old waitress from outside the Parkway Casino, where she had only worked for two nights. The young girl was driven to a hotel room where the men took turns raping her before dropping her home the next morning.

Murder Inc. had established their own control over a number of unions in the Brooklyn area, including Teamsters Local 138. A strike was called among Local 138 in November of 1939 and Tocci, along with the members of Murder Inc., began approaching employers and requesting a payoff to end the labor disruption or, as they put it, "a fee" for the right to negotiate with the union.

The extortion attempt was led by Tocci, representing the West Side waterfront; Abbandano; Maione; Buchalter henchmen Mendy Weiss, representing Buchalter's interests; and Max Becker, who was a friend of Joe Adonis, taking care of the Mafia's end. The group met on Thanksgiving of 1939 and set a minimum charge of $100 that would have to be paid from each individual truck operator before they were even allowed to enter into negotiations with Local 138. One furniture store in Brooklyn later confirmed that he had paid Tocci, Maione, and Abbandano $7500 to ensure labor peace at his business. The district attorney would estimate that it was possible that hundreds of thousands of dollars had been successfully extorted, but employers were not reporting the crime.

While Tocci was making money both on the West Side waterfront and with his new friends in Brooklyn, Murder Inc.'s world would come crashing down. A small-time gang murder that was loosely connected to the Brooklyn hitmen would set off a chain of events that would lead to a junior member of the gang implicating one of the group's leaders, Abe Reles, in the slaying. Facing the death penalty, Reles turned stool pigeon in January of 1940 and began providing details about hundreds of crimes, including dozens of murders and various union extortion schemes.

The remaining members of Murder Inc. were rounded up by police and a variety of other gangsters and corrupt union officials were charged as a result of the incriminating information that was provided. Tocci began to lay low as Reles would have been able to implicate him in a number of crimes, including the union extortion scheme that they had carried out together. All of the key members of Murder Inc. were convicted based on Reles' testimony and sentenced to die in the electric chair.

Tocci was wanted by authorities for questioning. Using the Dunn-McGrath Mob connections in Florida, Tocci was sent south to hide out. McGrath was in regular contact with Joe

Adonis and was told that Tocci would need to stay in Florida until further notice, as his involvement in the Murder Inc. extortion scheme could possibly be tied back to the Dunn-McGrath Mob and Adonis himself. With so many gangsters now cooperating it was hard to trust anyone who was picked up by police, Tocci included.

Tocci arrived in Fort Lauderdale in July of 1940. He rented a house at 1233 North Rio Vista Boulevard and bought himself a sporty 1938 Pontiac coupe. Life on the lam was not for Tocci, and he quickly grew bored with keeping a low profile. Within weeks of his arrival, he was making new friends in Florida, eating at popular restaurants, frequenting mob-controlled gambling houses, and betting heavily at the horse track. Tocci not only kept company with criminals, but also invited his wealthy neighbors for lavish parties at his rented home, where he would tell his guests that he was a millionaire sportsman from New York City.

It did not take long for Tocci to wear out his welcome. By September of 1940, he was forced to leave the area, as one prominent resident had reportedly attempted suicide by cutting her wrists after a failed relationship with Tocci, and another local man was extremely upset after he found that the New Yorker had bedded his wife. Tocci packed his possessions into his black coupe and headed to Miami on September 10, 1940. On September 14, 1940, he boarded a boat and headed to Havana, Cuba to enjoy the nightlife there. After a week in Havana, Tocci took the SS Cuba directly north to Key West and checked in at the La Concha Hotel under the alias H.C. Klein of Hollywood, California.

Detectives would later conclude that McGrath and company had heard about Tocci's problems in Fort Lauderdale and that McGrath and Henry "Buster" Bell traveled down to Miami to meet with him. Once McGrath and Bell arrived, they checked into a hotel on Biscayne Boulevard. Tocci called

McGrath from Key West early on September 21, 1940, and asked McGrath and Bell to get his car in Miami and then pick him up in Key West. The same day, a restaurant owner, who had given Tocci permission to leave his car in his parking lot during his trip to Havana, stated that he saw two dapper men get into Tocci's car and drive away.

A number of hotel employees who were working at La Concha stated that two men, who they identified as McGrath and Bell, arrived at the premises just after dinner and headed up to Tocci's room. Tocci came downstairs wearing an expensive suit in the company of McGrath and Bell. The three checked out of the hotel at around 6:25 PM and, according to witnesses, appeared to be laughing and joking together before starting the four-hour drive back to Miami. That evening, McGrath and Bell pulled up at their Miami hotel driving Tocci's car. Tocci was not with them. The next day the pair checked out, and again driving Tocci's car, left the area.

On September 23, 1940, a Key West fishing boat noticed something floating near the Card Sound Bridge, about forty-five miles from Miami. Pulled from the water was the body of an expensively dressed man with four bullets in his head. Within two days, the dead man was identified as Leo Tocci. Police believed that Tocci was likely lured out of the car on a quiet patch of road, shot in the head and then dumped into the water. Tocci's next of kin was contacted in New York City, and they were asked to claim his remains for burial, but there was no response from his family. The state of Florida waited two weeks, and then buried Tocci in a nameless pauper's grave. Tocci's behavior in Florida had made him a liability to the Dunn-McGrath Mob and other important gangsters like Adonis.

After the body was identified, the local district attorney got in touch with their New York City counterparts and the connection between Tocci and the Murder Inc. investigations was made. On September 28, 1940, Florida law enforcement traveled to New York City where they were briefed on Tocci's history and his criminal associates. Pictures of Dunn-McGrath Mob members were provided, and within days, both McGrath and Bell had been confirmed by hotel employees as Tocci's companions. The police in Miami also checked old records that contained McGrath's handwriting and found that it matched the documents of the two men who had taken a hotel room on Biscayne Boulevard in Miami. The search was on for McGrath and Bell.

The police focused on places outside of New York City where McGrath and Bell had connections such as New Hampshire, as they had discovered that Bell was on very friendly terms with a jockey who regularly rode at Rockingham Park Racetrack in Salem. The police were right about their New Hampshire lead and found McGrath watching the horse races in Salem. Police followed him in hopes that he would lead them to Bell, but when he didn't, he was arrested on October 12, 1940, at Hotel Westminster in Boston. McGrath had made no attempt to conceal his identity other than identifying himself to hotel workers as Richard Irvine of Pleasant Avenue, New York. Newspaper reporters caught up with McGrath as he was being taken to Charles Street Jail, but all he had to say was, "I never killed anyone. I never murdered anyone."

Shortly after McGrath's arrest, a first-degree murder indictment, which carried a possible death penalty, was sent from Florida. On October 22, 1940, it was announced that a grand jury would be convened in Dade County to further investigate the evidence against McGrath. McGrath's counsel advised that it would be a benefit for him to participate in the hearings investigating the crime, so on November 15, 1940, McGrath waived the extradition order against him and agreed to be sent to Florida. By November 16, 1940, McGrath was housed in his new home at the Dade County Jail.

The grand jury hearings began in December 1940, and McGrath was represented by local lawyer Bart Riley. According to reporters, McGrath appeared daily at the hearings well-groomed and wearing expensive suits; always with an expressionless look on his face. Fifteen witnesses testified about McGrath and Tocci's movements before the murder, and although the police were never able to locate the murder car, murder weapon, or Buster Bell, the first-degree murder charges against McGrath remained in place. On December 14, 1940, McGrath officially pleaded not guilty to murder in the first-degree and was remanded back to the Dade County Jail with a trial date set for January 20, 1941.

Prior to the trial starting, McGrath's lawyer, Bart Riley, made one final attempt to have McGrath set free. Riley argued that the evidence against McGrath was circumstantial and that there was not enough to support holding him without bail. On January 7, 1941, the Supreme Court of Florida found that "[. . .] after careful consideration of all the testimony the proof is not evident nor the presumption great that Edward J. McGrath committed the crime charged in the indictment." The Supreme Court decision was a huge blow against the existing evidence in the case, as the judge had essentially found that it was unlikely McGrath could be convicted. Not to be deterred, the district attorney delayed the original trial date and vowed to find new evidence.

Bail of $2500 was set for McGrath, and the next day he was given permission to return to New York City pending his trial. Elsewhere, Buster Bell remained in hiding around New York City but was no doubt breathing easier knowing the results of the Supreme Court decision. The decision was likely bittersweet as, although McGrath had been granted bail, he had just spent his longest stint in prison since being returned to Sing Sing in 1935, and a first-degree murder trial, with a possible death penalty, still hung over his head.

Coercion

THE LEO TOCCI murder had put an unwelcome spotlight on the gang, and there was a renewed police pressure following McGrath's return to New York City. Looking to put a damper on McGrath and his friends, the district attorney began a full-blown investigation of Varick Enterprises, which included placing undercover agents disguised as longshoremen in the West Shore Bar and Grill, dissecting Varick's financial records, and interviewing loaders.

Varick had openly controlled the loading racket under a cloak of pseudo-legitimacy, but after realizing that their operation was under scrutiny, the gang quietly withdrew. Connie Noonan no longer showed up at the West Shore Bar and Grill to give the daily orders, and the office was abandoned. The gang still continued to receive its usual share of loading tribute from the piers, although the money was now collected directly by their boss loaders. With the orchestrated decline of Varick, the gang's presence on the waterfront was less visible, even though the Dunn-McGrath Mob continued to leave no doubt in anyone's mind about who controlled the West Side.

After handling the Mutt Whitton problem, as described in the prologue, Squint Sheridan continued to have a busy year as the lead gunman for the gang. On February 7, 1941, Joseph Moran, a warehouse checker who had been speaking up about his concerns with Dunn and McGrath's union leadership, was unloading a truck with three co-workers at 508 West 14th Street.

As Moran and the others moved crates of cocoa, a new model car pulled up near them. Sheridan, with his cap pulled down low over his face, hopped out of the passenger seat and walked up to the group. Not wanting to make the same mistake he made when he shot the innocent John O'Hara, he asked: "Which of you is Moran?" Moran, who was standing near Sheridan, responded "Me." Sheridan drew a pistol from his pocket and shot Moran once in the forehead. Sheridan casually stepped forward and proceeded to shoot Moran twice more in the chest before putting his pistol in his pocket and walking back to the getaway car. The other platform workers who witnessed the killing were understandably tongue-tied when questioned by police.

The gang also attempted to make a pre-emptive strike when a longtime rival was released from prison in July of 1941. Francis "Buster" Smith, who had been arrested for violation of his parole after being twice shot by Dunn-McGrath Mob members during the West Side War, was one of the few members of the old Yanowsky Gang that had received only a short stint in prison. After Smith's release, he was in contact with jailed Yanowsky Gang member Albert Ackalitis who, although still incarcerated for at least five years, had maintained connections on the waterfront through his brother Willie, a Business Agent for an ILA local on the West Side. Ackalitis advised Smith that he could find work on the Hoboken waterfront in New Jersey, where the Yanowsky Gang still had connections, but instead Smith began to hang around his old West Side haunts.

One night, Smith was drinking in a dimly lit West Side bar on West 26th Street. As he sat at his table, he noticed John Dunn and Squint Sheridan enter and stand by the front door. While the gangsters remained locked in a stare, a third man, who was wearing gloves and dark glasses, burst into the room. Smith jumped up from the table as the man in the dark glasses drew a pistol and fired a shot at Smith's head, which blew off a chunk of his ear. Smith lunged forward as the shooter fired another shot that struck him in the shoulder. Grabbing the gun, Smith managed to wrestle it away and bolt toward the bathroom. He then shut himself in the toilet until Dunn, Sheridan, and the gunman were gone. Smith would later hear through a friend that the shooter had been either Buster or Ding Dong Bell.

Smith, who was not looking to start trouble since the eradication of the Yanowsky Gang, reached out to Arthur Biehler, a former hitman for Owney Madden who was a mutual friend of both he and the Dunn-McGrath Mob.

A meeting was scheduled by Biehler at an apartment in Jackson Heights, Queens. McGrath, who had been trying to lay low given his pending murder charges, had to return home from a trip to the horse races in Saratoga to deal with the matter. Not wanting to incite further violence during such a precarious time for the gang, McGrath offered Smith a cut of the loading money from one of the gang's piers as a show of good faith. Smith politely declined, as he was not interested in becoming involved with the gang that had now shot him on three separate occasions. McGrath and Smith decided that as long as Smith stayed away from the gang's territory then no harm would come to him. The gang kept their promise, and instead of becoming involved in the affairs of the waterfront, Smith followed his usual pattern of behavior and regularly remained in and out of prison for various hijackings and thefts.

While McGrath continued to try to keep his name off the police blotter, trouble on the docks was never far behind him. During the early 1940s, Pier 51, which was run by the Ryan Stevedoring Company, had been one of the busiest piers in the city. Though the company operated its business in the heart of the Dunn-McGrath Mob's territory, they often marched to the beat of their own drum, much to the chagrin of the gang.

In the summer of 1941, the Ryan Stevedoring Company

agreed to take on a new checker on their pier from ILA Local 1258. The hiring was made with the recommendation of the Business Agent for the local, who happened to be the Secretary-Treasurer of AFL 21510, Teddy Gleason. Taking on a new checker was nothing new for the company, but in this case, the man turned out to be none other then Dunn-McGrath Mob member John "Peck" Hughes. If the gang couldn't gain control of the pier, they were going to hit the company in the pocket books, and after only four weeks of Hughes being on the job, over $8000 of rice (or nearly $120,000 in modern value) was stolen from the pier. The Ryan Stevedoring Company was furious, but also reluctant to take action, as they knew the gang could organize a strike and shut down their operations at a moment's notice.

When Hughes wasn't ripping off goods from the dock, he was monitoring another problematic situation that was beginning to fester on Pier 51. The Ryan Stevedoring Company had previously rejected hiring a gang-friendly hiring boss and instead appointed Edward J. Kelly. Kelly was known around the docks as a slave driver with an anti-union stance. His attitude often caused trouble among the longshoremen, and Kelly had a reputation of ignoring union contracts, hiring non-union men illegally, and employing "short gangs" (fewer men than what was required by union rules to complete a given job). Kelly's attitude made him hated on the docks by longshoremen but a favorite of certain shipping companies who wanted to cut corners, increase profits, and circumvent the positive things that the ILA did for its members.

The situation on Pier 51 had deteriorated due to the hiring of Kelly, and the men were frustrated with his tenure as hiring boss. The longshoremen's anger finally boiled over on September 12, 1941, when, after a meeting of one hundred and fifty longshoremen at St. Veronica's church, a strike was called as a result of Kelly's tactics. The strike lasted until September 17,

1941, but the Ryan Stevedoring Company was still unwilling to remove Kelly from the position.

After Kelly called the afternoon shape-up on September 27, 1941, he and James Murphy, a timekeeper on Pier 51, headed to Bar Elmondo, which was located directly across the street from the pier. Within twenty minutes of arriving at the bar, Kelly downed six or seven glasses of whiskey. The bartender let Murphy know that he had a call from a checker on Pier 51 named George Donovan and that Donovan wanted Murphy and Kelly to come over to the West Shore Bar and Grill for a drink.

When Kelly and Murphy arrived at the West Shore Bar and Grill, they found that the small tavern was filled with about fifteen or so other men including George Donovan, who was standing at the bar along with Peck Hughes, and a third man who Kelly thought he recognized. When Kelly and Murphy joined Donovan and Hughes they were introduced to the third man—John Dunn. Dunn asked Kelly if he could have a private word with him.

Kelly followed Dunn into a small back room where Dunn's courteous demeanor changed. The first words out of Dunn's mouth were, "Are you going to play ball?" The drunken Kelly responded, "Not unless you explain yourself!" Dunn left the room and came back moments later with Eddie Thompson, who was the hiring boss on Pier 45 and the brother of Sonny Thompson, the owner of the West Shore Bar and Grill. Dunn angrily introduced Thompson to Kelly and informed Kelly that Thompson would now be providing him with instructions about the hiring at Pier 51. Kelly simply stated "no" and walked back out to the bar.

After leaving the back room, Kelly sidled back up against the bar next to Hughes, Donovan, and Murphy. Hughes turned to Kelly and told him that he should do what he is told, that Dunn controls the entire waterfront, and that Dunn could "make or break him." Kelly ignored Hughes and ordered another drink. As the bartender passed Kelly a whiskey, Dunn approached him from behind and said that if Kelly did not do what he was told then would get "a belt in the face." When Kelly ignored Dunn a second time, Dunn drew back his fist and punched Kelly square in the face. Kelly grabbed at Dunn and more punches were thrown at Kelly. The crowd in the bar broke up the fight as Dunn yelled to Hughes and Donovan to "tie Kelly up in the morning." Kelly was then thrown outside of the bar. Hughes stood over Kelly and forcefully told him to get a cab and to think about what had happened. Kelly yelled some profanities at Hughes and, instead of getting in a cab, turned to walk away. After walking about a hundred yards up West Street, Kelly felt a tap on the shoulder. When Kelly turned around, Peck Hughes dropped him with a right hook and walked away.

The next day, Kelly went down to the pier to conduct the daily shape-up as if nothing had happened. At the pier, Kelly found Teddy Gleason and Peter Hussey, who was also a Business Agent with ILA Local 1258. Gleason and Hussey told Kelly that the men were not going to shape-up for him today and that he should go home. When the Ryan Stevedoring Company found out what had occurred, they informed the ILA that Kelly would remain hiring boss and that he would be calling the shape-up the next day. Kelly turned up again on September 29, 1941, but found the pier empty. The men were on strike.

After a few days of striking, and with no end in sight, Ryan Stevedoring Company officials went down to the police station with Kelly and filed a report about the assault and the attempt to intimidate him. Meanwhile, the job action at Pier 51 had completely shut down business and also delayed a British freighter loaded with time-sensitive war supplies. The strike finally came to an end on October 10, 1941, after the Dunn-McGrath Mob caught wind that the investigation into the Kelly matter had been sent to the Rackets Bureau of the district attorney's office.

On October 16, 1941, Dunn, Hughes, Thompson, and Donovan were arrested and charged with coercion, which carried a prison term of up to three years. A rarely used charge, under New York State law coercion meant to use threats or violence to prevent someone from committing legal acts that they have the right to do. All were released on bail, but a trial was scheduled to begin within a few months. For the first time in the gang's history, both Dunn and McGrath were facing concurrent prison sentences.

While Dunn's arrest was big news on the waterfront, it was overshadowed by an event that would deeply affect the Dunn-McGrath Mob's operations and, more importantly, the entire world. Everything changed on December 7, 1941, when the Japanese bombed Pearl Harbor. Less than a week later, the US had entered the war, and the piers that the Dunn-McGrath Mob controlled changed substantially. Given that the Port of New York was the largest in the world, and geographically closer to Europe than other ports in the country, it would play an important role in aiding the war effort. The United States government needed to ensure that everything on the docks ran smoothly, and with that, they placed the War Department in charge of the waterfront.

The War Department now had the final say on what occurred on the docks, and they placed patrolling soldiers on the piers. If there was labor trouble, the government had also been given authority to step in and replace longshoremen with military personnel if needed. The shipping of many goods stopped due to rationing, and as a result, some docks were closed. The excess labor pool also diminished as many longshoremen enlisted to fight for their country.

The government's commandeering of the piers had both a

positive and a negative effect on the Dunn-McGrath Mob. The obvious negative effect was that many of the gang's money-making schemes were now earning substantially less. Although the gang's income was reduced, much of the attention that had been on them was now directed toward the war effort. Men like John Dunn, and other corrupt union leaders, seized the opportunity to further reshape themselves as labor leaders who worked in a rough business, but whose ultimate goal was to support the troops and ensure that goods were transported efficiently to the boys overseas.

Dunn did not have much time to adjust to the new powers on his waterfront, as on December 23, 1941, his coercion trial began. The trial ran until January 2, 1942, and throughout the proceedings, there were suggestions as to the extent of Dunn's real power on the waterfront even though he, Hughes, Donovan, and Thompson tried to argue that the event was nothing more than the usual longshoreman's brawl. Kelly rebutted the claims and his friend James Murphy corroborated the events. At the end of the trial, all the defendants were found guilty.

On January 16, 1942, Dunn was sentenced to an indefinite term in the New York City Penitentiary of up to three years. Hughes also received the same term while Donovan and Thompson got six months in the workhouse. Dunn immediately filed an appeal, but in the interim, he and Hughes were transferred to Rikers Island.

Dunn and McGrath had created a contingency plan in the event of a conviction, and within a week, the head of the Parole Commission started receiving some interesting letters that demonstrated just how far the Dunn-McGrath Mobs tentacles reached. The Commission was flooded with mail from some of the largest trucking firms in the US, who were all suddenly taking a keen interest in Dunn's plight. Eight of the letters all bore the date of January 29, 1942, and the general tone was that Dunn was an upstanding citizen who was an important part of their community. A second wave of correspondence was sent, this time from various prominent community members and politicians. On February 6, 1942, the Parole Commission even received a letter from George Holden Tinkerman, who was a member of the House of Representatives. Tinkerman stated that he was writing on behalf of a constituent who was close to Dunn and that he hoped that it was "possible to exercise clemency in this case."

Before the Parole Board could address Dunn's case, he was temporarily released from Rikers on February 4, 1942. He and Hughes successfully obtained a certificate of reasonable doubt pending a review of their case by the Appellate Division of the New York Courts.

At the time of Dunn's release, McGrath's case for the murder of Leo Tocci was thrown back into the spotlight. On April 25, 1942, Stanley Milledge, a candidate for State's Attorney in Florida, publicly questioned the current district attorney's office. Hinting at corruption during a debate, Milledge noted that "a gangster" like McGrath had not been brought to trial and that his accomplice Buster Bell was never actively sought. With renewed attention on the case, the district attorney responded that they were still trying to collect evidence and that they planned on bringing the McGrath case to trial within the next six months.

In Florida We Trust

IN DECEMBER OF 1942, McGrath was summoned back to Florida to stand trial on first-degree murder charges. Before the trial could begin, McGrath's lawyer, with McGrath present in the court, made a motion for a direct acquittal since it appeared that only circumstantial evidence existed to tie McGrath to the crime. The judge reviewed the evidence, and on January 2, 1943, announced that he agreed with the defense. The prosecution gave notice that they would not pursue an appeal and that McGrath was a free man. Within days of the judge's ruling, Henry "Buster" Bell suddenly turned himself into police in Atlantic City and informed them that he was wanted for a murder in Florida. The word came back from down south that they were no longer interested in Bell.

McGrath celebrated the verdict by checking himself into a luxurious beachfront hotel with a beautiful Chicago gang moll named Estelle Carey. Nicknamed "The Queen of the Dice Girls," Carey was known in the Windy City for her beauty and ability to manipulate men. A friend would describe Carey as someone who "dressed beautifully and had a tremendously attractive personality [but she was] naïve—almost dumb, really, but always eager to improve herself." Starting life out as an orphan, she became a nightclub hostess who won the attention of many suitors, including a number of Chicago Outfit mobsters.

In January of 1943, Carey traveled to Florida to help rid herself of a sinus infection and, while in the company of a mutual underworld connection, she met the recently acquitted McGrath. The two hit it off and McGrath invited Carey to stay in an adjoining suite.

What happened next between the couple would remain an unwanted footnote on McGrath's criminal resume. The two departed Florida at the end of January and both returned to their respective cities, which is where, on February 2, 1943, Carey's dead body was found in her apartment. She had been stabbed multiple times with a bread knife, struck over the head with numerous blunt objects including a rolling pin and a clothing iron, and finally, while still breathing, she was doused with a flammable liquid and set on fire.

Police had many different theories concerning the case, the main one being that Carey was killed because she knew too much about the Chicago Outfit's business. McGrath, who became known as Carey's last lover, was subject to a number of accusations, the most concerning being that he had accompanied Carey back to Chicago and murdered her as a favor to his underworld associates. To close friends, McGrath would vehemently deny that he was in any way involved in Carey's murder. McGrath was likely not lying, as witnesses could place him in New York City at the time of the crime, and Carey's phone records showed a call from her apartment to McGrath's residence at the Sheraton Hotel on the day of her murder.

The most probable solution to Carey's murder was much less sensational than the organized crime angle. Police arrested Thomas Stapleton, a known thief who frequented the same dice clubs as Carey and was well acquainted with her. Police believed it was possible that Stapleton was invited in, attempted to rob Carey, after which a struggle ensued and she was killed. The neighbor who had witnessed the man running from Carey's apartment initially identified Stapleton, but the statement was weak and charges against him were dropped.

McGrath would have likely enjoyed spending more time

away from the limelight, but pressing matters brought him back to New York. On January 25, 1943, the Court of Appeals declined to review the case of John Dunn and Peck Hughes, and they were both returned to Rikers Island. With his partner back behind bars, McGrath again began working the angles.

On February 1, 1943, War Department Officials traveled from Washington DC to New York City to meet with the senior members of the Parole Commission. Included in the contingent making the surprise visit was a Lieutenant, a Major, and the Chief of Materials from the Transportation Corps. The officers stressed to the Parole Commission that Dunn was extremely important to the war effort, that he had previously provided them confidential assistance, and that it was essential that he be released immediately. Whether Dunn actually aided the US government is unclear, but the military officials' intervention was either purchased or false promises were made concerning what Dunn could provide them in the future.

The Parole Commission, who was well aware of Dunn's reputation, wrote to the sentencing judge about the puzzling visit that they had received. They stated the following:

> "The matter of this inmate's case was thoroughly reviewed and we got into it very thoroughly, his criminal record was read to them and also the probation report giving all the facts and ramifications in connection with the activities of Dunn.
>
> After thorough examination and investigation, all the facts being stated, these officers who represent our government insisted that this man be released for the purpose of facilitating the movement of goods in connection with the successful prosecution of our war. They further stated that because of Dunn's connections with the labor unions and his influence over the men con-

nected therewith, he would be very necessary and that he had already done some excellent work in connection with the movement of supplies for our government and that they were positive he would be very necessary as a civilian in this connection."

Within two days, an official request came from Col. Frederick C. Horner, Chief of the Highway Division, Transportation Corps, in a letter dated February 3, 1943. Col. Horner addressed Dunn's conviction by writing "[. . .] in times such as these when there is a goal to attain, such an incident should not be the all-determining factor," and, adding an air of secrecy to the matter, he ended his communication with, "Nevertheless, consideration of the factors mentioned above and many others which I am not a liberty to divulge compels the decision to ask for his immediate release."

The Parole Commission had been outgunned, and on February 4, 1943, they voted unanimously to begin to prepare Dunn for release. Still wary of their own decision, they did add that they had come to the conclusion to release Dunn "[. . .] only because of the insistence of officials of the War Department." Before actually releasing Dunn, the Parole Commission checked with one last interested party—the Mayor of New York City. Mayor La Guardia, who campaigned on having a tough stance on crime, was furious when he heard about the interference of the war officials and consulted with New York City district attorney Frank Hogan about John Dunn's reputation.

On February 20, 1942, Mayor La Guardia sent a letter directly to the Secretary of War, Henry L. Stimson, detailing what had occurred in Dunn's case. On March 4, 1943, Stimson replied that he was unaware of the Dunn situation, but that he would be investigating it further. He concluded his letter with "[. . .] you may consider the request for Mr. Dunn's release as definitely withdrawn." Dunn's parole recommendation was immediately canceled and no details of Stimson's investigation were ever documented, although Col. Horner was relieved of his duties in September of 1944.

Dunn had been close to receiving a substantially early release with a little help from the US government, but he would have to wait until August 29, 1944, before being paroled. His latest conviction did nothing to stop his rise as a waterfront labor leader, as by September 16, 1944, Connie Noonan reinstated him as both the Vice-President and Business Agent of AFL Local 21510.

24

War Rations

DURING THE WAR years, many of the gang members began exploring new business ventures beyond their traditional scope on the waterfront. Some purchased bars and restaurants, and underlings who were put out of work due to the war were placed in no-show jobs, with men such as Barney Baker, McGrath's brother James Connors, and Danny Gentile, being added to the payroll of a company that made collections from vendors at West Side markets.

The numbers game, which had been running successfully for three to four years, experienced a steep decline in business due to the military's presence on the piers. The writing was on the wall for the operation and both McGrath and Dunn made it known that they were looking to get out of the business. When gang member Danny Gentile found out, he offered to buy the business from them, as he believed that he could keep it running. Gentile paid $3500 to McGrath and Dunn, and the operation was turned over to him, after which it declined and eventually shut down.

To make up for lost income, McGrath and Dunn, using their connection to Joe Adonis and Jimmy Alo, became heavily involved in the increasingly popular world of sports betting. Technology had improved to the point where a bookmaker was able to get live game results and also provide more consistent odds to potential players. Bookmakers were able to expand outside of the traditional realm of booking horses and were now taking bets on virtually every sport.

McGrath, with Dunn as an equal stakeholder, joined with an established bookmaker, Frank "Frank Mario" Bonfiglio, and his partner Louis Lepore. Bonfiglio, who lived with Lepore in an expensive West Side hotel, was a former Broadway night-club owner and good friend of crime boss Frank Costello. The group set up a bookmaking office inside Astor Motors, a car dealership that Mario and Lepore owned in Little Ferry, New Jersey, and McGrath, who enjoyed betting himself, would visit the offices almost daily.

McGrath, who was still the dominant criminal figure on the West Side and the de facto leader of the Irish Mob, quickly attracted a large pool of players using his influence on the waterfront. As one of the first in the area to establish a large-scale betting ring, McGrath's operation dwarfed the local bookmakers, who, in turn, began to lay off their own action to his much larger book. McGrath then assisted other members of his gang in establishing themselves as bookmakers on the piers, which led to further growth of his business.

When not running the rackets on the West Side, the members of the Dunn-McGrath Mob frequently enjoyed traveling to Florida during the slow winter season. One of their regular spots was Jimmy Alo's Colonial Inn casino in Hallandale. McGrath's longtime friend, Alo, had become hugely successful along with Meyer Lansky, and McGrath visited him numerous times a year. John Dunn and Squint Sheridan also frequently traveled to Florida, and the two men would often bring their families with them. During the war, when the waterfront profits were at their lowest, McGrath even arranged employment at the Colonial Inn for former Varick employees Barney Baker and Jackie Adams, where Baker worked as a security guard and Adams became a floor boss.

The most noteworthy news during this period was the

release of an old nemesis of the gang turned fragile new ally, Charlie "The Jew" Yanowsky. Yanowsky had kept his end of the deal, which was made prior to the murder of Mattie Kane, and returned to New Jersey following his release from Sing Sing. Like both Dunn and McGrath, the 1935 Waterfront War had built a reputation for Yanowsky, and he was able to reintegrate himself onto the New Jersey waterfront, in particular, the docks in Jersey City. Yanowsky created a new inner circle made up of old friends, which included a New Yorker named Eddie Polo and two career criminals from the Garden State named George "The Rape Artist" Donahue and Vincent "Cockeye" Brown (who always wore dark sunglasses as one of his eyes was even more cockeyed than John "Cockeye" Dunn's). Acting as frontmen for Yanowsky were his brother-in-law, Frank "Biffo" DeLorenzo, and Jersey City waterfront bar owner, Anthony "Slim" Lucey.

The piers in Jersey City had long been controlled by the famed and corrupt political dynasty of Mayor Frank Hague. Hague, who had been Mayor since 1917, had an iron grip on the city, and, through his crooked methods, he had his hands in the pockets of all of the important industries, which included the Jersey City waterfront. Hague had handpicked his own loaders and pier bosses and made it clear that men like Yanowksy were not welcome on the docks. Yanowsky found an ally in one of Hague's own ward leaders, John V. Kenny, a son of the same politician who cared for Connie Noonan and his family in the early 1900s. It is not clear if Noonan made the connection between Yanowsky and Kenny, but within a year of Yanowsky's release, there were reports that the two men were often seen driving around town together. A lawyer who was well acquainted with Kenny also told investigators that he frequently passed notes between Kenny and Yanowsky and that Yanowsky made comments that Kenny was "his man."

Although Mayor Hague remained in control of the Jersey

City docks for the time being, Yanowsky became an official of the ILA affiliated Marine Warehousemen's Union, and he established his own gambling and numbers operations on the New Jersey waterfront. Using his money and political connections, Yanowksy also muscled in on the Hoboken piers, where it was later discovered that he had bribed a collection of city officials for the right to operate in their city.

Within a year of his release, Yanowsky had solidified his control over the New Jersey waterfront. His new gang, the Dunn-McGrath Mob, and the Bowers Mob continued to cooperate in various rackets, which included sharing gambling ventures and also moving mob-friendly longshoremen between preferable piers in each other's territories. With the 1935 waterfront feud a thing of the past, and friendships blossoming between the groups, Yanowsky would be appointed Business Agent of AFL Local 21512, which was the New Jersey branch of the Dunn-McGrath Mob's own AFL Local 21510. Around the same time, Yanowsky, who kept his office in Jersey City, even hired Squint Sheridan's teenage daughter as his receptionist. The waterfront gangsters had gone from murdering each other in the streets to employing each other's family members.

With an improbable peace ensuing among the waterfront's most volatile criminals, the next source of conflict would come from an unexpected group—the legitimate longshoremen who the gangsters had successfully oppressed for decades.

The Rebels

ON MAY 8, 1945, it was announced that the Allied forces were victorious in Europe. Although the war in the Pacific raged on, people finally had hope that the end was in sight. As the victorious military personnel began to trickle home, the War Department began the process of gradually returning control of the piers to the city. Shipping companies started to lease the piers again, business returned to normal and, receiving no resistance, the Dunn-McGrath Mob placed their old boss loaders and hiring bosses back into their usual positions.

Although the gangsters easily resumed control over their old rackets, there was a different feeling on the waterfront following the end of the war. Longshoremen who had served overseas had seen combat, witnessed friends die, and taken lives themselves. The men returned home different than when they had left. Many longed for the simple things—a home for their families, steady work, and the freedoms that they had fought for; freedoms that they did not expect to be taken away by local hoodlums.

With longshoremen beginning to openly resent the rule of the gangsters and Joe Ryan, trouble began to brew in the heart of the Dunn-McGrath Mob territory at Pier 45. Prior to the War, both Pier 45 and Pier 46 were controlled by the owners of the West Shore Bar and Grill and Dunn-McGrath Mob members, Raymond "Sonny" Thompson and his brother Eddie Thompson. Sonny Thompson was the Business Agent for the neighborhood longshoremen's union, ILA Local 895, and Eddie Thompson was the hiring boss on Pier 45. Sonny Thompson was not popular with the men who lived around the pier, but when the United States entered the war, the pier was taken over by the Navy.

When the Navy vacated Pier 45 in 1945, shipping companies were hesitant to pick up the lease as they remembered the crimes that occurred under the Thompsons' rule. A group of ILA Local 895 men, led by a thirty-year-old named Johnny Dwyer, decided to take matters into their own hands. Dwyer, who was described as loyal and incorruptible, had just returned home from two years of service with the Navy and decided that together the local longshoremen could bring back business to Pier 45 by showing the shipping companies that ILA Local 895 was free from criminal influence. Helping Dwyer were other like-minded members of ILA Local 895, many of whom were also veterans, such as Pete Laughran, Jackie Mullins, John Barrieo, Vincent Kuscinski, Arthur Brown, and Eddie Barry. The Joe Ryan detractors became known around the waterfront as the "the rebels."

Joining Dwyer in the fight against corruption was a local Jesuit priest named Father John Corridan. Corridan, who would become the inspiration for the character of Father Barry in the Academy Award winning film *On the Waterfront*, was the son of an Irish-born police officer from Harlem. *On the Waterfront* writer Budd Schulberg described Corridan as a "tall, youthful, balding, energetic, ruddy-faced Irishman whose speech was a fascinating blend of Hell's Kitchen jargon, baseball slang, the facts and figures of a master in economics and the undeniable humanity of Christ." Assigned to work at the Xavier Institute of Industrial Relations, on Manhattan's West Side, Corridan recognized the problems that the men on the waterfront faced. Immersing himself in the world of the West Side longshoremen, he began to gain the trust of many of the cagey and street-hardened dock workers.

In September of 1945, the rebel group demanded that an election be held for the offices of ILA Local 895, as no one could even remember the last time one had occurred. The rebels announced that they would be running their own ticket against Sonny Thompson's and, with an election scheduled in two months, the fight for votes began. Word of their anti-Joe Ryan crusade spread along the waterfront, and many who had grown tired of Ryan's corrupt ways found acceptance with the group. With the rebels' numbers now swelling into the hundreds, the Dunn-McGrath Mob was limited in their ability to employ the same terror tactics that they had successfully used during the past decade.

Discontent was brewing all along the West Side piers, and the ILA Local 895 rebels found similar sentiment in ILA Local 791, a more powerful charter directly north of them in Chelsea. The local's business agent was a Joe Ryan antagonist named John J. "Gene" Sampson. Sampson was universally recognized within ILA circles as the chief rival of Ryan, and although Ryan openly resented Sampson, the Local 791 leader was largely untouchable due to the political backing of Sampson's brother Frank, a longtime Tammany Hall stalwart. Sampson, with his own agenda to steal the ILA away from Joe Ryan, capitalized on the growing dissatisfaction with Ryan's rule and became known as the "the spearhead of the rising insurgent movement."

In September of 1945, Joe Ryan had just finished negotiating a new contract for the ILA, but in typical Ryan fashion, many ILA members felt that the deal did not properly address their wages or increasing workload. With post-war shipping at its peak, the influential Sampson capitalized on the anger of many ILA members, and on October 1, 1945, he pulled ILA Local 791 off the docks in an unauthorized wildcat strike. The final provocation occurred when the shipping companies continued to increase the sling load, which was the amount of weight brought up each time from a cargo. Feeling overworked and unprotected by their new contract, the longshoremen decided that they would send a message to their leadership by walking off the job, although Sampson was quick to add that Joe Ryan's gangsterism and dictatorship rule had heavily contributed to the decision. By the second day of the work stoppage, the strike had grown to tens of thousands of longshoremen all over the city and shipping on the ports was reduced to a crawl.

The shadowy world of the waterfront was splashed across the pages of the dailies, and the reporters seemed genuinely curious about the divide in the powerful union. The attention benefited the members but was creating a big problem for the men behind the scenes. Police investigators later claimed that an informant advised them that the mob convened to discuss the potentially devastating strike and, on October 4, 1945, McGrath, Anthony Strollo, Albert Anastasia, Mickey Bowers, and others allegedly met to troubleshoot the wildcat strike. The first suggestion was that Sampson be murdered, but most agreed that he was too high profile and that his murder would only turn him into a martyr.

With the gangsters short on solutions, the strike came to an unexpected end when many of Ryan's longtime foes, such as the West Coast labor leader Harry Bridges and an assortment of communists, announced their support for the workers. To the striking longshoremen, there was no greater insult than being lumped in with communists, and various strike leaders made statements to clarify that this was strictly an internal membership dispute.

Joe Ryan was quick to state that the strike was due to a misunderstanding and that communists had been attempting to infiltrate his union. Ryan brought the membership's concerns to arbitration, where they successfully received a wage increase, Sampson stepped back from his role as a strike leader, and after eleven days the job action ended. In response to the upheaval, Ryan's group of largely handpicked ILA delegates voted overwhelmingly to keep Ryan as the lifetime President of the union. Disaster for Ryan and his cronies had been avoided, but the 1945 wildcat strike was the first time that the rank and file members of the ILA had so openly questioned his rule of the union.

In November of 1945, after much pressure from Johnny Dwyer and his friends, the ILA Local 895 election finally went ahead in the basement of St. Veronica's Church, which had become the unofficial meeting hall for Greenwich Village longshoremen. The rebels had been building on the momentum of the October strike and felt good about their chances in the election, but the day of the vote turned out to be a demonstration of the power that the mobsters still wielded on the waterfront. Before the voting could commence, hundreds of men that the rebels had never seen before turned up with ILA Local 895 membership cards in hand. Thompson and the Dunn-McGrath Mob had handed them out in bars across the city, paid the strangers a small fee, and then taxied them to the union hall to vote for Thompson's leadership ticket. Fist fights broke out around the church as the real members of ILA Local 895 fought to save the election. The votes were counted the next day by an ILA representative, and it was announced that Sonny Thompson and the rest of his ticket had been officially elected to five-year terms.

The core of the rebel faction was shut out of longshoremen work from Brooklyn to New Jersey and were labeled communists by the ILA leadership. It was a long and hard winter for the men in the neighborhood, as Pier 45 remained closed, and most of the members had to survive on unemployment insurance and odd jobs. It was common to see street skirmishes between the rebel group and ILA loyalists, and although Sonny Thompson's bar remained open, no one dared to sit by the windows as disgruntled longshoremen regularly hurled rocks and garbage cans through the glass.

Early in 1946, two shipping companies, The Alcoa Company
and McGrath Stevedoring (no connection to Eddie McGrath),
announced that they were ready to lease Pier 45 from the city,
and an offer was extended to the defeated rebels to return to
work and fall in line under the Thompson brothers. The rebels
discussed their options and, although hungry and broke, they
decided to hold out. With the men unwilling to work, Pier
45 remained closed.

The rebels turned to the Association of Catholic Trade
Unions (ACTU), a group whose mandate it was to fight com-
munism, provide support for Catholic union members, and
promote fairness in organized labor. George Donahue, the
longshoreman who dared to file charges against the Dunn-
McGrath Mob after receiving a beating in 1937, had become
a leader within the association and was keen to assist. The
ACTU announced their support for the rebels, and the counsel
for the ACTU, Ed Scully, began to provide legal services at
no charge. Scully felt the best course of action was for the
local membership to file official charges against the union
leadership, and hundreds of ILA Local 895 members put their
names on the official complaint. The men, who were sure to be
labeled as snitches, were willing to risk their jobs by signing
the court order that requested a new election. The stalemate
continued into the summer of 1946, when the courts finally
ordered that a new election be held under the supervision of
appointed monitors.

A second election was held in December of 1946. Sonny
Thompson recognized that it was impossible to win under the
watchful eye of the government, and he decided that he would
not even bother to run again. Instead, Thompson closed his
bar and moved to Miami where he found work as a bookie.
The rebel ticket won by a clean sweep. The Alcoa Company
signed the papers to lease the pier, and Johnny Dwyer was
asked to be the new hiring boss on Pier 45. Dwyer resented

Joe Ryan's favored shape-up system, but accepted the job and brought honesty to the position by establishing regular gangs of local union men that were rotated through fairly.

After defeating the gangsters using the legitimate legal means at their disposal, the rebel faction would continue to grow as a haven for those who wanted to fight the gangsters and Joe Ryan's control over the ILA. On the other side of the battle for Pier 45 was the defeated Dunn-McGrath Mob, who had been beaten at their own game for the first time. Although the waterfront was surprisingly calm following the rebels' victory, the upheaval that had occurred on Pier 45 would set off a chain of events that would forever change the face of the New York City waterfront.

26

61 Grove Street

ONLY WEEKS BEFORE being defeated in the December 1946 Local 895 election, the Dunn-McGrath Mob was cutting their losses and focusing on another West Side pier that appeared to be heading in the same direction as Pier 45.

In May of 1946, the Navy relinquished control of Pier 51 and a shipping company, States Marine, began to lease it. Designated as both the hiring boss and the loading boss was a seasoned dock worker, and known tough guy, named Anthony "Andy" Hintz. During the 1930s he had been employed as a bartender at a trendy nightspot named Maisie's Little Club, where he fell in love and married the owner, a former showgirl named Maisie LaMarr, whom he affectionately called "Daisy." When the bar went into the red, the newlyweds moved to Greenwich Village in the mid-1930s and Hintz found work on the piers as a member of the ILA. The blonde-haired and barrel-chested Hintz had earned a reputation as someone who was good with his fists if the occasion arose, a skill that was guaranteed to earn you respect on the waterfront.

After the piers began to open up following the end of World War Two, Hintz was an active supporter of ILA Local 895. During the months when the rebel group was finally starting to experience success on Pier 45, State Marine asked Hintz if he would take over the hiring and loading on Pier 51. Hintz took to his new role and was an immediate success with both the men and the shipping company. Running a clean pier, he was known to hire men fairly and divide loading proceeds evenly.

Although not close friends, Dunn-McGrath gofer Danny Gentile had known Hintz for years, so it was no surprise when the gangster approached Hintz at work one day. Giving his best sales pitch, Gentile told him that the Dunn-McGrath Mob wanted to partner up on Pier 51. All Hintz needed to do was share a portion of the loading, ensure that the right people were hired, and allow a little theft here and there. If he played by the rules, he would be making more in a week than he had in his entire life. Hintz told Gentile that he was not interested and that he was running his own operation on Pier 51. Shocked by Hintz's response, but not deterred, Gentile continued to visit, and each time he would let Hintz know that his fellow gang members were not happy with the situation. Hintz finally grew tired of Gentile's subtle threats and shortly before the Thanksgiving of 1946, Hintz was witnessed by other longshoremen chasing Gentile away while yelling, "You tell that cockeye bastard Dunn to keep his hands off this pier!"

Mysterious cars began to follow Hintz home while flashing their lights at him, and his friends and enemies alike suggested that he just play ball. Even though he was playing a dangerous game, Hintz wouldn't budge. The gang upped the ante when James "Ding-Dong" Bell and a couple of other thugs approached him on a street near his house. Bell told Hintz that he was now in charge of Pier 51 and that he could remain on the job if he started taking instructions from him, to which Hintz replied that Bell could go to hell. Without warning, Bell pulled out a pistol and shot Hintz in the thigh. Before leaving, Bell let the bleeding Hintz know that the next bullet would be in his head if he showed his face again on Pier 51.

Following the code of the waterfront, Hintz did not report the shooting to police, and instead Maisie drove him out to the countryside where she removed the bullet from his leg using a kitchen knife. A more prudent man would have known when to call it quits, but as soon as Hintz felt well enough, he drove back to his home, borrowed a gun from a friend, and went looking for Bell. Hintz found his target loitering outside of a bar in Greenwich and opened fire, grazing Bell in the head as he took off running. It was the fourth documented time that Bell had been shot. Hintz continued to let it be known that the only way he would be leaving Pier 51 was in a body bag.

The day after the Bell shooting, the longshoremen on Pier 51 saw an unusual sight, John Dunn and Squint Sheridan strutting slowly down the entire length of the dock. The two casually asked some longshoremen where Hintz was, but he had not turned up at work that day. The purposeful stroll was a show of force. With the gang's defeat in the ILA Local 895 election, their position on the waterfront had been openly questioned. Dunn regarded this as a personal affront and Hintz, who walked closer to the line that separated the legitimate longshoremen from the underworld, was fair game.

On January 8, 1947, Hintz was following his usual morning routine at his apartment at 61 Grove Street in Greenwich Village. Every morning Hintz would get up, eat breakfast, and wait to hear the honk of his driver's horn shortly before 8:00 AM. Hintz, who had been taking these precautions since running into trouble with the Dunn-McGrath Mob, would look out of his window to verify the car, give a signal to acknowledge his driver's presence, and then head down the steps of his building to the waiting car. On this day, Hintz's brother Willie and one of his friends had arrived to chauffeur Hintz to Pier 51.

Between the third and second floors of the low-rise building, Hintz turned the corner and found three waiting figures—John Dunn, Squint Sheridan, and Danny Gentile.

Hintz was not given a second to react as Dunn shouted: "Kill the rat!" Dunn then drew a pistol from his pocket and fired two shots into Hintz. Dunn and Sheridan ran up the stairs, and as Dunn passed Hintz's prone body, he fired another three shots. Hintz, who still had some fight in him, grabbed Dunn by the leg as he attempted to jump over him, but as he gripped tight, Gentile stepped forward and began to stomp on Hintz's face. Hintz lost his grip and Dunn and Sheridan ran up the stairs to the roof, crossed the rooftops to an adjoining building, and then ran downstairs to a waiting car on Christopher Street. Gentile separated from Dunn and Sheridan and ran out of Hintz's building and right past the waiting car containing Hintz's brother and friend, who barely had time to process what had just occurred.

Inside 61 Grove Street, Hintz lay in a pool of blood with a gunshot through his face and four bullets in his chest and abdomen, two of which had exited his body and two of which remained inside of him. Maisie had heard the shots and ran out to find the bloody Hintz, who just kept repeating "Daisy. . . Daisy. . . Daisy." Maisie asked him, "Who were the rats that shot you?" and Hintz mumbled over and over, "Johnny did it."

Two neighbors of the Hintzs', Dr. Tarlflau, a dentist, and a man named Mike Sullivan, ran out to assist Maisie and help bring Hintz back into his apartment. Dr. Tarlflau performed some basic first-aid while Mike Sullivan called for an ambulance. When Maisie was alone with Andy, she again asked who shot him and Hintz replied: "Johnny Dunn shot me." Moments later, when the first police officer arrived on the scene he asked the same question and Hintz replied: "I don't know." Hintz wanted his wife to know who attacked him, but keeping with the code of the waterfront, he had no intention of talking to police. Maisie told the police what Hintz had told her about John Dunn being the shooter, and the officer again asked Hintz, who responded with silence. Hintz arrived at St. Vincent's Hospital where surgery was attempted. One bullet was successfully removed, but the other could not be. Hintz was able to speak after surgery, but his vitals were extremely weak and the doctors did not know how long he would have to live.

Based on the information that Maisie had provided, the police detectives headed over to the gang's union offices, where they found a cooperative Dunn sitting behind his desk with a cup of coffee in hand. One of the detectives told Dunn about the Hintz shooting, and Dunn's first question back was, "Is he dead?" When questioned further, Dunn told the police that he took his children to morning mass, ate breakfast with his wife Anna around 8:30 AM, and then headed into the city. Unable to charge him with murder, the officers arrested Dunn as a material witness and the court set bail at $25,000.

At the same time that Dunn was being held, a young assistant district attorney named Bill Keating was being handed the file for the morning shooting. Known as a hardworking Assistant DA who did not blur the line between right and wrong, Keating had grown up blue collar and was fresh on the job having only recently completed law school.

Keating headed over to the station to question Dunn; he would later describe the gangster as detached and self-assured. The whole process seemed to be a minor nuisance to Dunn. As if he had already rehearsed his responses, he provided answer after answer without thought: "I don't know Anthony Hintz well," "No, I am not aware of any trouble," "Yes, I was at home at the time of the shooting."

Keating's next stop was to visit Dunn's wife, and Eddie McGrath's sister, Anna. Anna provided a basic alibi for Dunn saying that he did eat breakfast with her that day, but that she was unable to remember exact times, as she had taken sleeping pills the night before and was feeling drowsy that morning. When Keating worked out the distance between the shooting location and Dunn's home, he found that Dunn could have easily committed the murder at 7:45 AM and been back home by 8:30 AM.

With the day almost over, Keating made one last stop to the hospital to see if Hintz would be willing to provide information about the shooting. When Keating began to question Hintz, who had a swollen face, a gruesome bullet hole in his cheek, and a variety of tubes and lines in him, it became clear that Hintz might not live much longer. Despite Keating's pleas, Hintz refused to name Dunn and said, "What is the use of putting the finger on a guy if it ain't him?" That night Keating headed home dejected. He was dealing with another waterfront shooting that was about to go unsolved.

The next day, Anna Dunn and a bail bondsman turned up with the bail needed for Dunn's release. Keating was not willing to give up the fight and exercised his legal right, under the material witness law, to keep Dunn for forty-eight hours longer. The clock was ticking. Keating headed back to the hospital where he was introduced to a police officer named Lt. Joe Sullivan. Sullivan was wary of Keating, but after some conversation, the lieutenant realized that Keating might actually be trustworthy. He explained to Keating that he was a friend of Hintz and that his brother Mike was one of the men who first helped Hintz after the shooting. Sullivan told Keating that he lived in Greenwich, was a former longshoreman himself and, that despite what Keating might hear in the future, Hintz was one of the good guys on the piers. He provided Keating with the history of Hintz's problems, a rundown of what had been occurring on the waterfront, and also gave a brief lesson on the Dunn-McGrath Mob.

Lt. Sullivan told Keating that he would speak to Hintz privately about providing a statement, and on January 10, 1947,

Keating was informed by Sullivan that Hintz was ready to talk to him. The previous day, Sullivan had a long conversation with Hintz, Maisie, and his brother Willie and impressed upon them how dangerous it would be for them if Dunn beat this rap. Hintz was reluctant to cooperate, but, after urging from Maisie, he finally agreed. Keating headed back to the hospital with a stenographer by his side and again began to question Hintz about the shooting. Hintz named John Dunn, Andy Sheridan, and a "Danny" as the men who had tried to kill him. When asked who Danny was, Hintz said that he did not know any more about him.

In a dramatic moment, police rushed Dunn from custody to Hintz's bedside so that an official identification could be done. Dunn walked in calmly, looked at the bullet-ridden Hintz and simply said "Hello Andy," to which Hintz replied, "This is the man that shot me." Dunn responded with, "Andy, you know who I am?," after which he asked Hintz to tell the truth. Dunn asked Hintz if he was satisfied with himself, and Hintz replied by pulling down the top of his hospital gown to show Dunn his bullet wounds, saying, "I want to show him to see if he is satisfied." Hintz then closed his eyes and turned away. Dunn said, "I hope you get well Andy" and was escorted out of the room. Dunn was then taken back to jail and booked on the charge of felonious assault. Given Hintz's condition, the court decided to hold Dunn without bail.

A warrant was put out for Squint Sheridan's arrest that day. Police officers raced over to his apartment in Jersey City, but he was nowhere to be found. Hintz had not completely named Danny Gentile as the third man involved in the shooting, but through the Dunn-McGrath Mob's connections on the police force, they soon learned that Hintz had identified Dunn, Sheridan, and a "Danny." Gentile was at his home the day after the identification when he received a visit from Anna Dunn who only lived about six blocks away. She gave

Gentile a phone number to get in touch with McGrath, and Gentile was told to come to a meeting at Horn and Hardart's Automat at 58th Street and 6th Avenue.

Gentile headed right over to the Automat where McGrath was already waiting for him. McGrath told Gentile that his name had come up in the shooting and that he was to get out of town right away. Gentile told McGrath that he was hesitant to leave town, as it would make him look guilty, but McGrath told him that he did not have a choice and that he would be going shortly. The worried Gentile headed to a friend's home for a couple of days and then got in touch with the gang's regular lawyer, Joe Aronstein. Gentile told Aronstein that he wanted to turn himself in, but Aronstein said that he would need to speak to McGrath first.

Word came back from McGrath that Gentile was "to get going." Gang member Eddie Gaffney arrived, gave Gentile the keys to an apartment in St. Petersburg, drove him to the airport, and handed him a one-way plane ticket south.

According to the account provided in Keating's autobiography, *The Man Who Rocked the Boat*, during the evening of Dunn's arrest, Keating was approached by the Captain of the Homicide Squad, Dan Mahoney. Captain Mahoney, who held one of the most powerful positions in the NYPD, was a strong looking man who was held in high regard by the officers under his command. He also happened to be the same officer who had shot and killed McGrath's old friend George Achinelli in 1930. Mahoney asked Keating if he wanted to have dinner with him and discuss the case a bit further.

Mahoney and Keating were chauffeured to East 48th Street, New York's steakhouse row, but according to Keating's own statements, Mahoney began to make some unsettling remarks during the drive. Mahoney explained to Keating that Hintz was nothing but trouble and that, although Dunn had likely done the shooting, Hintz had it coming. He explained that

Dunn was a good guy who once helped a relative of his get a great job on the piers without even having to purchase a union book.

Mahoney's restaurant of choice that night happened to be the upscale Tiger Lily restaurant, which was owned by long-time Dunn-McGrath Mob stalwart Frank "U-Boat" Kelly. After they arrived, Mahoney told Keating that he wanted them to join a friend for dinner. Mahoney took Keating to a secluded table in the back where a well-groomed middle-aged man was sitting alone. Mahoney made introductions for the two and proudly announced that this was Eddie McGrath, brother-in-law of John Dunn. He then introduced Keating as, "the man who just locked Dunn up." McGrath smiled politely as Keating sat down.

Mahoney shared with Keating the story of how he met McGrath after arresting him. Mahoney laughed at how the world worked and how the two were now the best of pals. Mahoney and McGrath then began to talk about a handful of people who Keating had never heard of and nothing about the Dunn case was mentioned. After the meal, McGrath bade Keating a courteous goodbye and excused himself. Keating also left, but not before Mahoney exclaimed to him that he "[. . .] needed to get out more and meet the right people."

Although nothing illegal had happened with Mahoney and McGrath, the evening had left a bad taste in Keating's mouth. The dinner date had demonstrated why Lt. Joe Sullivan was cautious when he first met him, as it was now obvious to Keating that deep connections existed between the gangsters and law enforcement.

Keating approached Lt. Sullivan who informed him that he had continued his own unauthorized investigation into the Hintz shooting. Sullivan told Keating that Hintz knew that the Danny he previously identified was Gentile but that Hintz did not name him, as he thought Gentile was "a bum" who did not deserve credit for the shooting. After some coaxing, Hintz provided another statement, which again named Dunn and Sheridan, but now also included Danny "Danny Brooks" Gentile. Police put out a warrant for Gentile's arrest, but unbeknownst to them, he had already been sent to Florida by McGrath.

On January 14, 1947, the police officers who had been searching for Squint Sheridan had a breakthrough. A young girl named Edith Jansen, who was a close friend of Sheridan's daughter Cheri, had come forward and told them that she had been vacationing with the Sheridan family in Florida since mid-December of 1946. Jansen added that, on New Year's Day, Squint Sheridan had left them down south and returned to New York to attend to business.

Of interest to Keating was one other peculiar incident that the young Edith Jansen described. She said that a day or two before Squint Sheridan left, she and Cheri Sheridan were in the hotel pool when two men in swimsuits, who were introduced as John Dunn and Jimmy Alo, approached Cheri. Cheri seemed to know Dunn well, and Dunn asked her where her father was. Cheri told Dunn that her father had stepped out. Dunn asked Cheri to have Sheridan contact him at the Sheldon Hotel when he returned.

Investigators followed up on the lead and found that Dunn had also been in Florida for the last half of December 1946 and that he had shared an adjoining suite at the Sheldon Hotel with Alo's partner, Meyer Lansky. Phone records from the room were examined, and it was found that there were both outgoing and incoming calls made to McGrath, Mafia boss Frank Costello, Costello's New Orleans business partner "Dandy" Phil Kastel, Joe Adonis, Lansky's close friend Bugsy Siegel, and the Hotel Nacional in Havana, which was where the recently deported Lucky Luciano had been staying. Police investigating Lansky would theorize that Dunn may have been in Florida to discuss how his connections on the docks could be used to help facilitate the mob's growing drug smuggling business.

Jansen told police that Sheridan rejoined them again in Florida on January 13, 1947, which placed him in New York City at the time of the Hintz shooting. When Sheridan traveled back to Florida, he was accompanied by Jeff "Little Jeff" La Porte, a minor hoodlum with a lengthy criminal record, who began staying in the Sheridan family's hotel room. On the day the gangsters arrived, word got back to them that Hintz had named Sheridan as one of the shooters, so they hurriedly bundled Edith Jansen onto a train to Newark, New Jersey. Sheridan then told his family that he soon planned to head to California on business.

On January 15, 1947, an official request was sent from the NYPD to the Hollywood, Florida police to arrest Sheridan. Since they had provided Sheridan's exact address, the NYPD expected him to be picked up within the day, but no response was received from the Hollywood Police. Keating would later learn that when the officers in Florida received the request, they approached Jimmy Alo, who regularly paid-off their police department, and asked him what he wanted done with the warrant. Alo advised them to forget about it. In desperation, the district attorney's office in New York turned to the Miami Police Department and requested that they contact their neighbors in Hollywood and stress the importance of this case. No longer able to drag their feet, the Hollywood Police Department arrested Sheridan at his hotel on January 24, 1947. After searching the room, they found that Sheridan's suitcases had been packed and that he appeared ready to leave.

The police were unable to locate Sheridan's travel companion, Jeff La Porte, and after some digging, it was found that he had not been seen since January 15, 1947. An official missing persons report was filed, but the underworld rumor was that he was buried somewhere in Florida. Police speculated that La Porte may have known too much about Sheridan's crime and that once Sheridan heard he was wanted by police, he decided that La Porte would not hold up to police pressure.

After Sheridan's arrest, Robert "Barney" Baker, who had been spending the winter season working security at Alo's Colonial Inn, attempted to pay Sheridan a visit in jail to pass on information from New York. When Baker arrived at the jail, the Sheriff told him that he could not see the prisoner unless he was willing to help with the investigation. Baker intentionally gave false information that Danny Gentile was hiding out in rural New Jersey, which led to the FBI conducting a large search of the area. After failing to locate Gentile, the DA in New York City requested that Baker be picked up for questioning. Rather than turn himself in, Baker, with the help of Alo and Lansky, was shipped out west to stay at the Flamingo Hotel in Las Vegas.

On January 29, 1947, Hintz's condition deteriorated, and after nearly a month of lingering near death, he passed away. With Maisie by his side for his last moments, Hintz cried and told his wife that he knew that he was dying. He said goodbye over and over and kissed her one last time. Even while facing death, the hardened longshoreman still worried aloud about how his friends on the docks would view him since he "turned rat" during his last days.

Hours after Hintz's death, Lt. Sullivan approached Assistant DA Keating and told him that both Maisie and Willie Hintz were now willing to testify in court against Dunn, Sheridan and, if he was ever caught, Danny Gentile. Sullivan also had one more bombshell for Keating. Willie Hintz had actually seen Danny Gentile running from the scene of the crime that morning. He had not planned to tell anyone about what he witnessed, but after his brother's passing, he felt compelled to cooperate.

Sheridan was returned by FBI agents to New York City, and on January 31, 1947, the DA announced that the felonious assault charges against Dunn, Sheridan and, the still missing, Gentile were being upgraded to first-degree murder. With a possible death penalty looming, the trial was scheduled to begin in December of 1947 with or without Gentile.

The Trial

IN MARCH OF 1947, Gentile had a visit from Frank Kelly, who informed him that everything had been arranged so that he could turn himself in. Gentile, who had thought that Kelly had been sent to rub him out, was happy to board a plane to Newark. Once in New Jersey, Gentile was met by Eddie Gaffney, who drove him directly to the Hotel Lexington in New York City. At the hotel, Gentile received a call from McGrath who assured him that he had taken care of everything and that the state would never win a conviction. Gentile was then shuttled to the district attorney's office.

While Keating was preparing the case for trial, he received some unexpected news from a prisoner who was housed with the Dunn in the city jail. Intrigued, Keating arrived for the meeting with the mystery informant but was disappointed with the broken figure that sat in front of him, Anthony "Tough Tony" Tishon. Tishon's long criminal career began as an adolescent and mainly consisted of prison time due to his tendency to commit crimes while inebriated. One attempted robbery went very badly for Tishon after he was shot in the spine and left paralyzed from the waist down, and although he would gradually regain the use of his legs, he still walked with a permanent limp.

Tishon had been working on the West Side docks after his most recent release from Sing Sing, but one drunken night, he was arrested after robbing a sailor at gunpoint. In a desperate moment, Tishon attempted to hang himself in his cell. Like many things Tishon did, he was unsuccessful and guards managed to save his life. Now facing a lengthy sentence as a repeat offender, he turned to Keating to try to save himself. He told Keating that he and Dunn had served time together during a previous stint in prison and that he and Dunn often killed time gossiping about the people that they knew on the West Side. Keating was hesitant to accept anything Tishon said, but it soon became clear that he was aware of details of the Hintz murder that only someone who was involved would know.

Tishon stated to Keating that Dunn had told him that he had no worries about Sheridan, but that he was concerned about Gentile being unable to stand up to the pressure. Tishon had asked Dunn what went wrong with the killing, and Dunn told him that Sheridan claimed that his pistol had jammed. Dunn added that he thought that Sheridan had not actually drawn his weapon as, "those pistols McGrath gave us were no toys." Tishon exclaimed that maybe Sheridan was scared, but Dunn said no, Sheridan had committed lots of murders, and that he "[. . .] had handled Moran and others like an ace."

Keating made all the attempts he could to hide the fact that Tishon was snitching, but with the police force riddled with corruption, word traveled fast. Tishon was tasked with gathering more information from Dunn, but after a second secret meeting with Keating, Dunn approached Tishon near his cell and began a casual conversation. While he had seemed friendly at first, Dunn suddenly kicked Tishon's partially paralyzed leg, punched him in the face, and called him a rat. Prison guards, who were friendly with Dunn, then grabbed Tishon and took him away. When Keating heard of the beating, he had Tishon removed from the prison for his own safety.

On April 3, 1947, Keating had Teddy Gleason picked up as a material witness to the murder, as he stated that he believed

Gleason had information about the crime but could be intimidated by the culprits. In actuality, Keating was hoping that the legitimate Gleason, who had recently been promoted by Joe Ryan to the third highest position in the union, ILA General Organizer, would be more willing to work with the authorities. If Gleason knew anything about the Hintz murder, he was not sharing it, and on April 5, 1947, he posted $50,000 bail and was released.

In August of 1947, it was decided that the still inexperienced Keating would be left on the case, but that Assistant DA George Monaghan would handle the actual trial. Monaghan was unimpressed with the evidence that the crusading Keating had collected. He felt that due to unreliable parties like Maisie and Willie Hintz, a dead star witness, no murder weapon, and high-priced attorneys on the other side of the court, they would be in trouble come December. Keating asked Lt. Sullivan if there were any other possible witnesses to use, but Sullivan reported that although at least fifteen people had seen either Dunn, Sheridan or Gentile flee the scene of the crime, no one wanted to get involved. Monaghan, who was known for his ability to run a trial, put hours into prepping the witnesses and attacked Willie and Maisie's credibility at length. Both Maisie and Willie responded angrily toward Monaghan, but Keating assured them that the trial would be much worse and that Monaghan was only trying to prepare them.

The key elements to their case would be the dying declaration, Maisie Hintz's testimony supporting the declaration, a neighbor in a nearby apartment who overheard Andy telling Maisie that a man named "Johnny" had shot him, and Willie Hintz's identification of Danny Gentile. The young Edith Jansen would also testify to show that Sheridan was not in Florida at the time of the murder, and Anthony Tishon would take the stand to recount Dunn's prison confession. The DA planned to spend considerable time explaining the "code of the waterfront," as they wanted the jury to see why Hintz had initially refused to name his killers and cooperate with police.

Only days before the trial start date, Maisie Hintz disappeared, but the DA's worst fears were calmed when they were advised that she had fled to Florida. They learned that Maisie was being harassed by a private investigator hired by the Dunn-McGrath Mob, who had rented a room in her building to dig up dirt on her. Maisie explained that she had also been receiving regular hang-up phone calls and that the last straw came when a neighborhood patrolman told her that she was causing herself a lot of grief by testifying, as Dunn would get off anyways. The trial was delayed while the prosecution could figure out what to do about the problem, but after some time away, a tanned and calm Maisie returned and confirmed that she wanted to testify.

On December 12, 1947, the trial began. Although the Hintz shooting did not originally receive extensive media coverage, reporters picked up on the "labor killing" angle, and the daily events of the trial became front page news. One reporter commented that Dunn was the picture of calmness, Gentile looked slightly nervous, and that Sheridan looked completely bored. The trial went on for the better part of two weeks, and there were no shocking or dramatic moments. Willie and Maisie Hintz stood up to questioning and, as expected, Anthony Tishon was completely discredited during cross-examination due to his unsavory history. Tishon's testimony was the only time that McGrath's name was brought up during the trial, as he explained that Dunn had told him that McGrath had supplied the pistols used in the Hintz killing.

The defense's strategy consisted of continually poking holes in the reliability of the prosecution's witnesses. Various witnesses such as Sheridan's building manager, and members of Dunn's family including Anna Dunn and Dunn's oldest stepdaughter Eileen, were called by the defense to establish alibis for each man. The defense argued that although there were gaps in the time, it was still not possible for each man to have returned home by 8:30 AM when the shooting had occurred at 7:45 AM.

On December 30, 1947, the trial ended and the jury began deliberating. The prosecution, defense, and trial watchers all agreed on one thing—the verdict would likely be based on whether or not the jury believed the dying declaration of Anthony Hintz. Early on the morning of December 31, 1947, it was announced that a unanimous verdict had been reached. Family and friends rushed to the courthouse to hear the news. At 8:25 AM, the foreman proclaimed that they had found all the defendants guilty of first-degree murder. The color rushed out of Dunn's face, Sheridan finally showed some emotion as his jaw dropped open, and Gentile looked like he was about to faint.

The next month, a sentencing hearing was held and the court confirmed that Dunn, Sheridan, and Gentile would all receive the death sentence for the murder of Anthony Hintz.

Troubles

FOLLOWING THEIR CONVICTIONS for murder, Dunn, Sheridan and Gentile were all shipped directly to the death house in Sing Sing. While McGrath avoided the limelight and frequently moved between upscale hotels, he still wrote letters to Dunn regularly. To be sure that he did not incriminate himself, the communications consisted of simple pleasantries, and law enforcement believed that any updates of a criminal nature were communicated through visitors such as McGrath's sister and Dunn's wife, Anna.

The impending execution of the three senior Dunn-McGrath Mob members also resulted in immediate ramifications to the gang's business portfolio. The American Federation of Labor (AFL) had been watching the proceedings of the trial closely, given that Dunn, one of their own Business Agents, had been accused of first-degree murder. After the convictions were announced, the AFL President, William Green, sent a representative to New York City where the Dunn-McGrath Mob was stripped of their AFL 21510 and AFL 21512 charters.

In response, Joe Ryan quietly issued the mobsters a new ILA charter, which would officially become known as ILA Local 1730 Inland Platform and Terminal Workers. Gang organizer Connie Noonan remained President of the local, Teddy Gleason stayed on as Secretary-Treasurer, and Austin Furey, a former Teamsters Local 807 delegate who had been expelled from that union after pleading guilty to racketeering charges in 1940, took over Dunn's role as Vice-President.

While McGrath attempted to remain in control of the waterfront, his friends in the death house were becoming desperate. Only a week after being sentenced, Gentile called Assistant DA Keating and requested a confidential meeting at the prison. A desperate Gentile told Keating that he could give information on prior murders, but he needed to be assured that he would be granted an unconditional release. Keating offered to possibly have the death penalty commuted, but Gentile made it clear that he would only play ball for a discharge from prison. Keating declined Gentile's offer to cooperate and left the gangster to ponder his fate.

The Court of Appeals heard Dunn, Sheridan, and Gentile's case on June 3, 1948, and decided to uphold the murder convictions against the three. Lawyers had carefully poured over all of the testimony and tried to highlight its shortcomings, but it was found that no judicial errors had been made during the trial. The Dunn-McGrath Mob still had one more plan to try to get the convictions overturned and their lawyers began to prepare a final Hail Mary.

With Dunn and Sheridan off the streets, McGrath looked to cement his alliances along the waterfront. An opportunity to increase the gang's muscle presented itself on April 5, 1948, when former Yanowsky Gang member Albert Ackalitis was released from prison. Although relatively young at the time of his conviction during The West Side War, Ackalitis was seen as a serious customer on the docks, and according to his parole report, he had become a leader among inmates during his stays in Sing Sing and Clinton.

During his incarceration, Ackalitis had made it clear that upon his release he intended to take a piece of the action on the waterfront. To further strengthen his claim, Ackalitis was also set to be joined by his old friends from the original

Yanowsky group, as both Joseph "Heels" Murphy and Frank "Sonny" Campbell were scheduled for release in 1951.

The natural move for Ackalitis would have been to join Yanowsky in Jersey City; however, Ackalitis was still on parole for the next four years and he would not be allowed to leave the state. McGrath, through senior ILA member John "Chopsie" Plattner, secured a job for Ackalitis as a boss stevedore on Pier 32, the home of the shipping line owned by Bill McCormack — a close friend of Joe Ryan and one of Ryan's key political backers. The power-hungry parolee became an immediate force on the waterfront, and although he remained close to Yanowsky, he also began developing a relationship with the more influential McGrath.

The power base that the Dunn-McGrath Mob had built over the last ten years had been strong enough to fend off any up-and-coming gangsters who believed the gang's territory could be encroached on following the conviction of Dunn, but trouble soon began to brew on the other side of the North River.

Charlie Yanowsky was by far the most powerful gangster on the New Jersey piers, and with operations and political connections in both Jersey City and Hoboken, he had also become the richest. Not content with only controlling the waterfront, he began to branch into the northwest part of New Jersey. The manner in which Yanowsky expanded his rackets was simple, according to the testimony of a bookie who became a reluctant partner. Yanowsky had approached him and asked, "Do I shoot my way in and take it all over, or do I buy my way in for a third interest?"

One of the individuals who was unimpressed with Yanowsky's ways was a New Jersey Genovese member named Willie Moretti, who at that time was the number two man to then-boss Frank Costello and a business partner of McGrath's close friend, Joe Adonis. Yanowsky had been trying to force bookies who paid tribute to Moretti to instead pay a cut to him, which did not sit well with McGrath's Mafia friends. The message was sent to Yanowsky to stay on the waterfront, but Yanowsky continued to antagonize local gamblers.

One waterfront investigator who was monitoring the situation remarked that he knew trouble was brewing as Yanowsky "[. . .] was getting too big." Yanowsky recognized that the situation was reaching a boiling point, and he began to take extreme care with his movements. One of these extra precautions was to only surround himself with his closest associates, which included his waterfront gang in Jersey City and two newer friends named John De Biasio and Harold "Happy" Meltzer, who were helping him with his current expansion. De Biasio was a thirty-six-year-old veteran who had attended Notre Dame University and was a former physical education instructor, while Happy Meltzer was a more established criminal and a known narcotics dealer.

On July 14, 1948, Yanowsky was at the docks in Hoboken and was talking to a veteran longshoreman named Frank Williams. Yanowsky told Williams that he had been making big moves and that he was in the process of muscling in on one of Willie Moretti's gambling operations. Williams told Yanowksy, "Not to buck the gambling boys," but Yanowksy shrugged and replied, "I'll be alright, I'll be alright."

Two days later on July 16, 1948, Yanowsky and his two associates, Happy Meltzer and John De Biasio, ate dinner together at a Hoboken restaurant. An eavesdropping dinner guest, who was suspicious about the way the three men were acting, heard Yanowsky tell the other two that he had an appointment for 9:00 PM. Meltzer asked, "Do you know what you are doing Charlie?," and Yanowsky replied, "This guy is one hundred percent." Meltzer again asked, "Are you sure you know what you are doing?," but Yanowsky brushed him off with a simple, "Don't worry."

The next morning, Charlie Yanowsky was found dead in a field in Clifton, New Jersey. He had a dozen stab wounds in and around his heart. Yanowsky's wallet was missing, but a large expensive ring and a diamond-studded belt were still on his corpse. The detectives investigating the case knew why Yanowsky had been killed, but he had made so many enemies in the past year that they were unsure who had actually done the job.

Less than a month after Yanowsky's punctured body was found, another of his dinner companions, John De Biasio, met a similar fate. Just after midnight on August 10, 1948, De Biasio pulled his new car up to the front of his home in Elizabeth, New Jersey. While sitting in his car with the windows down, two men sprinted up to either side of the vehicle, stuck their guns into the car, and opened fire. Ten bullets were fired, and nine found their mark in De Biasio.

Harold "Happy" Meltzer, the last surviving member of the July 16, 1948 dinner, was picked up by police and questioned extensively about his friends' murders. Police asked Meltzer if Yanowsky and De Biasio had been killed over an unpaid $30,000 gambling debt, but Meltzer scoffed at the idea. He told police that only the month before the murders occurred, Yanowsky had received a $60,000 payment from his gambling operations. When asked who he believed committed the murders, Meltzer provided no information other than "Only some close friend of Charlie could have murdered him." After being released by police, Meltzer boarded a plane to Los Angeles where he would become associated with West Coast crime boss Mickey Cohen.

As is often the case in mob murders, it is best to start the list of suspects with those who were closest to the victim. Although the slaying would never be solved, the implication that McGrath, as a favor to his mobster friends, arranged for the demise of his old foe is strong. McGrath had only recently helped Albert Ackalitis obtain work on Pier 32 after his release from prison, and the two began to work hand in hand. Then immediately following Yanowsky's deadly meeting with someone he obviously trusted, Ackalitis suddenly assumed control of Yanowsky's old gang and ILA Local 1247 in Jersey City, while his territory in Hoboken was allotted to Edward Florio, a former bootlegger and Joe Ryan loyalist. There was no underworld response to Yanowsky's death, and no members of his Jersey City gang ever attempted to seek revenge. Investigators also found that Yanowsky's own brother-in-law, Biffo DeLorenzo, had begun to take orders directly from Ackalitis, who according to reports was someone he feared greatly. One does not have to look far to see who benefited the most from Yanowsky's death. McGrath had one of the biggest threats to his fragile leadership removed, while also strengthening his relationship with the Italians, and Ackalitis inherited his boss' waterfront empire. It was an unexpected underworld coup that proves that alliances can shift at the drop of a hat if a gangster's pocketbook is being affected.

29

Crime on the Waterfront

IN EARLY OCTOBER of 1948, the death row inmates of the Dunn-McGrath Mob made a final attempt to have the courts reconsider their convictions. To the surprise of everyone involved in the case, Andrew "Squint" Sheridan produced an affidavit stating that he was ready to take full responsibility for the murder of Anthony Hintz. The DA in New York City knew Sheridan had a reputation for being unstable, but they were awestruck when Sheridan's confession reached their desks.

Once Assistant DA Keating had a chance to dissect the documents, he realized it was a carefully constructed tale that could possibly destroy the prosecution's case. In the affidavit, Sheridan explained that he, and he alone, was the ruler of the West Side piers. Recounting real events, but leaving out anyone who was actually involved, he told of all of the trouble that Anthony Hintz had been causing his gang on Pier 51. Sheridan stated that Hintz was a cold-blooded killer himself and that the situation had escalated to kill or be killed. Sheridan stated that he discussed his deadly problem with two of his most loyal gang members: John Duff, a convicted armed robber and member of the Dunn-McGrath Mob, and the still missing Jeff Le Porte.

Sheridan claimed that he later received a call from Duff and Le Porte who told him that the problem with Hintz had been handled. To further distance Eddie McGrath from the case, Sheridan added that Duff and La Porte had gotten both guns and a getaway car from a friend of his named

Charlie Yanowsky. Sheridan said that while in the past he had some occasional union business with his co-accused, Dunn and Gentile, they were not criminals like him and were not involved with the murder. The lawyers for Dunn and Gentile argued that Duff and La Porte resembled their clients, which explained why there may have been errors in both Andy and Willie Hintz's identifications.

What Keating found interesting about Sheridan's confession was that no other member of the hit team was alive. La Porte was likely buried somewhere in Florida, Duff happened to be dead after he accidentally fell under the wheels of a commuter train on February 10, 1948, and Charlie Yanowsky had been slain that summer. Sheridan's confession was carefully crafted from a legal perspective, as his statement stressed that he had been scared of Hintz and that he had not actually been present during the murder. Keating knew that this was truly a last ditch attempt by the gang to avoid the electric chair, and he theorized that Sheridan was taking the blame in hopes of a new trial and to avoid the death penalty. The mumblings along the waterfront were that Sheridan had also been promised that his family would be financially taken care of for life if he made the statement.

On October 18, 1948, the motion for the new trial was heard. Dunn and Gentile's lawyer questioned Sheridan, who confirmed that the two men who sat beside him during the first trial were innocent men and that after he had talked to a priest in Sing Sing he was convinced to do the right thing. Assistant DA Monaghan had his shot at Sheridan, who despite being labeled as dimwitted, did not crack or make any errors during the retelling of his story. Highlights included when Monaghan asked Sheridan if it was easy for him to have someone murdered, to which Sheridan replied, "[. . .] just like ordering a cup of coffee." Monaghan questioned if Sheridan had any regrets about his life of crime. Without blinking, Sheridan calmly said, "I have no regrets."

The prosecution nervously awaited the judge's decision and was pleased to find that he denied the motion for a new trial. In his decision, he stated that the affidavit was based on the underworld's "[. . .] well-known trick of substituting guilty participants for dead men whose lips are sealed." Although the ruling had sunk the hopes of Dunn, Sheridan, and Gentile, the motion did give them one final chance as the decision could now be appealed for the last time to the New York State Court of Appeals. The guilty men received word back from the courts that their last appeal, the one that would decide their fates, would be heard on December 1, 1948.

While lawyers were still working on the Anthony Hintz case, another strikingly similar murder took place. Thomas Collentine was the hiring boss on Pier 92 and an associate of the Bowers Mob. Collentine had previously been friendly with Mickey Bowers and his boys, including Danny St. John, whom he used to work under. Things were good for a time, but the relationship soured when Collentine decided to branch off on his own and take Pier 92 with him. On April 29, 1948, Collentine approached his car and found that the back tires had been slashed. As he started walking down the street to the nearest subway station, a black sedan containing three men pulled up to the curb. A gunman, who was holding a handkerchief over his face, jumped out of the car, ran up to Collentine, and opened fire. Collentine dove to the pavement, but the gunman ran forward and emptied his gun into Collentine's back.

Like Anthony Hintz, Collentine did not immediately die from his wounds. He was taken to the hospital and questioned by police, but his only response was, "I don't know who shot me, and if I did, I wouldn't tell you." Collentine succumbed to his wounds eleven hours later. Given his insider knowledge and his obsession with uncovering the truth about crime on the waterfront, the case was given to Assistant DA Keating.

Keating was confident that the Bowers Mob was behind the murder, but unlike the Hintz case, he was unable to collect any solid evidence against them.

While Keating was working to find a break in the Collentine murder, an unusual occurrence was happening at the offices of *The Sun* newspaper. Waterfront murders had never received much media attention, but the Dunn, Sheridan, and Gentile trial had peaked public interest, and the paper noticed the similarities between the Hintz and Collentine murders. The editor asked Malcolm Johnson, one of their beat reporters, to do some poking around and see if he could gather enough information to write a couple of stories on the Collentine killing.

When Keating met with Johnson, he informed him that he could not provide much information on the Collentine murder since the investigation was still ongoing, but that the Anthony Hintz slaying had been an important waterfront crime and that he would be willing to give him all of his files about the case. Keating explained to Johnson in detail about the powerful organized crime figures that he felt controlled New York City's waterfront, the corrupt ILA officials that committed more crime than they did union business, and the greedy politicians and shipping executives that fueled the problem. Keating also introduced Johnson to a number of his connections on the waterfront, most of whom were part of the rebel faction.

Johnson soon realized that he had uncovered something big. In the past, newspapers dismissed waterfront murders as drunken longshoremen issues, but Johnson began to find that many of the killings were linked. What the reporter uncovered amazed him, and he asked his editors if he could do an entire series. Throughout the summer, he worked on his articles, which would eventually become a twenty-four part piece entitled "Crime on the Waterfront." Johnson knew that his writings would stir up controversy, as for the first time, the seedy world of the New York City waterfront would be exposed to the public. Johnson's editor agreed that the articles would surely blow the lid off the waterfront, and the first story was scheduled to be published on the front page of the November 8th edition.

Joe Ryan, the boss of the ILA, did not see the storm that was heading his way in the form of "Crime on the Waterfront"; instead, he was focused on more pressing matters. The ILA's contract with the New York Shipping Association was set to expire in November of 1948, and negotiations had been going on all summer. To outsiders, Ryan appeared to be aggressively advocating for the men of the ILA and an official strike seemed certain. With the deadline nearing, it was announced that the ILA had secured a contract that they recommended the membership ratify. Ryan excitedly announced the gains that had been made, but his rivals soon realized that the contract was virtually the same as a previous offer that Ryan had told the membership to reject.

Ryan basked in the positive attention garnered from avoiding a strike, but the wind was taken out of his sails on November 8, 1948, when *The Sun* hit newsstands with the headline "Mobsters, Linked to Vast International Crime Syndicate, Rule New York Piers by Terror; Reaping Untold Millions." The first piece provided a preview of what was to come and promised that the series would uncover, for the first time, the identities of the criminals who controlled the waterfront.

On the heels of "Crime on the Waterfront," the men of ILA Local 791, led by Joe Ryan's rival Gene Sampson, did not turn up for work the following morning. Father John Corridan, the waterfront priest, distributed ten thousand copies of an outspoken article he had written called the "Longshoremen's Case." Corridan's strong words explained to the ILA membership the numerous failings of the 1948 negotiations and called Joe Ryan's relationship with the Shipping Association, "joint criminal neglect." Ryan countered that Malcolm Johnson was a secret communist and that his propaganda and lies had caused the walkout.

What had started out as a wildcat strike among the rebel locals rapidly spread throughout the entire port. Ryan recognized that his cause was lost. On the second day of the wildcat strike, he made a last-ditch effort to save face and proudly announced to ILA membership that, "He would lead the strike!" and head back to the bargaining table. In the end, the strike would span eighteen days, paralyze the entire East Coast, and only end through government enforced mediation. Ryan's quick switch from a sellout to a strike leader had done enough to quell an all-out rebellion, but he was now on very uncertain ground with a growing portion of his membership.

To add to Ryan's problems, the nation was not only keenly aware of the labor dispute on the waterfront, but they were now feverishly reading Malcolm Johnson's "Crime on the Waterfront." The first articles mapped out which gangsters controlled each territory, and the rest of the series delved even deeper into the underbelly of the waterfront by covering topics such as cargo theft, the loading racket, payroll padding and kickbacks, biographies on John Dunn and other top organized crime figures, and details of Anthony Hintz's murder.

The November 26, 1948 article surely caught McGrath's attention, as his face was splashed across the pages of newspapers for the first time. Closing out the series, the December 7 and December 8, 1948 articles highlighted Joe Ryan's tainted leadership and pointed out all of the friendships he had with a variety of convicted criminals. Johnson called for an immediate response and asked that the government direct their attention to the waterfront.

The events of 1948 had put the focus on the waterfront, and

many felt that the Port of New York was a national embarrassment. In response to public concern, the NYPD shook up its waterfront squad and began investigating Johnson's stories, which would go on to win the Pulitzer Prize for Local Reporting the following year.

The embattled Joe Ryan had managed to maintain his position within the ILA following the 1948 strike and the Johnson articles, but now, more than ever, he was on shaky ground with his membership and many of his own loyalists.

The articles also did considerable damage to the reputation of McGrath, as prior to the series, the general public had never heard his name in connection with the waterfront. Although the stories could not hurt John Dunn, Andy Sheridan, or Danny Gentile's character any further, the timing of the articles was troubling, as their final appeal concerning Sheridan's confession of guilt was heard while papers were still rolling off the press. On February 24, 1949, the Appeals Court agreed with the previous ruling that Sheridan was not a believable witness, and the decision was upheld. Dunn, Sheridan, and Gentile's execution date was set for July 7, 1949.

30

Condemned

KNOWING THAT HIS death was now inevitable, the desperate Gentile renewed his efforts to make a deal with the government. He again sent word for Keating, who returned back to Sing Sing with the knowledge that he now had significant leverage over the doomed gangster. Gentile provided some tidbits about waterfront crime, and he told Keating that if he could get his death sentence commuted, he would give him information on murders. Keating informed Gentile that he would need him to cooperate fully first, and then he would try to assist him. After a few days, Keating called Sing Sing to make a second appointment, but word came back that Gentile no longer wanted to meet — he claimed that he had made his peace with God and that he had nothing left to tell.

A more curious request to the DA's office came shortly after Keating interviewed Gentile. John Dunn sent word that he wanted to talk to Assistant DA Monaghan, but that he would not speak to Keating, whom he hated. Monaghan visited Dunn in Sing Sing in March of 1949, where Dunn played coy with Monaghan and told him that, "I can make you governor with what I know," but that he first needed a stay of his death sentence. Another meeting was scheduled for later in the month, and Keating supplied Monaghan with a list of murders to question Dunn about. Keating, who estimated that the Dunn-McGrath Mob had been responsible for more than thirty killings, included on the list many that he knew Dunn had personally been involved in. When Monaghan returned to the office from the second meeting, Keating reviewed the interview notes and found that Dunn had lied about the circumstances of all the murders and denied his own involvement in any. Dunn was attempting to win a reprieve without supplying real information.

Monaghan again met with Dunn, who promised that he could name a wealthy New York businessman, nicknamed "Mr. Big," who controlled the entire waterfront. Although the DA could not confirm it at the time, "Mr. Big" was no doubt Bill McCormack, who had often manipulated ILA affairs through his financial and political support of Joe Ryan. Dunn said the level of corruption would amaze the entire city, but that Monaghan needed to get his sentence changed to life before he would start talking. The newspapers somehow caught wind that Dunn had been meeting with the DA regularly, and gangsters, ILA members, politicians, and businessmen all waited nervously to see what would come next.

Monaghan let Dunn sweat it out for a few days, and then sent word to Sing Sing that he was ready for another discussion about getting his sentence commuted. There was no response from Dunn. Monaghan contacted the prison again, but word came back that Dunn, like Gentile, was done talking and that he had accepted his fate.

The last of the trio, Squint Sheridan, never showed any signs that he was troubled about his upcoming date with death. During a visit, Sheridan's wife noticed a priest sitting with one of Sheridan's fellow death row inmates, Santo Bretagna, who was scheduled to be electrocuted the next day. She asked Sheridan what was happening, and Sheridan replied: "They are fireproofing the Dago for tomorrow." On another occasion, Sheridan joked with a guard that he was sure the electric chair would cure his case of the shakes.

On July 6, 1949, the day before the execution, the men had final visits with their families. There was nothing notable about the goodbyes, but when lunch approached, Sheridan told his wife and daughter, "Now, you go on uptown and have a nice lunch. When you get back, we'll have a nice talk." Sheridan watched them go and then called to the guard, "Phone the warden's office. Have him tell my wife and daughter not to come back, that no more visitors will be admitted. When I last saw them they were smiling and I was smiling. That's the way I wanted it to be. No weeping stuff."

While the men were counting down their last hours, backroom politicking was taking place all the way to the Governor's office. Later in the day, a shocked Danny Gentile received word that his sentence was being commuted to life in prison by Governor Dewey based on a recommendation from Keating's boss, District Attorney Frank Hogan. Dewey stated that the last minute change in the sentence was due to Gentile's important cooperation in waterfront investigations. In front of both Dunn and Sheridan, Gentile was swept out of the death house and moved into protective custody at an undisclosed location. DA Hogan then sent word to Dunn that if he decided to talk he would get the same treatment as Gentile. The small fry was being used as a pawn to convince the gang boss to cooperate. Dunn sent word back that he had nothing to say.

Dunn went to the chair first, shortly after 11:00 PM, on July 7, 1949. A mask came down over his face, buckles were applied, guards attached electrodes to his arms and legs, and a low humming buzzed as the machine charged. The switch was flipped and a powerful surge of electricity flowed through Dunn's shaking body. The machine was turned off and a physician put a stethoscope to Dunn's chest and said: "This man is dead." Guards removed Dunn from the chair, placed his body on a gurney, and wheeled him into the adjacent autopsy room. Sheridan entered the room next at 11:08 PM. As he was being strapped to the chair, he silently looked up at the bright overhead light and caught sight of a moth fluttering above. His eyes tracked the moth intently until a guard brought the mask down over his face. The switch was flipped, Sheridan shook violently, and then all was still. By 11:11 PM, Sheridan's body lay next to Dunn's in the autopsy room.

The following day, the bodies were prepared for release to the families, but prison officials found that Squint Sheridan had made one more unusual request before his death—he wanted his badly damaged eyes to be donated to New York's Eye Bank so that doctors could advance their techniques on how to treat injuries like his.

Under Pressure

WITH THE EXECUTION of his brother-in-law and the release of "Crime on the Waterfront," McGrath had been publically exposed as the gangster who ruled the West Side piers of New York City. The directive came down from the Governor to do something about the problems on the waterfront, and McGrath became an active investigation target of multiple law enforcement agencies.

On April 17, 1950, investigators followed McGrath and his Mafia backer Joe Adonis to Hot Springs, Arkansas. The two checked into a shared suite at the Arlington Hotel, where two other guests happened to be Arthur Samish, one of the most powerful lobbyists in California, and Harry Stromberg, better known as "Nig Rosen," a Philadelphia gangster who ran one of the largest numbers rackets in the city. The officers tailing Adonis and McGrath believed that the meeting may have been concerning the possibility of Samish pushing for the legalization of gambling in California.

Law enforcement later learned that the visit to Hot Springs may have served an additional purpose. Senator Estes Kefauver of Tennessee had noticed the attention that organized crime was receiving, and planned to demonstrate to the world that a national crime syndicate existed. The public hearings would officially be known as the Special Committee to Investigate Organized Crime in Interstate Commerce, or more commonly the Kefauver Committee. Hearing dates were set within the year, and gangsters across the country began to receive subpoenas to testify, which was something that men like Adonis and McGrath hoped to avoid. A month later, Adonis made his way back to his New Jersey home, where he was served with a date to testify in December; however, when US Marshals searched New York City, they found that Eddie McGrath hadn't returned from Arkansas. He had disappeared.

Adonis appeared before the Kefauver Committee on December 12, 1950, and was a hostile witness who repeatedly refused to testify, citing his right against self-incrimination under the Fifth Amendment of the United States Constitution. Adonis was questioned about his relationship with McGrath, his visit to Hot Springs, his role on the waterfront, and his knowledge about why the now deceased John "Cockeye" Dunn had visited Meyer Lansky in Florida. Some of the highlights of Adonis' testimony concerning McGrath included:

> *Halley (Committee Member): What is the basis of your friendship with McGrath?*
> *Adonis: He is a nice fellow, and I like him.*
> *Halley: What was the occasion of you and McGrath going to the Arlington Hotel at Hot Springs last April?*
> *Adonis: For the baths.*
> *Halley: You both felt in need to take baths for 3 weeks?*
> *Adonis: Yes, sir.*
> *Halley: Are you still on friendly terms with McGrath?*
> *Adonis: Yes, sir.*
> *Halley: Are you on friendly enough terms to know where he is now? The committee is looking for him.*
> *Adonis: No, sir.*
> *Halley: We have a subpoena out for him and we have not been able to find him.*
> *Adonis. Oh, you have? I didn't know.*

Due to public interest, the committee's hearings were televised live to the homes of Americans, many of whom were provided with their first look into the underworld. Most were shocked to hear about the existence of organized crime, and the committee received two hundred thousand pieces of mail from a viewing audience that was estimated to be at over thirty million.

For Adonis, the Kefauver Committee was the beginning of his downfall. He was initially charged with contempt for not cooperating during the hearings and later arrested after the bust of one of his gambling rooms. Sentenced to two to three years in prison, the U.S. Department of Justice would then discover that he had never properly applied for citizenship. After a lengthy legal battle, Adonis left for his native Italy on January 3, 1956. Despite leaving the country, Adonis would allegedly remain an influential crime figure until he died of a heart attack on November 26, 1971.

After the Kefauver Hearings finished, the NYPD expected that McGrath would turn up, but after months of waiting, he was still nowhere to be found. One report stated that due to increased police attention he had decided to leave New York for good. The other possibility that police could not rule out was that McGrath had become a victim of his notoriety and that he had been murdered by his own friends.

Blowing Up

THE SCRUTINY THAT followed "Crime on the Waterfront" and the Kefauver Hearings had led many of the gang bosses to temporarily withdraw into the shadows, but what should have been a period of quiet on the waterfront was instead marred by violence as other power-hungry criminals attempted to fill the void. The violence, which might have been minimized if McGrath had not been missing, resulted in 1951 being one of the bloodiest years in the history of the waterfront.

The problems started on the other side of the Hudson in 1950, where Albert Ackalitis had become overlord of the Jersey City docks following Charlie Yanowsky's murder. Traditionally, many of the plum waterfront operations had been controlled by longtime Mayor Frank Hague, but Ackalitis was able to expand his reach when John Kenny, the man who was raised alongside Connie Noonan, became Mayor after a surprise victory over Hague's successor. Bolstering Kenny during the election was the longshoremen's vote, which was delivered after endorsements from the leadership on ILA Local 1247—Ackalitis' frontman Biffo DeLorenzo and Anthony "Tony Cheese" Marchitto, a Genovese crime family member who operated on the Jersey City waterfront.

Following his win, Kenny loosened the traditional Hague grip on the piers and instead opened the doors for his criminal backers. Ackalitis, who was still unable to travel to Jersey City, would call DeLorenzo from Joe's Tavern on the West

Side and supply him with regular orders. To the displeasure of the ILA leadership in New York, Ackalitis wasted no time in removing the old Hague stalwarts from their positions on the waterfront, even though many were friends of Joe Ryan.

Ackalitis recognized that Joe Ryan and the old guard of the ILA were losing power fast, and like many others, he began to buck their rule. On October 9, 1950, Ackalitis arrived at his Staten Island home to find police officers waiting for him, armed with a warrant to search his house. In Ackalitis' cellar, they found a large number of stolen goods that were missing from Pier 32. Booked for violation of his parole, he was sentenced to an additional year in prison. Ackalitis openly told his associates that he believed ILA leadership had tipped off the police, as they resented that he was not following their directives.

The wolves began to circle after Ackalitis was temporarily removed from the waterfront, as Biffo DeLorenzo was regarded as a stooge that lacked the toughness needed to maintain control of the volatile Jersey City piers. On December 5, 1950, a reporter at *The Jersey Journal* received a call from Ackalitis associate George Donahue stating that a spontaneous election had been held at ILA Local 1247 and that DeLorenzo and his associate, Anthony "Slim" Lucey, had resigned from their positions. Donahue explained that Vincent "Cockeye" Brown remained President of ILA Local 1247, but that Anthony "Tony Cheese" Marchitto was the new Business Agent and that he, Donahue, had been made Trustee.

The paper later discovered that only minutes before the call, Donahue; Brown; Marchitto; and Morris Manna, a Jersey City resident and member of the Genovese family, had conducted their own hostile takeover of ILA Local 1247. Manna had longed to control the Jersey City waterfront, and with Ackalitis in prison, he saw his opportunity. After plotting the double-cross, Donahue, Brown, Marchitto and Manna walked into the union headquarters on Grand Street and informed DeLorenzo and Lucey that they were out of the job and needed to write their resignations. When the two refused, Donahue pulled out a gun and pointed it at DeLorenzo's head, who then complied and wrote his resignation. Lucey would not agree as easily, so Manna pistol-whipped him and knocked out his front teeth. Lucey was then ordered to open the union safe, but he still held out. The group then pulled off his shoes and began to put matches out on his feet until he cooperated. After the assault was over, the new ILA Local 1247 leadership called the media to announce their promotions.

After the takeover of the union, DeLorenzo began to make some very loose statements to police about his forced resignation, and the local longshoremen demanded that an election be held. Joe Ryan, who was trying to appear democratic and did not want further details about the ugly incident to come to light, approved a vote for March 5, 1951.

With the upcoming election, Manna and Marchitto began to work closely with Anthony "Tony Bender" Strollo, their Genovese counterpart across the Hudson. To gain the muscle needed to support their rule, the Mafia opened the floodgates and began importing ex-cons from New York City to work for them on the waterfront. The local Jersey City longshoremen, who had their own group of bad apples, resented the New Yorkers taking the best jobs and calling the shots. Even the most casual of waterfront observers knew what was coming next.

The first pre-election outburst occurred early in January 1951, when Morris Manna's house was riddled with bullets in a drive-by shooting. Next, on January 28, 1951, George Donahue was starting his car when a hidden grenade exploded. Donahue was relatively unharmed, but his car was destroyed.

On March 3, 1951, two days prior to the election, a green car with two men pulled up to the ILA Local 1247 union offices. One man walked up to the open window and hurled a grenade into the room. The explosive rolled across the floor and settled under a table, where a number of supporters of the new leaders of ILA Local 1247 were sitting. The grenade exploded, shooting shrapnel into Local 1247 President Vincent "Cockeye" Brown, new Secretary-Treasurer Armand Faugno, and three other of their supporters. The table likely saved their lives, and no one was seriously injured except Faugno, who had a significant leg injury that resulted in a long hospital stay.

Mayor Kenny and the police in Jersey City were quick to blame the bombing on the outsiders from New York, and many of the most troublesome out-of-towners were held as material witnesses. Another suspect was Albert Ackalitis, who many thought was ordering revenge attacks from behind bars. Although no one was ever convicted of the audacious crime, the evidence strongly points to Marchitto's leadership rivals from within the union, men who were born and bred in Jersey City.

The election was delayed due to the grenade attack, but when it went ahead, the Marchitto candidates capitalized on the chaos and triumphed with a contentious win. Morris Manna, the man who had orchestrated the move against DeLorenzo, would not get to enjoy his new power, as he would be returned to prison and subsequently pass away in 1953. ILA Local 1247 would remain under the control of Anthony "Cheese" Marchitto for the next two years, until he was overthrown in the next election by an all Jersey City longshoremen ticket. Upon Ackalitis' re-release from prison, he was welcomed back into the waterfront fold and even became close with Marchitto, who after losing Local 1247, was relegated to controlling a smaller New Jersey ILA union that consisted of warehouse workers.

Although less explosive than the events in Jersey City, the Manhattan side of the North River remained in a state of flux after McGrath's disappearance. Flying bullets were not a rare occurrence on the waterfront, but gang members and friends began to turn their guns on each other—a dangerous situation that would never have been allowed with McGrath in town.

On May 18, 1951, William Vanderwyde, a Dunn-McGrath Mob associate who was gaining a reputation as one of the most violent hoods on the waterfront, called on Benjamin "Barney" Dietz at his Greenwich Village home. Dietz, who was the gang's long-serving hiring boss on Pier 32, came out of his house as Vanderwyde yelled, "I thought you were supposed to be the tough guy!" Vanderwyde then drew a revolver and plugged Dietz five times in front of multiple witnesses. In a strange twist, which shows how small the West Side waterfront can be, the first cop on the scene was Lieutenant Joseph Sullivan, who only two years prior had helped Assistant DA Keating crack the Anthony Hintz murder case. Vanderwyde attempted to flee as Sullivan opened fire and struck him once in the side. Vanderwyde was taken to hospital and stabilized, but would later get the electric chair for the slaying.

The strife of 1951 occurred during a time when the public was paying close attention to waterfront issues, and instead of the gangsters maintaining a low profile, the media was now reporting on hostile union takeovers, murders, and the grenade throwing. Joe Ryan's usual detractors sensed that he was losing control of the ILA, and while Ryan was trying to downplay the violence that was occurring, he was also in the process of negotiating a new contract with the New York Shipping Association.

On October 8, 1951, Ryan proudly announced that an agreement was reached, although the contract's gains were significantly less than what was initially promised. Less than a week later, ILA Local 791, led by Gene Sampson, refused to attend work. What would again start out as a small job action would grow to encompass over thirty-thousand men, and would lead to a twenty-five day strike that would become the costliest job action in the history of the port. All of Ryan's usual foes, including Sampson; Father Corridan; John Dwyer of ILA Local 895; and former Assistant DA Keating, who had recently resigned from his position to accept an appointment at the newly created New York City Anti-Crime Committee, were active in fueling the anti-Ryan fires.

Although the 1951 strike initially appeared to be identical to the 1948 job action, it soon became clear that something very different was occurring on the waterfront. Resentment of Ryan's rule had been slowly building over the past decade, and although the longshoremen had publicly aired their grievances before, there always appeared to be a reluctance to remove Ryan. After all, he was the only leader most had ever known. The problems that the ILA leadership faced in 1951 were now too numerous and too severe to ignore. Ryan's criminal backers also began to doubt the benefits of his presidency. After being exposed in "Crime on the Waterfront," he had drawn too much attention to organized crime's waterfront activities, and he had clearly lost the confidence of the members of the ILA. Joe Ryan was becoming expendable, and the mob began to plan for a future without him.

The normal battle lines drawn between Ryan's ILA and the rebels became blurred, as instead of running to aid Ryan, some gangsters began to argue that the aging union leader had outgrown his usefulness. The exodus was not limited to the criminal element, as Ryan's former crony, Teddy Gleason, also lined up against him. Ryan responded by firing Gleason from his position as ILA General Organizer, but he was unable to do anything about his elected positions within other ILA locals, such as McGrath's own union, ILA Local 1730.

Even from prison, Albert Ackalitis, who held Joe Ryan responsible for his parole violation, was joining in the strike movement. When his former rival for ILA Local 1247,

Anthony Marchitto, was dragging his feet about pulling his longshoremen from the docks, Ackalitis sent the following letter to his brother Willie, who was an ILA delegate:

> *Hello Willie: Call Joan and tell her to get Tony Cheese's phone number and call him and say I said to get those men off those Jersey piers and go on strike.*
> *Ackie*

Marchitto listened to the order and the Jersey City men were off the piers by the next day.

Federal mediators were sent in to see if they could end the strike, but word came back to President Truman that the two sides were not close to a resolution. On October 28, 1951, Johnny Dwyer and Gene Sampson wired President Truman and informed him that they would call off the wildcat strike if he would investigate the longshoremen's grievances. Ryan sent off his own telegram that countered with "We'll have the harbor working tomorrow" and "We'll go through them [the rebels] and over them but never around them." Sensing looming violence, Father Corridan headed down to the rebel headquarters and led a now famous public prayer for peace among longshoremen. The prayer reinforced to watching journalists that the rebels were not communists who were trying to incite problems but instead were honest workers with legitimate concerns. That day, many papers predicted that Ryan's downfall was imminent as the strength of the wildcat strike seemed to be growing.

In October of 1951, Edward Corsi, who was the Commissioner of the New York State Industrial Board, started an inquiry into the events that led up to the strike. On November 9, 1951, Corsi presented his final report, and strike leaders were persuaded to return to work after he submitted it to Governor Thomas Dewey. The damaging investigation explained to

Dewey that the ILA was not democratic, that they failed to hold elections, and that they did not have proper accounting procedures. What became known as *The Corsi Report* had extended beyond its original mandate, and had drawn attention to the plight of the anti-Ryan movement. Dewey responded by ordering the newly created New York State Crime Commission to conduct a series of public hearings, and a full investigation, into the crime and corruption that plagued the waterfront.

A New Life

GOVERNOR DEWEY DESCRIBED the problem on the waterfront as "pervasive corruption" and promised that the New York State Crime Commission would begin the cleanup process. The hearings were sure to be a spectacle and were scheduled to take place at the New York City County Courthouse from December 3, 1952 to January 30, 1953, with the questioning of ILA President for life, Joe Ryan, as the finale. The waterfront had already been receiving considerable media attention, but after the announcement of the investigation, the public was salivating at the opportunity to see the shadowy criminals and corrupt officials in person.

While the Crime Commission began to interview prospective witnesses, dissect financial documents, and examine police reports, there was still no trace of Eddie McGrath. It would be months before an informant would advise police that McGrath was alive and living in a new luxury apartment in the South Florida neighborhood of North Bay Village. FBI agents followed up on the tip and confirmed that a forty-five-year-old white male with the same name was residing in Apartment #1, Sun God Apartment Hotel, 7911 East Drive, Harbor Island, North Bay Village, Florida. The arriving agents surveilled the residence and found a low-rise apartment building with an expensive blue Packer Pontiac parked out front. After about an hour of waiting, the agents saw McGrath, who was dressed in a light sweater and crisp slacks, climb into his car and drive away.

It did not take long for them to discover that the once cagey gangster had become a creature of habit. Every day McGrath would leave his apartment around noon, pick up a copy of the Miami Daily News from the Normandy Isle Delicatessen, then drive to the Normandy Shores Golf Club. McGrath would usually eat a light breakfast there and would either spend the afternoon in the card room, enjoy a game of golf, or leave to attend the horse races. McGrath's evening usually consisted of a nice restaurant or a bar, where he was often seen in the company of large groups of middle-aged men and much younger women.

Agents turned up empty-handed when they began asking questions about McGrath at his hangouts. All they found was that McGrath was claiming to be a recently retired union organizer from New York City. Members of the golf club were interviewed, but they did not have any information on McGrath other than that he was, "a pretty good golfer."

Law enforcement remained suspicious about the newly retired McGrath, as they found that his neighbors at 7911 East Drive included a first cousin of Joe Adonis and a convicted criminal named Victor Piantedosi, alias Vic Allen, a minor hoodlum from Boston who appeared to constantly be in McGrath's company.

When McGrath's phone records were checked for the period during the 1951 ILA strike, it was revealed that regular calls had been made to the offices of ILA Local 1730; Teddy Gleason; Jackie Adams; Jimmy Alo; Meyer Lansky; and also to Henry "Buster" Bell, who had just become President of ILA Local 1804—a new charter that was created by Joe Ryan for Bell in 1951. Helping Bell run the charter was a good friend of his named Harry Cashin, a West Sider who, prior to having his conviction overturned on appeal, had been sentenced to death for the murder of a police officer during a bar robbery in the 1920s.

Police in New York City checked on McGrath's old rackets and found that his regular loaders were still on the piers, ILA Local 1730 was operating business as usual, and his bookmakers appeared to be active. Word continued to trickle in from sources in New York that McGrath had been hiding out in Florida the entire time, but prior to deciding to permanently stay there, he had made secret visits to the city to meet with Connie Noonan, Buster Bell, Albert Ackalitis, and his bookmaking partner Frank Mario. While it appeared that McGrath had decided to leave the state and run his rackets through proxies, the Crime Commission anxiously awaited their opportunity to return him to New York and question him about his recent activities.

34

Crime Commission

AFTER A FLURRY of subpoenas were sent to the who's who of the waterfront, the New York State Crime Commission opened their hearings to a frenzy of media attention on December 3, 1952. Inside the hallways of the courthouse, photographers frantically snapped pictures of the witnesses, many of whom tried to hide their faces. For the last two years, the public had been hearing how the port was New York City's greatest shame, and for the first time, the culprits would be revealed.

The Crime Commission called nearly two hundred witnesses from New Jersey and New York. They included shipping company executives, who were questioned extensively as to why they would agree to hire so many known criminals; legitimate longshoremen, who told of the problems that they faced every day on the waterfront; and also a select few criminals who agreed to cooperate with law enforcement. One ex-con named Dominick Genova, who had been a close friend of Bowers Mob member John Applegate, explained that he had been expelled from his position on West Side docks after refusing to murder a Hell's Kitchen milkman, Vincent Wice, after Wice had sliced Applegate's face with a broken bottle during a barroom fight. Despite Genova's refusal to help kill Wice, the brawling milkman was later machine-gunned to death while walking near his home.

Many of the key waterfront racketeers were marched in front of the Commission and publicly questioned about their backgrounds, finances, roles on the docks, and criminal activities. Most invoked their charter right to not incriminate themselves, and instead of providing answers, responded to questions with, "I refuse to answer on the grounds it may tend to incriminate me." For the labor gorillas that lacked the intelligence of some of the dock bosses, small cards with the sentence written on it were provided to them by their legal counsel so that they could read it over and over. The counsel for the Commission was met with hostility and defiance, and Mickey Bowers even refused to provide his age.

Highlights of the testimonies, which newspapers across the country printed on their front pages, included a shipping executive who covered the cost of the wedding for the daughter of Michael Clemente, the overlord of the East River piers (an event that was attended by Joe Adonis, Teddy Gleason, and Joe Ryan); regular "goodwill" payments that were made to ILA officials from shipping companies; $25,000 being paid to Timothy O'Mara who did nothing but promise "labor peace" for the Grace Line; numerous letters from shipping officials offering convicts jobs on the docks to satisfy their parole restrictions; and an exposé of the loading racket, which the Commission estimated cost the industry over $5,000,000 annually in unnecessary fees.

Dunn-McGrath Mob members Connie Noonan, Eddie O'Connell, Nick Tanzella, and Frank Kelly all testified at length; however, they were uncooperative, especially when asked about McGrath. Also forced to testify were Teddy Gleason and McGrath's half-brother, James Connors. Gleason admitted to being friends with McGrath, but insisted that he did not know a thing about his companion's criminal businesses because "friends don't ask friends about those things."

The Commission had two surprise witnesses for the members of the Dunn-McGrath Mob. Brought in from undisclosed locations were Danny Gentile and Francis "Buster" Smith.

Gentile, who since avoiding the death penalty was now looking for an early discharge from his life sentence, spoke about Varick Enterprises, the numbers operations, the loading racket, and McGrath's bookmaking business. Smith's reasons for informing were due to a lengthy prison sentence that he had received for hijacking, and in an attempt to get some years shaved off his time, he decided to provide information to the Commission about the men who had shot him three times. Although he could not offer any concrete evidence against McGrath, he spoke about the Dunn-McGrath Mob's violent takeover of the docks in the mid-1930s and the multiple attempts on his life.

On January 26, 1953, a smiling and tan McGrath, who had only recently arrived from Florida, appeared at the courthouse dressed in a dark suit and hat with lawyer Joe Aronstein by his side. McGrath moved quickly past the photographers but made no attempt to hide his face, and his picture was plastered across the pages of a number of papers the next day. Articles about McGrath's appearance described him as "handsome," "sharp-featured with a high color and graying hair," "dapper," and "robust."

McGrath sat down at the witness table and asked if he could read a prepared statement. The Commission denied his request and the usual rapid-fire questioning began. McGrath was asked about his employment history, his family, his criminal activities, and his role in the ILA; then, a lengthy list of his criminal associates was read for the record. The interrogation lasted over forty minutes, but to almost every question, and a total of one hundred and fifteen times, McGrath answered along the lines of "I decline to answer on the grounds that the question is unreasonable and not within the scope of the investigation, and on further grounds that the answer will tend to incriminate and degrade me." Even when asked who his mother was, he replied with the same answer.

When counsel asked McGrath for his financial statements

during the period he was employed with the ILA, they added: "But you haven't got any, is that so?" McGrath thought for a second and then replied: "That is so." One particular question from the Commission was phrased like a statement, and it appeared that McGrath might actually respond. After pausing, McGrath asked: "Are you asking me a question?" Counsel replied "Yes" so McGrath quickly spurted out, "I decline on the ground that the answer will tend to incriminate and degrade me."

At the conclusion of his testimony, McGrath again asked if he could read a statement. The Commission, who had heard nothing but the same sentence over and over, agreed. McGrath read off a piece of paper:

> "I, Edward McGrath, refuse to answer any questions this committee or any member thereof shall put to me upon the grounds that any answers made by me will tend to incriminate me.
>
> For the past fifteen years I have been continuously under investigation by the Federal authorities, by the State authorities, and by private investigations instituted by committees. My name has been published in newspapers, magazines, over the radio and on television and I have been depicted as a criminal, racketeer and gangster. I am still under Federal investigation, by local organizations and by State and City authorities.
>
> I, therefore, believe that any answers I give to questions that will be put to me will invade my constitutional privilege against self-incrimination."

For their final question, the Commission asked, "Are you in fact a racketeer, criminal or gangster?" McGrath tucked away his statement and calmly said: "I refuse to answer on the grounds that my answer might tend to incriminate me."

After being dismissed, McGrath walked calmly out of the courthouse and again disappeared from New York City.

Joe Ryan was the last witness dragged before the Commission, and loudly and defiantly he met them head on, although the deck was stacked firmly against him. He was shown pictures of himself attending the Teddy Gleason Testimonial Dinner with the boys from Varick Enterprises, and another photograph from one of his own events, which featured Mickey Bowers, Harold Bowers, and John Keefe. When Ryan was asked about McGrath specifically, he brushed it off by explaining that Teddy Gleason had known a man who was suited for the ILA Organizer job, but that it turned out to be McGrath. Ryan denied knowing McGrath's past but noted that he had done a good job in the position.

The Commission hammered Ryan about his finances, and after closely examining ILA financial records, they accused him of misappropriating certain funds. When asked about the money, Ryan said, "In these troubled times we're out fighting these Commies. We had to take money from the international treasury and then I had to pay some of those expenses."

The following day, the news labeled Ryan's testimony as "evasive" and "unresponsive," and many predicted that his downfall was inevitable. Although based on the evidence collected by the Commission, there were no grounds to prosecute the waterfront gangsters, the hearings had succeeded in airing out the Port of New York City's dirty laundry. The lawlessness of the waterfront could no longer be ignored.

War Zone

AS THE GOVERNMENT carefully considered what legislative action to take on the waterfront, the ILA was busy planning a counterattack against the onslaught that they were about to receive from the powerful American Federation of Labor. A number of unions were upset that the ILA's reputation was hurting the labor movement, while others recognized that there was now an opportunity to take control of the lucrative waterfront. David Beck, the President of the powerful Teamsters union, announced that with the support of other groups within the AFL, he would clean up the New York waterfront.

On February 3, 1953, George Meany, the President of the AFL, drafted an order that directed the ILA to clean house by April 30, 1953 or face being kicked out of the AFL and stripped of their legitimacy as a trade union. Meany stated that to meet the "[. . .] the minimum standards of trade decency," the ILA would need to remove all of their top officers and end the shape-up system. Meanwhile, behind closed doors, the AFL believed there was little hope for Joe Ryan's ILA, and along with the Teamsters and the Seafarers unions, they began to raise funds to support the creation of a new AFL union to succeed the ILA in New York City. Despite mounting pressure from the AFL, the mob, and a handful of his own senior delegates, the stubborn Ryan announced that he would not resign. Ryan planned to lead the fight against his adversaries until the bitter end.

While internal strife wreaked havoc on the ILA,

longshoremen around New York City waited anxiously for over three months to hear the official findings of the Crime Commission. Many, who had lived through dozens of failed cleanups and investigations, believed that although the waterfront's dirty secrets had been exposed, they would still be abandoned. Change, which would forever alter the waterfront, did finally come on May 20, 1953, when a report, known as The New York-New Jersey Waterfront Compact, was delivered.

The Compact supported the abolishment of the shape-up system in favor of employment centers; the registration of all longshoremen, in an attempt to end the casual nature of the work on the docks; the banning of men with criminal convictions; the power to bar anyone from the docks who the government identified as a danger to the public; the creation of a state division to monitor the waterfront; the banning of public loading unless performed by a licensed company with liability insurance; and new legislation that would make it mandatory for the union to keep sound financial records. The ILA and the New York Shipping Association were bitterly opposed to the proposed changes and referred to them as "total government control." On June 22, 1953, both New York and New Jersey enacted legislation based on the Crime Commission's recommendations, and the Waterfront Commission of the New York Harbor was created to oversee the piers.

By November 18, 1953, all men working on the docks were forced to register with the newly created Waterfront Commission. Some longshoremen with minor criminal convictions had reviews and were allowed to continue their employment, but two hundred and twenty-five men were permanently barred. Most of the gangsters did not even bother applying for licenses, but the few who did, such as Timothy O'Mara, Danny St. John, John Keefe, Albert Ackalitis, Nick Tanzella, Mickey McLoughlin, Frank "Sonny" Campbell, John Applegate, and Frank Kelly, were all denied.

In response to the forced registration of longshoremen, Teddy Gleason and another senior ILA official, Captain William Bradley, made a last ditch effort to stir up a fight. The two made their rounds on the piers and threatened work stoppages wherever they went. Bradley, who was now being positioned as the successor to Joe Ryan, was a portly man with thick glasses who always had a disheveled look about him. He was a real Captain, having worked as part of an obscure ILA tug boat charter for years. The reason for Captain Bradley's sudden rise in the union was because he was close to shipping magnet Bill McCormack, had been a friend of Joe Ryan, and, most importantly, had not been involved in any of the previous allegations of corruption.

The moment that the ILA was dreading came on September 22, 1953, at the AFL's annual convention in St. Louis. While Joe Ryan was in the lobby of the hotel trying to drum up support for the floundering ILA, AFL President George Meany was at the podium announcing that the ILA was being kicked out of their federation, as Meany had given up hope that the ILA would "[. . .] ever live up to the rules, standards and ethics of a decent trade union." Meany then outlined the AFL's plans to launch their own union, with the aid of the Teamsters and the Seafarers, which he hoped would replace the ILA. Ryan pushed through the crowd of reporters, and when asked to comment, he angrily responded: "We'll hold on to what we got!"

The AFL quickly organized their new union, which they named the International Brotherhood of Longshoremen, and Meany told reporters that a vote would be held sometime before Christmas. The current members of the ILA would head to the polling stations and choose if they wanted to remain in the ILA or if they wanted to be succeeded by the new AFL union. If the AFL won then the longshoremen would transfer their membership, and the ILA would effectively cease to exist in New York City.

With the waterfront in turmoil, law enforcement kept close tabs on the criminal element. Police found that McGrath had registered at a hotel in New York City near the end of September and that secret parlays had been held with various high-ranking mobsters. Although unsuccessful in tracking these meetings, except for one brief rendezvous between McGrath and Ackalitis, police had heard from reliable sources that the waterfront gangs had decided that they would need to work together if they were going to beat the AFL in the upcoming election. Even with the gangsters banned from officially working on the docks, there was still significant money to be made, and they all knew that an ILA defeat would mean the end of their waterfront rackets. Irish and Italians alike all banded together for one final push to save their illegal interests.

Ignoring what had happened at the AFL convention, the ILA began a feverish attempt to negotiate a new contract with the New York Shipping Association, and John Lyon, the President of the Association, told reporters, "We don't care much what goes on in St. Louis."

While the ILA was attempting to finalize negotiations, AFL organizers from around the country arrived in New York City and began their campaign for votes. Tensions ran high with longshoremen's allegiances divided, and both the AFL and ILA could be found on the piers handing out pamphlets, colorful posters, and buttons. Threats of violence against the AFL men were frequent, but the Teamsters and the Seafarers were no strangers to union scuffles and came prepared for a fight. One man, who was associated with the Seafarers, had his car pulled over and police discovered over twenty sawed-off baseball bats and forty other blunt instruments in the backseat.

The NYPD sent fifteen hundred policemen around the docks daily, and for the most part, the officers managed to contain the violence to small individual skirmishes. While there were initially no large clashes, one event in late September of 1953 caught the attention of many election observers. Michael Brogan, one of hiring bosses on Pier 32 and a member of ILA Local 895, had recently declared his support for the new AFL union. Brogan's choice was a dangerous one as Pier 32 was still the domain of Albert Ackalitis, who at that time had continued working on the dock, as his ban would not be finalized until two months later. Brogan had told friends that he had been having problems with Ackalitis as a result of his support for the AFL and that "The big fellow [Ackalitis] wants me off the docks."

On September 28, 1953, the members of ILA Local 895 held their own internal vote and decided that they, as a charter, would join the new AFL union. ILA organizers, who had heard about ILA Local 895's decision, headed down to Pier 32 and attempted to get the men to sign cards that re-pledged their loyalty to the ILA. Brogan gave the ILA organizers a hard time about being on the pier, and they eventually left. The next day was Brogan's birthday, but he was nowhere to be found. Two ILA longshoremen reported to police that they last saw Brogan drunk on the dock after the morning shape-up, but his friends in the AFL did not believe it.

On October 20, 1953, Brogan's body was pulled from the waters near Pier 32. There were no clear signs of trauma, but police found it odd that his corpse was discovered so close to Pier 32, as, due to the river's current, it should have washed up much further south. The case went cold, but Brogan's friends in the AFL were confident that he had died as a result of foul play and that his death was meant to scare others from speaking out against the ILA.

Only a few other incidents marred the lead up to the voting, most of which were centered in the Brooklyn area. An undetonated bomb was found near a pier that was frequented by AFL members, and on November 12, 1953, a two hundred man melee broke out between police and ILA members, which included members of Tony Anastasio's crew, after the ILA put up a picket line in front of a freight company that had exclusively hired AFL men.

While chaotic scenes dominated the New York waterfront, the last hope that Joe Ryan had of clinging on to his ILA Presidency was dashed away when, based on financial documents that were subpoenaed by New York State Crime Commission, Ryan was indicted on charges that he misused $11,390 of union funds. The embezzled money had been used for Ryan's personal taxes, golf club memberships, expensive dress shirts, life insurance premiums, and payment for a relative's funeral. Even Ryan recognized that if the ILA had any chance of surviving its upcoming fight with the Dewey government and the AFL, it could not have a leader who had just been charged with misappropriating union money.

On November 16, 1953, during a key point in the lead up to the election, a special convention of the ILA was held in Philadelphia. With hundreds of loyal members present, Ryan took to the podium and called the men to order. Ryan denied any corruption, said he would fight the criminal charges against him, and proclaimed that he had always done what is best for the greatest labor union in the United States. Ryan predicted that the ILA would not only survive the fight with the AFL, but also would thrive. Ryan then announced his long-awaited resignation, and as he bowed to leave the stage, thunderous applause filled the venue. As expected, Captain William Bradley was announced as Ryan's replacement, and during Bradley's own rallying speech he singled out Teddy Gleason as the man most responsible for his appointment.

For resigning, and playing his part to the end, Ryan was rewarded with a $10,000 annual salary as President Emeritus. Following his resignation, Ryan disappeared from the waterfront scene and refused to comment on any of the ongoing issues. In 1955, he was convicted of embezzling union funds, and he served six months in prison, after which he again remained out of the public eye until his death from natural causes in the early 1960s.

The National Labor Relations Review Board (NLRB), who would be responsible for refereeing the ILA versus AFL referendum, set the dates for voting as December 22 and December 23, 1953. Father Corridan, who was actively supporting the AFL union, was concerned that some of the AFL's own supporters had caused them to lose momentum. Teamsters President David Beck caused a stir when he proposed that his own union would take over the role of public loading and ensure it was done properly. Longshoremen were already nervous about the choice they had to make, and Beck's comments made many feel that their waterfront jobs were now being threatened by outside unions. However, despite Beck's rash comments, most were still confident that the AFL had the upper hand going into December.

The December 22nd voting went smoothly at the main polling station at Prospect Hall in Brooklyn. The NLRB placed voting monitors around the location and police had cordoned off a whole block, which was designated as a "No Campaigning Area." On December 23, 1953, the day that most men were likely to vote, the waterfront mobs turned out in full force in an attempt to rout an AFL victory. Joining together, the West Side gangsters and the Italian mobs headed to Brooklyn in large numbers and began to aggressively campaign for the ILA. Staten Island overlord Alex DiBrizzi loaded up buses of voters from his jurisdiction; Albert Ackalitis, Mickey and Howard Bowers, Danny St. John, Sonny Campbell, and John Keefe were all seen around the polling stations talking to groups of ILA men. At one point, an NLRB election monitor caught Tony Anastasio and two of his top men, Anthony "Spanish" Calvo and Joseph Colozzo, inside the polling stations handing out ILA pamphlets. Calvo was allegedly heard telling one voter, "You know there isn't going to be any police protection after today."

At 10:30 AM, another monitor saw Ackalitis, Campbell, St. John, and Leslie Bell standing on a street corner surrounded by a gathering of fifty ILA men. Ackalitis started to yell directions to the group, who then ran forward and began to attack six members of the Seafarers who were handing out leaflets for the AFL. The six AFL men were kicked and stomped down the length of the entire block, and when the police finally broke up the beating, they found that three of the Seafarers were suffering from stab wounds. After the brawl, the Ackalitis group began to hand out ILA literature and was repeatedly heard saying to voters, "You know what you need to do." Danny St. John would later be held as the man who had wielded the knife during the melee, and a warrant would go out for Ackalitis' arrest, since he had initiated the violence. Due to the confusion that took place during the beatings, St. John would be acquitted, and Ackalitis was released with a slap on the wrist.

When the votes were tallied, it was announced that the ILA had defeated the AFL nine thousand and sixty votes to seven thousand five hundred and sixty-eight. While the ILA celebrated and proclaimed victory, the government and AFL both put forward complaints that the results should be voided based on the intimidation and violence that had occurred at the polling stations. To the anger of the ILA, the NLRB announced that hearings would take place on February 17, 1954, to determine if the election results would remain valid.

The docks were just waiting for a single incident to spark a revolt, and that occurred on February 26, 1954. On the trouble-some Pier 32, a cousin of Michael Brogan, Billy McMahon, continued to actively rally AFL men, as he remained confident that the election results would be overturned. When the ILA heard that McMahon was acting as an AFL representative on the pier, they threw up picket lines and demanded that the shipping company fire him. In sympathy of McMahon and the AFL, Teamsters Local 807, who were responsible for the truck drivers that transported goods along the waterfront, ignored ILA picket lines and continued with their deliveries.

In response to the Teamsters' actions, Teddy Gleason, who had again been appointed ILA General Organizer after Captain Bradley became President of the ILA, announced a boycott of all Teamster trucks in New York City. Fearing a city-wide delivery shut down, a federal judge issued an order to the ILA that no Teamsters' trucks were to be interfered with. Three ILA delegates, who turned out to be none other than Harold Bowers; Albert Ackalitis' brother, William; and William P. Lynch, a longtime Gleason associate, continued to order their men to block Teamster trucks. As a result, the federal judge found that the three ILA men had violated his order, and on March 9, 1954, they were charged with contempt.

The ILA called an official strike and headed to the Federal Courthouse to picket against the charges. Captain Bradley told the media that the ILA would continue their walkout until they had a contract with the Shipping Association and the ILA was properly recognized as the winner of the December 1953 election.

AFL members began to attempt to break the ILA's strike to show the public that, unlike the ILA, they were willing to work. The longshoremen in New York were more divided than ever before, and the docks turned into a war zone. Brawls broke out on the piers, anonymous death threats were being made, vandalism was rampant, AFL buses were pelted with stones and bottles by throngs of ILA men, and nails were regularly thrown in the way of oncoming Teamster trucks. Tension again boiled over when, to the delight of the AFL, the NLRB announced on March 26, 1954, that the first election was being overturned due to the violence that had occurred at the polling station. A new election would be held in May. The AFL longshoremen had been given renewed hope and began to fight back even harder against the striking ILA.

After the announcement of a new vote was made, nearly six-hundred ILA men got on buses, headed to Washington DC, and began picketing outside of the White House. Carrying signs that read "We served you in 41 now serve us in 54" and "Heroes in 44 and Hoodlums in 54," angry ILA members marched in circles for hours. An end to the strike appeared to be nowhere in sight, so the NLRB took the drastic step of threatening to remove the ILA from the May re-vote ballot unless the ILA longshoremen returned to work. The ILA again proclaimed that they were being bullied by the government, and they reluctantly returned to work twenty-nine days after their job action began.

On the date of the election, the longshoremen headed to the polling stations, and it was evident by their body language that the events of the previous month had taken a toll on both sides. Compared to the previous vote, nothing of relevance occurred, and the NLRB announced it had been the most peaceful vote in memory.

Although the ballot counting appeared to be going in favor of the AFL union, the final tally had the ILA as victors by a mere three hundred and nineteen votes. The AFL longshoremen, who had fought so long and hard against the ILA, were devastated by the results. The newspapers commented that, unlike the last vote, this defeat was "undeniably real." In a final blow to the AFL, the ILA also confirmed that they had secured a new contract with the New York Shipping Association and that it was a "closed shop union contract," which meant that only men who were members of the ILA would have the right to perform work for the Shipping Association. Any hopes of an AFL resurgence died with the new contract. To the disgust of many of the rebels on the waterfront, the

AFL bitterly declared the Port of New York City a lost cause and abandoned the waterfront as fast as they had arrived.

Following their victory, the ILA recognized that, if they had any hope of maintaining control, they would need to stabilize their union immediately. Some of the key rebels were quietly shunned and found other work in various unions, but the ILA leaders knew what was best for business and allowed the losing AFL men to come back under the ILA banner. Many of those who had been vocal supporters of the AFL accepted defeat, and most, who simply needed to work, gradually returned back to the ILA under the same leadership that they had fought so hard against.

36

"Like Water Off My Back"

THE WATERFRONT CONFLICT of the early 1950s remained a hot topic, even as the struggle for control of the port ended. With so much attention on the ILA, Captain William Bradley and Teddy Gleason had to ensure that the public was seeing their attempts to reform the union. Waterfront Commission employment centers opened, charters offered training classes for shop stewards, the union cooperated with industry groups, and copies of collective bargaining agreements were provided to all longshoremen. By 1959, George Meany, the President of the AFL, even welcomed the ILA back into the AFL, offering the simple explanation that the ILA had cleaned up their union.

With ex-cons banned from the docks, a new breed of presentable and articulate ILA leaders came to prominence. There were men like Fred Fields Jr., an East River ILA delegate who had quickly ascended in the union where Michael Clemente had once held office; and Anthony Scotto, a college educated Brooklyn ILA official and son-in-law of Anthony Anastasio. Although unknown at the time, the rise of men like Fields and Scotto had been carefully orchestrated by their backers, and many years later, both would be convicted of crimes relating to their own illegal union activities.

Even the wild Hell's Kitchen's ILA Local 824 was making changes. The eventual new leader of the local was Mickey Bowers' own son, John, who had no criminal record and was a veteran of World War 2. After obtaining his new position, the younger Bower could regularly be found at the side of his new mentor, Teddy Gleason.

The relationship with the Teamsters and the ILA improved after the now famous Jimmy Hoffa was elected President of the Teamsters. Besides the numerous organized crime connections between Hoffa and the crime-ridden ILA, Eddie McGrath would also later admit to being a good friend of Hoffa's. Robert "Barney" Baker, McGrath's former enforcer who had never returned to New York after being wanted in the Anthony Hintz murder investigation, would even become a Teamsters official and bodyguard to Hoffa.

The waterfront was experiencing an unusual period of calm, but the newly created Waterfront Commission and police were suspicious about the positive changes on the docks that the ILA was championing. On December 2, 1954, the Waterfront Commission received a report that a meeting had been held at the Rivera Hotel in Cliffside Park, New Jersey, which was the headquarters of Newark gangster Abner "Longy" Zwillman. The meeting was attended by high-level gangsters including McGrath; Zwillman, who along with Jerry Catena represented the Genovese crime family's interest in the Newark piers; and Albert Anastasia, the boss of the Gambino family. At the meeting, it was decided that maintaining a low profile was necessary. It was also reinforced that the gangsters' original territories would remain the same, but that New Jersey would be the domain of the Genovese family.

While the Mafia was growing more powerful, McGrath's gang was declining due to attrition brought on by age, changing West Side neighborhoods, and the new waterfront laws that banned criminals from the docks. Jackie Adams was in poor health, Ding-Dong Bell reportedly suffered from a chronic illness and spent his days pickling his liver in local watering holes, and ex-loaders Tommy Burke and Tony Deliss had died from natural causes. Ruled off the waterfront were

Nick Tanzella, John "Peck" Hughes, Frank Kelly, Eddie Gaffney, and Mickey McLoughlin, while the aging Timothy O'Mara was busted by waterfront investigators and sentenced to three years in prison for falsifying his income taxes.

Remaining active were gang stalwarts Connie Noonan and Henry "Buster" Bell. Noonan remained President of ILA Local 1730, along with Austin Furey as Vice-President and Teddy Gleason as Secretary-Treasurer, while Bell became the overseer of most of the gang's remaining New York rackets, as well as maintaining his position as President of ILA Local 1804. Bell, who was not barred from the waterfront as he only possessed a minor criminal record, was considered a leader for the dwindling number of younger West Side hoodlums looking to make a name for themselves. Others, like Leslie Bell, Albert Ackalitis, Sonny Campbell, and Joseph "Heels" Murphy, took various waterfront jobs that tied them to the docks but were outside of the scope of the Waterfront Commission.

The Bowers Mob also had their own problems during the 1950s, as Mickey Bowers, John Ward, and John Potter were all indicted for not filing correct tax returns relating to their Allied Stevedoring loading company. The case went to trial, and they were all sentenced to two to five years in federal prison. Mickey Bowers' cousin Harold would die of stomach cancer, while the remaining members of the gang, such as John Keefe, John Applegate, and Danny St. John, were placed in jobs that were loosely associated with the docks. As the power and numbers of both the Bowers and McGrath gangs diminished, they began to cooperate, and the divisions among the gangsters in Greenwich, Chelsea, and Hell's Kitchen began to blur into one large West Side entity.

With the ILA stabilized, McGrath settled back into the life of a wealthy retiree. The government actively audited McGrath's income, but McGrath still maintained that the luxuries in his life were earned through horse winnings, and the FBI did find that McGrath was a sizeable bettor who could be found almost daily at the track's $50 dollar betting window.

It would not be until around 1960 that law enforcement would find that McGrath had trusted the remnants of his bookmaking operation to one of the last major Irish operators in New York City. Born in 1908, Hugh "Hughie" Mulligan was an unassuming gambler who wore thick rimmed glasses, and though well-dressed, could not hide the fact that he was balding and significantly overweight. Mulligan, who had always been friendly with a variety of McGrath's associates, had been a bookmaker on the Lower West Side and had run one of the city's biggest craps games in the Garment District. Like so many of his West Side neighbors, Mulligan moved to Queens in the 1940s.

Trustworthy and low-key, Mulligan had the unique ability to stay on good terms with everyone in the underworld. As aging gangsters died off or gradually backed away from their rackets, they turned to men like Mulligan to manage their interests. As one officer who investigated Mulligan put it, "He took care of everybody and in return everybody loved him. He was the original Godfather." Mulligan also had a reputation as a corrupter of policemen, and he once told an associate that he believed that providing regular payments to police was better than any other insurance policy in the world. Using codenames for the police officers, Mulligan's subordinates made anonymous payments to policemen all over the city.

Daily, Mulligan could be found at Gallagher's Bar and Grill at 39-33 Queens Boulevard, Long Island City, Queens (the same bar where Tommy Protheroe had his last drink before being murdered in 1935, although it was now under a different name and ownership). Mulligan did not, by definition, have his own gang, but due to his success and underworld connections, he was surrounded by an assortment of leftover West Side hoodlums. His right and left hand were a duo of stocky gamblers from Queens, Joseph "Red" McGinnity and Cornelius "Big Moe" Mahoney, while enforcement was left to a rough ex-con named Thomas Callahan and Michael "Mickey" Spillane, a younger gangster who Mulligan trusted. McGrath put Albert Ackalitis, Frank "Sonny" Campbell, and Joseph "Heels" Murphy in business with Mulligan, and Bowers' gangsters Danny St. John and John Ward ran their own bookmaking and loansharking rackets that were directly linked to Mulligan. Mulligan and McGrath would speak weekly by phone, and surveillance reports from the Florida FBI found that Mulligan made regular trips to Florida.

The NYPD and the FBI believed that there was a connection between Mulligan and McGrath but were not initially able to establish what illegal ventures the two shared. After urging from the Waterfront Commission and the NYPD, the Miami office of the FBI confirmed that they would investigate McGrath to see if they could find out if he was exerting his criminal influence on the ILA.

The FBI continued to investigate McGrath, and they sent scattered reports to New York that began to pique the interest of some of the Bureau's top brass. McGrath had made trips to New York, and in Florida he had been seen with Jimmy Alo, Albert Ackalitis, Genovese gangster Joseph Tortorici, and his old bookmaking partner Frank Mario. Based on the surveillance reports, in 1957 McGrath was added to the New York FBI office's brand new "Top Hoodlum Program." The initiative placed twenty-six of the state's most powerful mobsters under constant investigation, as the FBI was still playing catch-up after long denying the existence of a national organized crime syndicate. Also on the list with McGrath were his old friends Jimmy Alo, Frank Costello, and Meyer Lansky.

It did not take McGrath long to realize that he had become an active target of the FBI. Agents began to follow him daily to the golf course, interview people he knew in Florida, sit in cars outside of his favorite restaurants, and open and reseal his mail. McGrath proved to be a difficult target, as agents soon found that he did not conduct business over the phone and did not regularly meet with his closest criminal associates.

The FBI continued to surveil McGrath for the better part of two years but didn't even come close to laying a charge or identifying any criminal activity. Even the agents who were assigned to work the case were beginning to wonder if McGrath was only a figurehead being used by his old criminal associates.

Top Hoodlum?

ON OCTOBER 13, 1958, a supervisor in the FBI's Miami office wrote to his counterparts in New York City that "For the past seven years, subject [McGrath] has led the life of a retiree in North Bay Village, Florida. He golfs frequently, plays cards at the Normandy Shore Golf Course, and frequents nightclubs in the area. No violations of any criminal statutes have been developed in this investigation." The report noted that McGrath still appeared to be involved in union activity, but that "[. . .] it is recommended that no further investigation be conducted in this matter and that the case be closed."

McGrath's strategy of lying low had proven effective, but the actions of some of his criminal associates would again turn the spotlight back on him. The Waterfront Commission received information from an ex-convict named Fred "The Whale" Baron that men like Albert Ackalitis, Sonny Campbell, Joseph "Heels" Murphy, Danny St. John, John Keefe, and John Applegate were still actively influencing ILA matters and that they did so on behalf of the "old mob." Baron also explained how gangsters who did not have criminal convictions, such as Henry "Buster" Bell and Harry Cashin, held official titles within ILA.

The Waterfront Commission asked the FBI to check in on McGrath, and on the first day of their surveillance, McGrath was found eating dinner at Luau's Restaurant in Miami with the second most powerful man in the ILA, Vice-President

Patrick "Packy" Connolly. The surveillance of McGrath was immediately restarted.

The FBI put a considerable amount of effort into their renewed investigation and, to assist with their spying, an undercover agent rented an apartment in McGrath's building. The FBI then broke into McGrath's apartment and installed an illegal eavesdropping device behind the wall near McGrath's phone. On February 10, 1961, the bug was activated, but agents monitoring the device found a nearly silent wire. The FBI concluded that McGrath still did not talk business on the phone, and within two months the bug was removed.

On July 26, 1961, agents approached McGrath at the clubhouse of the Normandy Shores Golf Club and, in a bold proposition, asked if he would be interested in a working relationship with them. McGrath admitted that he probably knew everyone that the FBI could ask him about in one way or another, but that he did not have any information. McGrath firmly stated he would never be an informant and that he could never be friendly with anyone in the FBI. In a veiled threat, McGrath added that the agents would never want to sit down to dinner with him, and neither would the Kennedys. When the agents asked McGrath if he was concerned about being seen with them, he said that he had been under investigation his whole life, but that "it runs off my back like water," and that "you [the FBI] are trying to put me in the penitentiary, and I am not about to help you do it." Now ranting, McGrath said that he was fifty-five years old and just trying to "live out my time," without trouble, and that if he had "eight dollars to spend on a golf game or a broad it would be a lot." McGrath then walked away.

The FBI's near-constant monitoring of McGrath again slowly ceased, but in August of 1961, his old cronies in New York City again kicked the hornets' nest. A letter to the Miami office of the FBI was sent from the Director's Office to notify them that agents working a case against Michael Clemente, the boss of the East River piers and a Genovese family soldier, had developed important information from a bug that was placed in an office Clemente used. During a recorded conversation, Clemente complained to two fellow Genovese gangsters, Saro Mogarevo and Peter DeFeo, that he was having problems with his Gambino family rival from Brooklyn, Anthony Anastasio, over disputed territory that straddled the East River and Brooklyn waterfront. Clemente explained that the problem could only be solved if he reached out to Jimmy Alo, who would speak to McGrath, who could then get the ILA leadership to intervene on Clemente's behalf. He then added that McGrath was one of the only gangsters who still had a direct line to the ILA leadership and that he was only to be consulted as a last resort. Clemente ended the discussion by saying that "He [McGrath] is the ILA."

Based on the information that the Clemente bug had provided, another wiretap on McGrath's Florida home was approved on March 13, 1962. This time, agents put the bug in the same place, but knowing that McGrath did not conduct business on his home phone, they also installed a microphone that would pick up conversations that occurred in McGrath's living room.

On one of the first few days of the bug being live, McGrath was picked up raving about the Kennedy family, whom he believed was responsible for the continued investigations into organized crime. McGrath was recorded telling his then girlfriend, Jeanne Dobbins, that the FBI in Miami had gone to the home of Gil Beckley, a bookmaker and McGrath associate, to tell Beckley's significant other that Beckley had been staying in New York with a girlfriend. McGrath fumed:

> *"What is this Russia, you know what they did, they went over to Gil's and said do you know that Gil is living with a*

girl in New York City, why don't they come in and say this to me? I'll say since when is it a fucking federal offense, and if it is a federal offense I want the President of the United States [John F. Kennedy] indicted because I know he was whacking all those broads Sinatra brought him out. If I could just hit Bobby Kennedy . . . some kind of bomb that will explode . . . I would gladly go to the penitentiary for the rest of my life, believe me."

A week later a very intoxicated McGrath reminisced about the old times in New York City. He talked about how Jimmy Alo had been sent to help him after being released from prison, how he was good with guns and owned many, and how he and his bootlegging partners had made big money before he had been sent to prison.

By June 8, 1962, the bug was again removed. The FBI found that McGrath did not talk about business in his house, and that crime was only ever mentioned during his regular rants about the government. McGrath remained untouchable in Florida; so instead, the FBI turned their attention to some of his closest associates in New York City.

38

The Daily Grind

AFTER A FAILED attempt to bug a restaurant that Buster Bell regularly frequented, the FBI received authorization to place a listening device in the office of Connie Noonan, on the 14th floor of 265 West 14th Street. The FBI not only hoped to gather information on Noonan, who had been allowed to remain President of ILA Local 1730 since he had no criminal convictions, but also to investigate the increasingly influential Teddy Gleason, who despite his rise to prominence as the number three man in the ILA, still remained Secretary-Treasurer of ILA Local 1730.

The monitoring of the microphone began in October of 1962 and the listening agents soon found that Noonan and Austin Furey, the ILA Local 1730 Vice-President, were far more talkative than McGrath. Although the two mostly talked in cagey street code, frequently using nicknames and hand signals during their conversations, they often gossiped like the aging union officials they were. Noonan and Furey enjoyed holding court at the office, and a parade of ex-cons, friendly police officers, and longshoremen visited daily to discuss topics ranging from the state of the waterfront, potential real estate deals, the size of the "Christmas presents" that they received from shipping companies, favorite places to eat, finding jobs for friends, and how to purchase a stolen color television for Noonan's heart specialist. More importantly, the FBI was able to conclude that McGrath was still involved in waterfront matters, as Noonan regularly mentioned that he would need to check with "the big guy down in Florida" or "Eddie."

The bug also provided information about the changing leadership on the waterfront, as McGrath's number two, Buster Bell, had run into his own legal trouble. During the early 1960s, Teamsters leader Jimmy Hoffa had been indicted for taking kickbacks from a trucking company in Tennessee. Bell, who had financial interests in a horse racing farm in Nashville, had learned about a local gambler who was good friends with a juror, and Bell agreed to attempt to arrange a bribe. The trial ended in a hung jury. One of Hoffa's close associates later turned government witness and provided information about the jury tampering; as a result, on May 21, 1963, Bell was arrested. The day after the arrests, Noonan and Furey remarked that Hoffa "[. . .] should pay [for Bell's defense] as Bell did it for him, and it is going to cost Buster a good chunk." Bell would later be convicted and sentenced to more than five years in federal prison, which also meant being removed from his high-level position in the ILA. With Bell behind bars, McGrath lost his most powerful associate.

Talk of the upcoming ILA Convention dominated Noonan and Furey's conversations during the summer of 1963, as Teddy Gleason, their fellow ILA Local 1730 official and longtime rising star in the union, was planning to run against Captain Bradley for the position of President. Noonan and Furey remarked on how Gleason had been buttering them up to secure votes from the Greenwich and Chelsea areas and that he had been to Florida and convinced "the big guy" to support his bid. Both men agreed that Teddy Gleason was a lock to win the election now that he had secured the backing of "the crowd."

On July 16, 1963, Gleason was elected President of the ILA after Captain William Bradley voluntarily withdrew from the race during the annual convention in Miami. Completing the winning ticket was Mickey Bowers' son, John, as Vice-President and Fred Fields as the General Organizer. Noonan would later be caught on the bug explaining that Bradley had withdrawn from the race after being pressured by Mike Clemente and that Gleason sweetened the pot by offering him a $20,000 salary as President Emeritus.

As the FBI intently monitored the wheeling and dealing that was taking place in the union, the bug also finally established their first definitive connection between McGrath's waterfront associates and his gambling operations with Hughie Mulligan. After Albert Ackalitis and Sonny Campbell visited the ILA head offices in September of 1963, they were unknowingly tailed by the FBI to Gallagher's Bar in Queens. Conducting undercover reconnaissance inside Gallagher's, an agent found large posters that read:

> *"Boys from Gallagher's Outing: Gallagher's 39-33 Queens Blvd. The Boys from Gallagher's Outing and Bus Ride to Thunder Mountain Lodge, Shepherd Lake, Ringwood, NJ. Baseball and Swimming. No children permitted. $10 each ticket. Buses leave at 8:30 AM."*

The local NYPD attachment was asked about the posters, and the FBI was told that the outing was actually a gambling event that Mulligan had been running annually. The previous year it had been held at the Sundance Lodge and over one thousand people attended, with more than two hundred guests playing dice games at sixteen different casino tables. The 1963 event took place on September 8, and police followed a car that contained Sonny Campbell, Joseph "Heels" Murphy, and Mulligan. After the three arrived at the Thunder Mountain Lodge, FBI agents also spotted the familiar faces of Mulligan man Red McGinnity and Bowers Mob member John Ward. FBI agents were also surprised to discover that ILA President Teddy Gleason was present, and they watched as he mingled his way around the large group and stopped for a prolonged conversation with Sonny Campbell.

The investigation had been consistently turning up ties between the gangsters and what was supposed to be the cleaned up ILA. On January 17, 1964, the new ILA General Organizer, Fred Fields, visited with Noonan and Furey. The three complained that Teddy Gleason had become power crazy since taking the title of ILA President and that he had too many loyalties, which caused him to alienate some people. Fields asked Noonan "[. . .] if things were okay with Eddie [McGrath]," and Noonan replied that Eddie was the only one who could deal with the Italians. Furey added that he just saw Eddie during the ILA convention and that "[. . .] everything was good with Eddie and Jimmy [Alo]."

February 11, 1964, proved to be an interesting day for the bug, as according to Noonan, "a very bad individual" had been around the offices looking to see Gleason. The very bad individual in question proved to be Albert Ackalitis, as the wire later picked up the gangster meeting with Teddy Gleason. At the beginning of the conversation, an obviously nervous Gleason suggested to Ackalitis that, going forward, Noonan should be used as the liaison as "he doesn't want the world to know" about their relationship. In code, Ackalitis then demanded money from Gleason to help pay for Sonny Campbell's lawyers' fees, as Campbell had an upcoming extortion case. Gleason attempted to deflect the issue, but Ackalitis snapped back that Gleason was lying about the availability of the money. After Gleason promised to help, Ackalitis made small talk and related how two men had been bothering him lately, so he threatened to throw them out of a window. Gleason nervously laughed along.

Although it was unclear if the FBI had just heard an extortion attempt or a tense conversation among friends, the FBI was surprised to have found that the most powerful man in the ILA remained acquainted with one of the most influential West Side gangsters. In their report, the FBI agents assigned to the case wrote that the bug was providing important information and that future indictments, which would reach the upper echelons of organized crime and the ILA, were likely.

The FBI waited patiently to hear about the fallout from the Gleason and Ackalitis conversation, but Connie Noonan's office went quiet. The agents drove around Noonan's usual haunts, but he was nowhere to be found, and they later discovered that Noonan had possibly suffered a heart attack. Noonan did not return to work until April 30, 1964, and as they listened to the bug, the usually boisterous and talkative racketeer appeared tired and disinterested. Like an aging prizefighter, a reflective Noonan reminisced with Furey about how things had changed on the waterfront and that they would never be the same. As Noonan spoke of the old gang, he told Furey, "It was a good feeling having the tough guys around. I never killed anyone, but I sat in on a lot of judgments where a lot of guys were killed."

Shortly after Noonan returned to work, he again disappeared from his usual routine, and to the disappointment of FBI agents, it turned out that he had been admitted to the hospital in Jersey City and diagnosed with terminal lung cancer. Investigators asked the hospital about who had been visiting Noonan but were told that only his sister and brother came regularly. The one interesting visitor had been Charlotte Moyer, a known prostitute at the Hotel Warwick in Philadelphia, who made noisy demands in Noonan's room for $225 and repeatedly asked who would pay her rent. On November 16, 1964, Noonan died, and with him so did the FBI's budding investigation into the West Side gangsters' involvement with the ILA.

At Noonan's funeral, a combination of NYPD officers and FBI agents camped out in front of the location with cameras in hand. Noonan's brother was a high-ranking officer of the Jersey City Police Department, and a number of squad cars arrived on the scene.

Two Jersey City officers and a funeral home employee angrily approached the NYPD officers and FBI agents. The funeral home employee yelled at the officer taking the photographs, "How would you like a bullet in your head? Go mind your own business." Chief Smith of the Jersey City Police then had the NYPD and FBI escorted back to New York City, telling the FBI agents that "You are no better than they fucking are [the NYPD]."

The FBI later reviewed their photographs and confirmed that McGrath had attended Noonan's funeral. Following McGrath's return to Florida, FBI agents in Miami noticed a rare sight — caught sitting together in a parked car outside the Normandy Shores Golf Club were McGrath and Jimmy Alo. McGrath appeared to be getting his affairs in order, as shortly after his parking lot meetings with Alo, he was again spotted in New York City dining at the Capri Restaurant with Hughie Mulligan and Mulligan's muscle, Thomas Callahan.

After the New York visit, McGrath, who was now sixty years old, became less and less active according to the agents assigned to him. They noted that most of his friends were now either retired or dead, including one of the last West Side waterfront bosses and the king of the Hell's Kitchen docks, Mickey Bowers, who had recently perished in a fiery car accident. The Florida FBI office reported to the New York Office that McGrath was now living alone and that he often suffered from a bad back that would cause him to stay in his apartment for days. In their last surveillance report, the FBI agreed with what McGrath had been trying to preach to them for years — that he was retired from crime.

39

A Tangled Web

WHILE THE FBI had given up any hope of building a case against McGrath, the NYPD was still focusing on his rackets in New York City and Hughie Mulligan. During the late 1960s, detectives had been operating around the clock surveillance on Mulligan and had tapped the phone lines that he used at home and at Gallagher's Bar and Grill. The wires proved what the officers already knew, Mulligan was running a nationwide bookmaking and loansharking operation, and even more concerning, he had a large number of cops in his pocket.

McGrath and Mulligan had still been speaking on the phone weekly, with McGrath calling on various phones around the Miami area. Although the coded language that the two used prevented the NYPD from determining the extent of McGrath's criminal involvement with Mulligan, it was obvious that Mulligan still deferred to McGrath. While police continued to build their case, one of Mulligan's connections on the police force leaked information to him that his phones were tapped, and on July 29, 1969, Mulligan told McGrath that their conversations had likely been recorded for at least a year.

McGrath asked Philip "The Stick" Kovolick, a member of Meyer Lansky and Bugsy Siegel's gang who had relocated to Florida, to visit with Mulligan during one of his trips to New York City. McGrath instructed Kovolick to tell Mulligan to use his police connections to do everything he could to have the ongoing investigation ended. Police caught wind of the plot when Kovolick made a phone call to an associate of Mulligan's, whose phone was also being tapped by the NYPD. An angry Kovolick repeated over and over, "I want this killed [the investigation], I don't care, I want this killed."

The NYPD detectives who had been building the case against Mulligan knew that they did not have enough concrete evidence to guarantee a conviction against him. Instead, they deployed a new tactic that law enforcement had recently been using to hamper organized crime figures. Prior to 1970, the charge of criminal contempt was a relatively minor offense, but the state of New York had recently upgraded the charge to a felony, which now carried up to two years in prison. Police knew that if a grand jury was ordered to investigate the possibility of laying criminal charges, they would be able to call the gangsters to testify. If anyone refused to cooperate, the DA could then file criminal contempt charges against them. In April of 1970, a grand jury was ordered to investigate the activities of Mulligan, his associates, and the police that they had in their pocket.

The police officers who were called to testify were no more cooperative than the gangsters, except for one detective, John Keeley. Detective Keeley had been caught red-handed speaking to Mulligan on wiretaps and admitted to the grand jury that he had taken bribes, or "suits," and that he had also facilitated payments to a large number of fellow cops. Most shockingly, Keeley told the grand jury that he had even arranged for former Chief Inspector Thomas C. Renaghan, who at the time was one of the highest ranking members of the NYPD's uniform force, to take a bribe from Mulligan for his assistance in moving a mob-friendly cop to the Narcotics Division.

As the grand jury neared to a close, seven NYPD officers and a number of Mulligan associates, including Joseph "Red" McGinnity, Connie "Big Moe" Mahoney, Edward Kerrigan, Mickey Spillane, and Danny St. John, were indicted for contempt, while dozens of other police officers were implicated for their involvement. On October 15, 1970, Mulligan himself appeared before the grand jury but refused to answer any of their questions, which led to his arrest on November 23, 1970, for twelve counts of criminal contempt.

On February 16, 1971, subpoenas were sent to Florida for McGrath and Philip Kovolick. When McGrath's attorneys reviewed the information, it was evident that McGrath was facing more serious questioning from the grand jury than first thought. The extradition paperwork stated that McGrath would be questioned about his role in Mulligan's bookmaking and loansharking activities, as well as his involvement in a conspiracy to murder a government witness.

McGrath's role in the plot to kill an informant was a tangled scenario, and possibly an innocent one on his part.

Like most criminal capers it started with a simple idea that ballooned into something much larger and more dangerous. The originator of the plot was a down on his luck criminal named John Pierce, who worked on Pier 90 and was loosely connected to Hughie Mulligan. In January of 1964, Pierce had noticed that an armored car had been driving around Paterson, New Jersey and that it appeared to be making regular cash pickups in secluded areas.

Pierce told Charles Roberts, another West Side ex-con, about his findings, and they brought the job to Albert Ackalitis' partner, Sonny Campbell, who had let it be known that he was looking for a quick score as he needed money to pay his legal fees for his upcoming extortion trial. Pierce suggested that a fourth man for the heist could be Tom "The Greek" Kapatos, the same individual who likely stabbed Mattie Kane to death in the late 1930s. Kapatos had served twenty-two years in prison and now appeared to be trying to make up for lost time, as he rarely turned down a job.

After looking the truck over, the foursome of Pierce, Roberts, Campbell and Kapatos liked the prospect of the robbery and came to the conclusion that they would need two cars, one to block the truck from the front and other to carry the robbers that would ambush the guards. Needing more bodies, Thomas Callahan, one of Hughie Mulligan's main enforcers, and Callahan's friend Henry "Speedy" Speditz were also brought into the conspiracy.

In March of 1964, the gang carried out two failed robbery attempts, the first of which was aborted after losing sight of the truck and the second after spotting a cop car. Kapatos proved to be a difficult co-worker, as after the second failed attempt, he had a meltdown and berated his fellow robbery crew. Roberts and Campbell decided that due to Kapatos' temper and the two failed jobs, which they viewed as bad omens, they no longer wanted to participate in the robbery. Kapatos apologized to both men and asked that they reconsider, but Roberts and Campbell declined. Not long after, Campbell died of a heart attack on October 4, 1964.

Kapatos was unwilling to give up the job and began to reconsider the gang's options. He found that the armored car stopped at a number of churches, and he began conducting reconnaissance while disguised as a beggar at the soup kitchen at St. Anthony's Catholic Church in Paterson, New Jersey. On December 21, 1964, three men wearing plastic flesh-colored masks stormed into the church at 8:50 AM. The robbers handcuffed and duct-taped the mouths of three priests and threatened to shoot one in the head when he tried to run away. When the armored car guard entered the church, he was ambushed at gunpoint. The three robbers then unloaded $511,000 worth of cash into a waiting station wagon.

Within months of the heist, an undisclosed informant told the FBI all of the details of the robbery. The information was confirmed by law enforcement when they found that the suspects had all bought new flashy cars and had been spending large amounts of money in local bars.

FBI agents decided to try to drive a wedge between the members of the robbery crew, so they approached Thomas Callahan, whom they viewed as one of the most dangerous members of the gang. Intentionally tipping their hand, the agents concluded their chat by leaving Callahan with the clear impression that they already had a cooperating witness in the case. The agents' goal was to make the robbery crew nervous, get them to start turning against each other, and then apply pressure to one of the weaker members in an attempt to get them to cooperate. However, the agents grossly underestimated the steps that men like Callahan and Tom Kapatos would take to stay out of prison.

On November 8, 1965, Charles Roberts was walking along 12th Avenue, near 25th Street, when a hooded man approached and shot him at close range in the arm and the chest. Roberts managed to run away and was lucky to survive the attack. At the hospital, FBI agents visited the wounded gangster and promised him safety if he would cooperate. Roberts hinted that he knew about the robbery, but told agents that he was not interested in becoming a government witness. Although the hit on Roberts had failed, the house cleaning continued in December of 1965, as both Pierce and Speditz were reported missing by their significant others. The bodies of the men were never found, but the FBI agents learned that the men had been murdered.

Charles Roberts remained the one loose end that could tie Callahan and Kapatos to the crime, and it was clear that the West Side gangsters felt that there was unfinished business with him. On August 7, 1967, Roberts and his wife got into their car, which was parked near their home in the Bronx. As Roberts turned on the ignition, a powerful blast ripped through the automobile and Roberts and his wife were thrown from the car. Both survived the blast, but each lost one of their legs and Roberts' wife was left with severe scarring on her face.

Surprisingly, at the hospital, the maimed Roberts was still uncooperative with police. NYPD officers, who at the time had active wiretaps on Hughie Mulligan and his associates, heard various phone calls that mentioned the bombing. On one call, Mulligan was heard talking to his close associate Mickey Spillane, and, without mentioning Roberts specifically, Mulligan asked Spillane if he could "[. . .] try to deal with that thing that just happened." Spillane said that he could try. When FBI agents showed Roberts what they had uncovered with their wiretaps, he finally agreed to testify about the robbery.

The FBI was never able to build a case against Callahan or Kapatos for the murders and attempted killings that took place after the heist, but on December 18, 1968, the two were charged with robbery, and as result of Charles Roberts' testimony, they were convicted and sentenced to ten years in prison.

McGrath's connection to the case arose after the indictment was brought down against Callahan and Kapatos, and was only due to a single slip-up after years of being careful and elusive. During a recorded conversation with Mulligan, Roberts' cooperation with law enforcement came up. Perhaps it was age or complacency, but McGrath responded to Mulligan by saying, "I would come up there to New York and shoot him in the head myself." While McGrath was simply posturing, given the attempts on Roberts' life, the statement became very real.

After being served in Florida, McGrath's lawyers attempted to block his extradition to New York. His lawyers argued that McGrath was actually an investigation target and that he would be charged with various crimes when he arrived in New York City, which is not the legal purpose of witness extradition. McGrath waited anxiously for the courts to make a decision concerning whether or not he would be forced to return to his home state.

Back in New York City, Mulligan was convicted on October 4, 1971, of criminal contempt and sentenced to three years in prison. The government's victory was short-lived, as while Mulligan was out on bail pending his appeal, he died of natural causes in July of 1973.

On March 17, 1972, McGrath was ordered extradited to New York to testify for up to seven days about violations of gambling laws, bribery of public officials, bribery of labor union representatives, criminal usury, grand larceny by extortion, and conspiracy to commit murder. The DA in New York City had originally requested Philip Kovolick's presence from Florida, but would soon find that he was no longer available. On April 29, 1972, his decaying body was found in a barrel after he had been murdered by a younger criminal who he had been extorting.

McGrath finally testified before the grand jury on February 20 and February 21, 1973. The Assistant DA, who conducted the questioning, later reported to the FBI's Miami office that on the first day of testimony McGrath "[. . .] looked like a broken down bartender with a red face and baggy rumpled trousers and not the well-known hoodlum [that he was supposed to be]."

The following day, McGrath looked considerably improved in a fine suit, and he answered questions for about three hours concerning the Mulligan investigation. During McGrath's appearances, he was granted transactional immunity, which meant that his statements could not be used against him and that he would be required to provide full answers or possibly face contempt charges. McGrath was subjected to a lengthy interrogation and answered all questions under protest. Most of his answers constituted a refusal to respond, and what information he did provide was vague and evasive.

On May 18, 1973, McGrath was arrested on two counts of criminal contempt for refusing to answer the grand jury's questions. For the first time since 1940, Eddie McGrath was facing prison time.

McGrath's indictment began a litany of motions from his legal team to suppress evidence or delay his trial. After almost three years of pre-trial matters, the case went ahead, and on September 20, 1976, McGrath was convicted of criminal contempt after a short jury trial. The judge allowed McGrath to remain out on bail in Florida pending what would likely be a lengthy appeal. The case was scheduled to be heard by the Supreme Court, but stayed a number of times, as McGrath was having heart issues. On May 6, 1980, after six years of legal proceedings, the People v. Edward J. McGrath was finally decided, and the court unanimously affirmed McGrath's conviction.

The seventy-four-year-old former overlord of the waterfront was ordered to turn himself into Rikers Island to serve a ninety-day sentence for contempt.

Police had been investigating McGrath actively since 1938 and had been unable to obtain a conviction until he finally slipped up during an unassuming phone call. After forty-two years of investigations, the end result was a ninety-day sentence.

A Dentist, a Stockbroker and a Gangster

WHILE THE GRAND jury was investigating Eddie McGrath in the 1970s, he almost entirely disappeared from all police reports. One briefly mentioned that he still attended the Normandy Shores Golf Club, where he enjoyed playing Gin and Hearts with other native New Yorkers; McGrath's name also occasionally appeared in the FBI file on Jimmy Alo, who had remained active in the Genovese family's affairs. Both McGrath and Alo continued to live in Florida and, according to sources, maintained the friendship that had started during their bootlegging days in the 1920s. Alo, who like McGrath had outlived most of his criminal contemporaries, would pass away from natural causes on March 9, 2001 at the age of ninety-six.

Back in New York City, the ILA remained the leading waterfront union in the country under the leadership of McGrath's old friend Teddy Gleason. However, by the 1980s the ILA would have been unrecognizable to McGrath. The number of men working on the piers continued to significantly decline as the world became less reliant on water-based transport, and containers and automation drastically changed the shipping industry.

As the docks disappeared so did the waterfront gangsters, and most of McGrath's generation either died off or moved on to new rackets. Albert Ackalitis was one of the last holdouts, but even he shifted his interests away from the waterfront before eventually passing away in 1984. By 1987, the age of the average dock worker in New York was fifty-eight, and from 1966 to 1977, the ILA's membership decreased from one hundred and sixty-five thousand to fewer than sixty thousand.

Gleason remained President of the ILA until 1987, serving six consecutive terms; he is remembered by the membership as their most popular leader, and as the man who led them back to prominence as one of the top unions in the country. In the 1960s, Gleason negotiated what was, at the time, the longest lasting ILA contract in history, and put in place important initiatives involving guaranteed annual income and job security.

During Gleason's tenure as leader, he had difficulty distancing himself from the ever present corruption allegations that often surrounded his union. Five years of intensive investigation by the FBI between 1977 and 1981, in a case they entitled UNIRAC (which was short for union racketeering), led to fifty-two convictions involving ILA union officials across the country. UNIRAC also proved that the Genovese and Gambino crime families controlled large portions of the ILA throughout the late 1960s and 1970s and that corruption was still teeming at every level of the union. Despite the feeling by some law enforcement that Teddy Gleason had to be aware of the criminal behavior within his own union, he was unscathed by the massive indictments.

In Gleason's old age, he began to speak more freely about the former criminal influences that were part of the ILA, and he admitted that when he first started working on the docks, it was a different time. When asked about the mob and if he was ever complicit with the criminal activity that had occurred, he stated, "There's no way I could be tied up with the Mafia, I'm Irish." Gleason added with a smile, "I believe in the Seventh Commandment [Thou shall not steal]." When asked about McGrath, he would always volunteer that he had been a friend at one time. Gleason passed away on December 24, 1992, at the age of ninety-two, and his life was celebrated during a large mass at St. Patrick's Cathedral.

Further demonstrating the factional nature of the ILA, the next ILA President following Gleason's death was John Bowers, a longtime Gleason supporter and the son of the notorious Mickey Bowers. During Bowers' tenure as President, which lasted until 2007, the number of longshoremen actually working on piers in New York continued to plummet, with much of the valuable waterfront real estate being converted into condominiums and parks.

Although the New York City waterfront is a ghost of itself, waterfront shipping remains an important industry in many places, including New Jersey. The ILA is still recognized as one of the leading labor unions in the country, and they now have upwards of sixty-five thousand members in over two hundred locals across the United States, Canada, and Puerto Rico.

The leadership of the ILA has never left the West Side, and the current President is Harold Daggett, who happens to be the nephew of McGrath's former associate George Daggett (although it should be noted that George died more than a decade before Harold was born). According to the Waterfront Commission, the relationship between the mob and the ILA remains unchanged, and there have been a number of large investigations and cases over the years concerning corruption within the union. The Justice Department has described Daggett as "[. . .] a longtime Genovese family associate," although they have been unable to prove this allegation in court.

In 2005, Daggett and a number of other longshoremen officials were charged with fraud, but the jury accepted that the union boss had been a victim of the mob's extortion tactics rather than a participant. Daggett's lawyer during the 2005 trial, his cousin George Daggett, recently stated that, "the mob on the waterfront is a myth" and that the Waterfront Commission thinks that, "we're still in the '50s."

Regardless of the extent of the current level of the mob's influence on the docks, the days of the West Side long-shoremen shaping-up at the piers, gathering in waterfront taverns, fishing bodies out of the North River, and rubbing elbows with the neighborhood gangsters have passed, and surnames like Bowers and Daggett are now only a reminder of days gone by.

Eddie McGrath outgunned and outmaneuvered his gangster friends and foes alike, and he was one of the few mobsters to be able to enjoy his riches during his golden years. McGrath's past crimes during the lawless years on waterfront continued to follow him well into his old age, and although he was not behind bars, he was tailed, spied on, and monitored by law enforcement for the majority of his life. Desperate to remain out of jail, McGrath chose to become a recluse, and he reluctantly cut himself off from many of his old friends. His ninety-day sentence for contempt was a symbolic victory for law enforcement, as although McGrath had fought tooth and nail, and spent hundreds of thousands of dollars to fight the short prison sentence, he was unable to stymie his conviction.

McGrath, who often seemed angry and annoyed at law enforcement, was evidently happy to have never been caught, but in many of the wiretapped conversations, there always seemed to be a hint of nostalgia for the old days. The FBI or the NYPD never heard McGrath speak about his prior crimes, but he seemed happiest when he would wax poetically about the exciting days of Prohibition, the cars that he drove, the women that he bedded, and the money that he spent.

McGrath passed away on April 15, 1994, in Florida, at the age of eighty-eight.

Prior to his death, McGrath lived like any other retired senior citizen. He had medical issues, followed a mundane daily routine, and spent his days enjoying leisure activities.

If you had happened to catch sight of him at the Normandy Shores Golf Club, you would not have been able to guess which elderly card player was the former stockbroker, which was the retired dentist, and which was the gangster suspected in over thirty murders.

ACKNOWLEDGEMENTS

What started out as a childhood curiosity with Prohibition mobsters somehow grew into this book. I remember the surprise and excitement when I discovered that, through Freedom of Information laws, I could obtain investigative reports on all of the seedy underworld stories that had long fascinated me. For one reason or another (which I can barely remember at this point), I filed a request with the FBI about Eddie McGrath, and to my wonderment, I received a voluminous response. Still in my teenage years, I poured through pages and pages of information on McGrath, but at the time, I never would have dreamed of writing this book. Only after the research became more complete did I decide that there was an untold story that needed to be shared.

Fast forward to more than ten years later; I still feel the same excitement when I receive a package from the archives or find a document for which I have been searching. Prior to writing this book, I told myself that my research about crime on the waterfront was complete, but one file leads to another, and that file leads to even more questions, and so the search continues. None of this would have been possible without the archivists and librarians who tirelessly serve the public, keep history alive, and embrace the interests of their visitors.

I am in indebted to the staff at the New York State Archives who have constantly accommodated my often large requests (which I frequently feel guilty about) and have gone above and beyond to help me with my searches. I would also like to thank Ken Cobb and the staff at the New York City Municipal Archives, who have dug out many a court record and DA Case File; Ellen Sexton at the Lloyd Sealy Library, the staff at the National Archives, particularly Joseph Sanchez in San Francisco, Lori Cox-Paul and Sarah LeRoy in Kansas, Carol Swain in the Motion Picture Branch, and William Davis at the Center for Legislative Archives; the librarians at the New York State Library, Robarts Library, and the New York Public Library; the New Jersey, Florida, and Pennsylvania State Archives; the Freedom of Information Unit at the Executive Office for United States Attorney; and the FBI's Records and Information Dissemination Section.

In addition, I would like to thank the many people who have provided their own insights and stories. Your accounts were invaluable when I was learning about the West Side waterfront.

I appreciate the assistance of Carole Stuart and Carmela Cohen at Barricade Books for taking on this project and providing their guidance throughout the process. Also, I owe my gratitude to author Scott Deitche for offering helpful advice.

Last, thank you to my family and friends who have always encouraged my "unique historical interests" and put up with my hours of research and writing. I likely would not have started this book without your love and support, and this would not have been possible without you.

SELECTED BIBLIOGRAPHY

Books and Articles

Block, Alan A. *East Side-West Side: Organizing Crime in New York 1930–1950*. Transaction Publishers, 1983.

Carter, Richard, and William J. Keating. *The Man Who Rocked the Boat*. Harper & Brothers, 1956.

Coffey, Joseph, and Jerry Schmetterer. *The Coffey Files: One Cop's War Against the Mob*. St Martin's Press, 1992.

Cort, John C. *Dreadful Conversions: The Making of a Catholic Socialist*. Fordham University Press, 2003.

Davis, Colin John. *Waterfront Revolts: New York and London Dockworkers, 1946-61*. University of Illinois Press, 2003.

English, T.J. *Paddy Whacked: The Untold Story of the Irish American Gangster*. William Morrow, 2005.

Feder, Sid, and Burton B. Turkus. *Murder Inc.: The Story of The Syndicate Killing Machine*. Da Capo Press, 2003.

Fisher, James T. *On the Irish Waterfront: The Crusader, the Movie, and the Soul of the Port of New York*. Cornell University Press, 2009.

Freeman, Joshua B. *Working-Class New York: Life and Labor Since World War II*. The New Press, 2001.

Goddard, Donald. *All Fall Down: One Man Against the Waterfront Mob*. Times Books, 1980.

Goewey, David. *Crash Out: The True Tale of a Hell's Kitchen Kid and the Bloodiest Escape in Sing Sing History*. Crown, 2005.

Goldstein, Joseph. "Along New York Harbor, 'On the Waterfront' Endures." *The New York Times*. January 6, 2017.

International Longshoremen's Association Local 38–79. "The Truth about the Waterfront : I.L.A. States its Case to the Public ." *International Longshoremen's Association*. 1936.

Jacobs, James B. *Mobsters, Unions, and Feds: The Mafia and the American Labor Movement*. NYU Press, 2007.

Jensen, Vernon H. *Hiring of Dock Workers and Employment Practices in the Ports of New York, Liverpool, London, Rotterdam, and Marseilles*. Harvard University Press, 1964.

Johnson, Malcolm. *On the Waterfront: The Pulitzer Prize-Winning Articles That Inspired the Classic Film and Transformed the New York Harbor*. Chamberlain Bros., 2005.

Kimeldorf, Howard. *Reds or Rackets?: The Making of Radical and Conservative Unions on the Waterfront*. University of California Press, 1992.

Lardner, James, and Thomas Reppetto. *NYPD: A City and Its Police*. Henry Holt and Co., 2000.

Larrowe, Charles P. *Shape-up and Hiring Hall; A Comparison of Hiring Methods and Labor Relations On the New York and Seattle Waterfronts*. Berkley: University of California Press, 1955.

Long, Joseph. "On the Waterfront: Irish Life in Chelsea & Greenwich Village, Part I." *New York Irish History Roundtable Journal, Volume 26*. 2012.

Maas, Peter. *The Valachi Papers*. William Morrow Paperbacks, 2003.

May, Allen R. *Gangland Gotham: New York's Notorious Mob Bosses*. Greenwood, 2009.

Nown, Graham. *Arkansas Godfather: The Story of Owney Madden and How He Hijacked Middle America*. Butler Center for Arkansas Studies, 2013.

Ogg, Elizabeth. *Longshoremen and Their Homes: The Story of a Housing Case Study Conducted Under the Auspices of Greenwich House*. Greenwich House, 1939.

Raymond, Allen. *Waterfront Priest*. Henry Holt & Company, 1955.

Schulberg, Budd. *On the Waterfront: A Novel*. Open Road Media, 2012.

Van MacNair Jr., John. *Chaplain on the Waterfront; The Story of Father Saunders*. Seabury Press, 1963.

Correctional Records/Reports

Albert Ackalitis, New York State Archives (NYSA)

Andrew Sheridan, NYSA

Benjamin Dietz, Connecticut State Archives

Charles Yanowsky, The National Archives

Daniel Gentile, NYSA

Edward McGrath, NYSA

Edward O'Connell, NYSA

Francis Smith, NYSA

Frank Campbell, NYSA

Frank Peraski, Pennsylvania State Archives

George Achinelli, NYSA

Henry F. Bell, Federal Bureau of Prisons

James Skinner, NYSA

John Dunn, NYSA

John Keefe, NYSA

John McCrossin, NYSA

John Oley, The National Archives

John O'Mara, NYSA

John Whitton, NYSA

Joseph Murphy, NYSA

Joseph Potter, Pennsylvania State Archives

Leo Tocci, Pennsylvania State Archives

Leslie Bell, NYSA

Matthew Kane, NYSA

Michael Bowers, The National Archives

Patrick Ahearn, NYSA

Percy Geary, The National Archives

Philip Sheridan, NYSA

Stewart Wallace, Pennsylvania State Archives

Thomas Adobody, NYSA

Timothy O'Mara, NYSA

Thomas Protheroe, NYSA

William Vanderwyde, NYSA

Court Documents/District Attorney Case Files

Arrow Laundry v. Edward T. McCaffery, Commissioner of The Department of Licenses of the City of New York. 1949.

Dr. Harry Gilbert v. Ernest Cole, Commissioner of Education of the State of New York. 1943.

National Labor Relations Board Case Number 02-RM-000556. 1954.

New York State District Attorney. *Annual Report of the Chief Clerk to the District Attorney, County of New York.* 1942.

New York State District Attorney. *Annual Report of the Chief Clerk to the District Attorney, County of New York.* 1947.

The Application of Edward Falvey v. The Waterfront Commissioner of the New York Harbor. 1954.

The Application of Nicholas Tanzella v. The Waterfront Commissioner of the New York Harbor. 1955.

The People of the State of New York v. Edward McGrath. 1931.

The People of the State of New York v. Edward McGrath. 1977.

The People of the State of New York v. Hugh Mulligan. 1971.

The People of the State of New York v. James Skinner. 1935.

The People of the State of New York v. John Dunn etc. all. 1941.

The People of the State of New York v. John Dunn etc. all. 1947.

The People of the State of New York v. John Whitton and Patrick Ahearn. 1923.

The People of the State of New York v. Joseph Butler. 1928.

The People of the State of New York v. Joseph Murphy etc. all. 1937.

The People of the State of New York v. Matthew Kane. 1927.

The People of the State of New York v. Robert J. Sullivan. 1933.

The People of the State of New York v. Tony Deliss. 1917.

The People of the State of New York v. Victor Patterson. 1927.

The State of Florida v. Edward J. McGrath. 1940.

The State of New Jersey v. James Bell etc. all. 1937.

United States of America v. Allied Stevedoring. 1956.

United States of America v. Charles Yanowsky. 1936.

United States of America v. Harry Gross and Cornelius J. Noonan. 1960.

United States of America v. Henry F. Bell. 1963.

United States of America v. Thomas Callahan and Thomas Kapatos. 1971.
United States of America v. Timothy J. O'Mara. 1954.

FBI Files

Albert Ackalitis
Allied Stevedoring
Charles Yanowsky
Cornelius J. Noonan
Edward J. McGrath
Henry F. Bell
Hugh Mulligan
John M. Dunn
Michael J. Bowers
Owney Madden
Thomas W. "Teddy" Gleason
Timothy O'Mara
Varick Enterprises
Vincent Alo

Hearings/Hearing Records

Investigation of Improper Activities in the Labor or Management Field. Hearings Before the Select Committee on Improper Activities in the Labor or Management Field, Eighty-fifth Congress. 1957–1958.

Investigation of Organized Crime in Interstate Commerce. Hearings Before a Special Committee to Investigate Organized Crime in Interstate Commerce, United States Senate, Eighty-first Congress. 1950–1951.

New Jersey-New York Waterfront Commission Compact: Hearing Before Subcommittee No. 3 of the Committee on the Judiciary, House of Representatives. 1953.

New York State Crime Commission Records. Columbia University. 1951–1953.

Public Hearings (no. 5) Conducted by the New York State Crime Commission Pursuant to the Governor's Executive Orders of March 29, 1951 and November 13, 1952. 1953.

Records of the Subcommittee Investigating Waterfront Racketeering
    and Port Security. The National Archives. 1953.
Records of The United States Senate Special Committee to Investigate
    Crime in Interstate Commerce. The National Archives. 1951.
*Waterfront Corruption: Hearings before the Permanent Subcommittee on
    Investigations of the Committee on Governmental Affairs, United States
    Senate, Ninety-seventh Congress.* 1981.
*Waterfront Investigation: Hearings Before a Subcommittee of the Committee
    on Interstate and Foreign Commerce, United States Senate, Eighty-third
    Congress.* 1953.

Historical Newspapers/Magazines/Serials

Albany Evening News
Albany Morning Herald
Auburn Free Press
Binghamton Press
Brooklyn Daily Eagle
Brooklyn Standard Union
Brooklyn Daily Star
Click, The National Picture Monthly
Daily Labor Report
Geneva Daily Times
Harper's Magazine
ILA Newsletter
ILWU Dispatcher
Jersey Journal
Life Magazine
Lockport Union Sun Journal
Long Island Daily Press
Long Island Star Journal
Miami Herald
Monthly Labor Review
Mount Vernon Daily Argus
New York Evening Post

New York PM Daily
New York Sun
New York Tribune/Herald Tribune
Newsday
Ossining Reminder Weekly News
Poughkeepsie Evening Star and Enterprise
Poughkeepsie Daily Eagle
Rochester Democrat Chronicle
St. Petersburg Times
Syracuse NY Journal
The Boston Globe
The Longshore News
The Miami News
The New York Times
The New Yorker
The Palm Beach Post
The Wall Street Journal
Time Magazine

Other

Crime Inc: The True Story Of The Mafia. Thames Television Ltd. 1984.
Eugene Canevari Papers. Lloyd Sealy Library. 1927–1951.
Hollstein, Brian R. Interview of Former Special Agent of the FBI Graham J. Desvernine. Society of Former Special Agents of the FBI. October 4, 2006.
International Longshoremen's Association. *Proceedings of the Annual Convention.* 1935–1956.
On the Waterfront. Dir. Elia Kazan. Columbia Pictures Corp. 1954.
Slaughter on 10th Avenue. Dir. Arnold Laven. Universal International. 1957.
The Mary Heaton Vorse Collection. Walter P. Reuther Library. 1966.

INDEX

FOR A COMPLETE LIST OF BARRICADE TITLES
PLEASE VISIT OUR WEBSITE: WWW.BARRICADEBOOKS.COM

A COP'S TALE: NYPD THE VIOLENT YEARS
Jim O'Neil and Mel Fazzino

A Cop's Tale focuses on New York City's most violent and corrupt years, the 1960s to early 1980s. Jim O'Neil–a former NYPD cop –delivers a rare look at the brand of law enforcement that ended Frank Lucas's grip on the Harlem drug trade, his cracking open of the Black Liberation Army case, and his experience as the first cop on the scene at the "Dog Day Afternoon" bank robbery. A gritty, heart-stopping account of a bygone era, *A Cop's Tale* depicts the willingness of one of New York's finest to get as down-and-dirty as the criminals he faced while protecting the citizens of the city he loved.

$24.95 – Hardcover – 978-1-56980-372-1
$16.95 – Paperback – 978-1-56980-509-1

BLACK GANGSTERS OF CHICAGO
Ron Chepesiuk

Chicago's African American gangsters were every bit as powerful and intriguing as the city's fabled white mobsters. In this fascinating narrative history, author Ron Chepesiuk profiles the key players in the nation's largest black organized crime population and traces the murderous evolution of the gangs and rackets that define Chicago's violent underworld.

$24.95 – Hardcover – 978-1-56980-331-8
$16.95 – Paperback – 978-1-56980-505-3

BLOOD AND VOLUME: INSIDE NEW YORK'S ISRAELI MAFIA
Dave Copeland

Ron Gonen, together with pals Johnny Attias and Ron Efraim, ran a multimillion-dollar drug distribution and contract murder syndicate in 1980s New York. But when the FBI caught up, Gonen had to choose between doing the right thing and ending up dead.

$22.00 – Hardcover – 978-1-56980-327-1
$16.95 – Paperback – 978-1-56980-145-1

BRONX D.A. TRUE STORIES FROM THE DOMESTIC VIOLENCE AND SEX CRIMES UNIT
Sarena Straus

If you dealt with violence all day, how long would it be before you burned out? Sarena Straus was a prosecutor in the Bronx District Attorney's office, working in an area of the Bronx with the highest crime and poverty rates in America. This book chronicles her experience during her three-year stint with the Domestic Violence and Sex Crimes Unit, combating crimes and women and children and details how and why she finally had to give up the job.

$22.00 – Hardcover – 978-1-56980-305-9

CIGAR CITY MAFIA: A COMPLETE HISTORY OF THE TAMPA UNDERWORLD
Scott M. Deitche

Prohibition-era "Little Havana" housed Tampa's cigar industry, and with it, bootleggers, arsonists, and mobsters–plus a network of corrupt police officers worse than the criminals themselves. Scott M. Deitche documents the rise of the infamous Trafficante family, ruthless competitors in a "violent, shifting place, where loyalties and power quickly changed."

$16.95 – Paperback – 978-1-56980-287-8

CONFESSIONS OF A SECOND STORY MAN: JUNIOR KRIPPLE-BAUER AND THE K&A GANG
Allen M. Hornblum

From the 1950s through the 1970s, the rag-tag crew known as the K&A gang robbed wealthy suburban neighborhoods with assembly-line skills. Hornblum tells the strange-but-true story thru interviews, police records and historical research, including the transformation of the K&A Gang from a group of blue collar thieves to their work in conjunction with numerous organized crime families helping to make Philadelphia the meth capital of the nation.

$16.95 – Paperback – 978-1-56980-313-4

DOCK BOSS
Eddie McGrath and the West Side Waterfront

Neil G. Clark

At a time when New York City's booming waterfront industry was ruled by lawless criminals, one gangster towered above the rest and secretly controlled the docks for over thirty years. *Dock Boss: Eddie McGrath and the West Side Waterfront* explores the rise of Eddie McGrath from a Depression Era thug to the preeminent racketeer on Manhattan's lucrative waterfront. McGrath's life takes readers on a journey through the tail-end of Prohibition, the sordid years of violent gang rule on the bustling waterfront, and finally the decline of the dock mobsters following a period of longshoremen rebellion in the 1950s. This is the real-life story of the bloodshed that long haunted the ports of New York City.

$17.95 – Paperback – 978-1-56980-813-9

DOCTORS OF DEATH
TEN TRUE CRIME STORIES OF DOCTORS WHO KILL
Wensley Clarkson

These mystifying and spine-tingling stories are just what the doctor ordered and they are all true. *Doctors of Death* presents ten hair-raising real life accounts of killing and mayhem in medical training ultimately causing others to die. With a sharp eye for the sort of detail that only true cases can have, they are woven together with some of the most horrifying killings that ever occurred.

$17.95 – Paperback – 978-1-56980-806-1

FRANK NITTI: THE TRUE STORY OF CHICAGO'S NOTORIOUS "ENFORCER"
Ronald D. Humble

Frank "The Enforcer" Nitti is arguably the most glamorized gangster in history. Though he has been widely mentioned in fictional works, this is the first book to document Nitti's real-life criminal career alongside his pop culture persona, with special chapters devoted to the many television shows, movies and songs featuring Nitti.

$24.95 – Hardcover – 978-1-56980-342-4

GAMING THE GAME: THE STORY BEHIND THE NBA BETTING SCANDAL AND THE GAMBLER WHO MADE IT HAPPEN
Sean Patrick Griffin

In June 2007, the FBI informed the NBA that one of its referees, Tim Donaghy, was the subject of a probe into illegal gambling. With Donaghy betting on games he officiated, a trail unraveled that led to the involvement of Donaghy's childhood friend and professional gambler Jimmy Battista. Researched with dozens of interviews, betting records, court documents and with access to witness statements and confidential law enforcement files, this book is a "must-read" for any NBA fan.

$16.95 – Paperback – 978-1-56980-475-9

GANGSTER CITY: THE HISTORY OF THE NEW YORK UNDERWORLD 1900-1935
Patrick Downey

This is an illustrated treasure trove of information about New York City's gangsters from 1900 through the 1930s. Told in depth are the exploits of Jewish, Italian and Chinese gangsters during New York City's golden age of crime. No other book delivers such extensive detail on the lives, crimes and dramatic endings of this ruthless cast of characters, including Jack "Legs" Diamond and the sadistic Dutch Schultz.

$16.95 – Paperback – 978-1-56980-361-5

GANGSTERS OF HARLEM: THE GRITTY UNDERWORLD OF NEW YORK'S MOST FAMOUS NEIGHBORHOOD
Ron Chepesiuk

Author Ron Chepesiuk creates the first comprehensive, accurate portrait of Harlem gangs from their inception, detailing the stories of the influential famed gangsters who dominated organized crime in Harlem from the early 1900s through the present. In this riveting documentation, Chepesiuk tells this little known story through in-depth profiles of the major gangs and motley gangsters including "Nicky" Barnes, Bumpy Johnson and Frank Lucas.

$16.95 – Paperback – 978-1-56980-365

GANGSTERS OF MIAMI: TRUE TALES OF MOBSTERS, GAMBLERS, HIT MEN, CON MEN AND GANG BANGERS FROM THE MAGIC CITY
Ron Chepesiuk

Miami has been the home for a colorful variety of gangsters from its early days to the modern period. These include the notorious smugglers of the Prohibition era, famous mobsters like Al Capone and Meyer Lansky who helped make Miami a gambling Mecca, the Cuban Mafia which arrived after Cuba fell to Castro, the Colombian cartels during the cocaine explosion, the Russian mafia after the fall of the Soviet Union, and the street gangs that plagued Miami after the advent of crack cocaine.

$17.95 – Paperback – 978-1-56980-500-8

I'LL DO MY OWN DAMN KILLIN': BENNY BINION, HERBERT NOBLE AND THE TEXAS GAMBLING WAR
Gary W. Sleeper

People know of the notorious Benny Binion for opening the Horseshoe and becoming the most successful casino owner in Las Vegas. But before he became the patron saint of World Series Poker, Binion led the Texas underground in a vicious, nefarious gambling war that lasted over fifteen years. Author Gary Sleeper presents the previously unseen details of Benny Binion's life leading up to his infamous Las Vegas days, when he became the owner of the most successful casino in the world.

$16.95 – Paperback – 978-1-56980-321-9

IL DOTTORE: THE DOUBLE LIFE OF A MAFIA DOCTOR
Ron Felber

The inspiration for Fox TV's drama series, "Mob Doctor," **IL DOTTORE** is the riveting true story of a Jewish kid from the Bronx who became a Mafia insider and physician to top NY Mafia dons such as John Gotti, Carlo Gambino, Paul Castellano, and Joe Bonanno. Eventually, he had to make a choice between loyalty to the mob and remaining true to his Hippocratic Oath, all under the watchful eye of New York's top federal prosecutor, Rudolph Giuliani.

$16.95 – Paperback – 978-1-56980-491-9

JAILING THE JOHNSTON GANG: BRINGING SERIAL MURDERERS TO JUSTICE
Bruce E. Mowday

This is the inside story of the dedicated law enforcement team that brought to justice serial murderers Norman, David and Bruce A. Johnston Sr. For more than a decade the Johnston Gang terrorized communities throughout the East Coast of the U.S. by stealing millions of dollars worth of property. But in 1978, fearing that younger members of the gang were going to rat them out, the brothers killed four teenagers and nearly killed Bruce Sr.'s own son.

$16.95 – Paperback – 978-1-56980-442-1

LUCKY LUCIANO: THE MAN WHO ORGANIZED CRIME IN AMERICA
Hickman Powell

He was called the Father of Organized Crime. Born in Sicily and reared in poverty he arrived with his family on New York's Lower East Side in the early 20th century. He grew up among Irish Jewish and Italian youths dedicated to crime, some of them going on to become world class thugs. This book is written by a top investigative reporter who followed Luciano's trial from its inception to the jury verdict. He not only interviewed Luciano but also the assorted prostitutes and pimps who testified against him.

Lucky Luciano was responsible for the infamous Atlantic City gathering of the nation's top mobsters that included Al Capone, Meyer Lansky and Frank Costello and where they were persuaded to run crime as a business.

$16.95 – Paperback – 978-1-56980-900-6

MILWAUKEE MAFIA: MOBSTERS IN THE HEARTLAND
Gavin Schmitt ★NEW★

Milwaukee's Sicilian underworld is something few people speak about in polite company, and even fewer people speak with any authority. Everyone in Milwaukee has a friend of a friend who knows something, but they only have one piece of a giant puzzle. The secret society known as the Mafia has done an excellent job keeping its murders, members and mishaps out of books. Until now.

$16.95 – Paperbackr – 978-0-9623032-6-5

MURDER OF A MAFIA DAUGHTER THE LIFE AND TRAGIC DEATH OF SUSAN BERMAN
Cathy Scott ★NEW★

Susan Berman grew up in Las Vegas luxury as the daughter of Davie Berman, casino mogul and notorious mafia leader. After her father died she learned about his mob connections. Susan then dedicated her life to learning about Vegas and its underworld chiefs. When Kathie Durst - the wife of her good friend, Robert Durst, mysteriously disappeared Durst was a prime suspect but the case was never solved. After the Kathie Durst case was reopened, the DA wanted to question Susan about what she knew regarding a phone call Kathie supposedly made to her medical school dean saying she was sick and wouldn't be at school. Soon after the Kathie Durst case was reopened, Susan Berman was found dead, shot in the back of head. No forced entry, no robbery, nothing missing from her home.

$17.95 – Paperback – 978-0-934878-49-4

SHALLOW GRAVE
THE UNSOLVED CRIME THAT SHOOK THE MIDWEST'
Gavin Schmitt

NEW

An upright citizen kidnapped in public and dumped in a shallow grave. A police chief's wife arrested for murder. A mobster kidnapped and threatened by the FBI. And an ongoing corruption probe looking at everyone from the lowest bookie all the way up to judges and prosecutors. What is going on in small town America? Follow the exploits of the police, FBI and Bobby Kennedy himself as they try to put together the pieces and catch the bad guys... if they can.

$17.95 – Paperback – 978-1-56980-808-5

STOLEN MASTERPIECE TRACKER: INSIDE THE BILLION DOLLAR WORLD OF STOLEN MASTERPIECES
Thomas McShane with Dary Matera

Legendary undercover FBI agent Thomas McShane is one of the world's foremost authorities on the billion-dollar art theft business. For thirty-six years, McShane matched wits with some of the most devious criminal masterminds of the 20th and 21st centuries. Here he presents a unique memoir that gives readers a thrilling ride through the underworld of stolen art and historical artifacts. Written with veteran true crime author Dary Matera, this captivating account is as engaging as it is informative.

$17.95 – Paperback – 978-1-56980-519-0

TERRORIST COP: THE NYPD JEWISH COP WHO TRAVELED THE WORLD TO STOP TERRORISTS
Mordecai Z. Dzikansky with Robert Slater

Terrorist Cop is a colorful, haunting and highly graphic tale of retired New York

City Detective First Grade Morty Dzikansky. Dzikansky first patrolled Brooklyn streets with a yarmulke on his head. A rise through the ranks would eventually bring him to Israel, monitoring suicide bombings post 9/11. It was part of Commissioner Ray Kelly's plan to protect New York from further terrorist attacks, but it led to Morty becoming a victim of post traumatic stress disorder.

$24.95 – Hardcover – 978-1-56980-445-2

THE JEWS OF SING SING
Ron Arons

Sing-Sing prison opened in 1828 and since then, more than 7000 Jews have served time in the famous correctional facility. The Jews of Sing-Sing is the first book to fully expose the scope of Jewish criminality over the past 150 years. Besides famous gangsters like Lepke Buchalter, thousands of Jews committed all types of crimes—from incest and arson to selling air rights over Manhattan—and found themselves doing time in Sing-Sing.

$22.95 – Hardcover – 978-1-56980-333-2

THE LIFE AND TIMES OF LEPKE BUCHALTER: AMERICA'S MOST RUTHLESS RACKETEER
Paul R. Kavieff

This is the first biography of the only organized crime boss to be executed in the United States. At the height of his power, Louis "Lepke" Buchalter had a stronghold on the garment, banking and flour tracking industries. As the overseer of the killing-on-assignment machine known as "Murder Inc.," his penchant for murder was notorious. This impeccably researched book traces the story from childhood, through the incredibly sophisticated rackets, to his ultimate conviction and execution. All the names, dates and brutal murders are described here, in a unique history of labor unrest in turn-of-the 20th century New York. In the end, it was an obscure murder that led to his conviction and execution.

$16.95 — Paperback — 978-1-56980-517-6

THE MAFIA AND THE MACHINE: THE STORY OF THE KANSAS CITY MOB
Frank R. Hayde

The story of the American Mafia is not complete without a chapter on Kansas City. "The City of Fountains" has appeared in the **The Godfather**, **Casino**, and **The Sopranos**, but many Midwesterners are not aware that Kansas City has affected the fortunes of the entire underworld. In **The Mafia and the Machine**, author Frank Hayde ties in every major name in organized crime—Luciano, Bugsy, Lansky —as well as the city's corrupt police force.

$16.95 — Paperback — 978-1-56980-443-8

THE PURPLE GANG: ORGANIZED CRIME IN DETROIT 1910-1946
Paul R. Kaveiff

In Prohibition era Detroit, a group of young men grew in power and profile to become one of the nation's most notorious gangs of organized crime. **The Purple Gang**, as they came to be called, quickly rose to power and wealth leaving law enforcement powerless against the high-profile methods of the gang. During the chaos of the Prohibition era, the fearless "Purples" rose to the highest ranks of organized crime and then shattered

it all with bloodthirsty greediness and murderous betrayal.

$16.95 — Paperback — 978-1-56980-494-0

THE RISE AND FALL OF THE CLEVELAND MAFIA
Rick Porrello

This is the fascinating chronicle of a once mighty crime family's birth, rise to power, and eventual collapse. The Cleveland crime family comprised of the notorious Porrello brothers, was third in power after New York City and Chicago, had influence with mega-mobsters like Meyer Lansky, and had a hand in the development of Las Vegas. At center stage of this story is the Sugar War, a series of Prohibition gang battles over control of corn sugar, a lucrative bootleg ingredient.

$16.95 — Paperback — 978-1-56980-277-9

THE SILENT DON: THE CRIMINAL UNDERWORLD OF SANTO TRAFFICANTE JR.
Scott M. Deitche

For thirty years he was Tampa's reigning Mob boss, running a criminal empire stretching from the Gulf Coast of the U.S. into the Caribbean and eventually, the island paradise of Cuba. After the fall of Batista and the rise of Castro, Santo Trafficante, Jr. became embroiled in the shadowy matrix of covert CIA operations, drug trafficking, plots to kill Castro and ultimately, the JFK assassination. Trafficante's unique understanding of the network of corrupt politicians, heads of state, non-traditional ethnic crime groups, and the Mafia enabled him to become one of the pivotal figures in the American Mafia's powerful heyday.

$16.95 — Paperback — 978-1-56980-355-4

BARRICADE BOOKS TRUE CRIME

THE VIOLENT YEARS: PROHIBITION AND THE DETROIT MOBS
Paul R. Kavieff

In **The Violent Years**, author Paul Kavieff has once again masterfully fused the historical details of crime in Detroit with the true flavor of the Prohibition era. For those found with new prosperity after World War I ended, it became a status symbol in Detroit to have one's own personal bootlegger and to hobnob with known gangsters. Numerous gangs scrambled to grab a piece of the profit to be made selling illegal liquor which resulted in gruesome gang warfare among the many European ethnic groups that were involved.

$16.95 – Paperback – 978-1-56980-496-4

THIEF! THE GUTSY, TRUE STORY OF AN EX-CON ARTIST
William Slick Hanner with
Cherie Rohn

William "Slick" Hanner delivers action-packed drama just as he lived it: as an outsider with inside access to the Mafia.

Here's the gutsy, true story of how a 1930s Chicago kid with street smarts and a yearning for excitement catapults into a crime-infested world. Cherie Rohn details all of the hilarious, aberrant, exhilarating details of Hanner's adventures in this sharp, insightful biography about secrets of the Mafia.

$22.00 – Hardcover – 978-1-56980-317-2

For more information, contact:
Carole Stuart at 201-266-5278 or
Email: cstuart@barricadebooks.com
Order through your National Book Network rep or directly from:
National Book Network
15200 NBN Way
Blue Ridge Summit, PA 17214
Phone: Customer Service:
1-800-462-6420
Email: Custserv@nbnbooks.com
Fax: 1-800-338-4550